No. 2650
$21.95

SERIOUS
PROGRAMMING IN
BASIC

HENRY SIMPSON

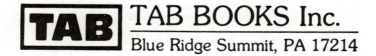

TAB BOOKS Inc.
Blue Ridge Summit, PA 17214

FIRST EDITION
FIRST PRINTING

Library of Congress Cataloging in Publication Data

Simpson, Henry.
Serious programming in BASIC.

Bibliography: p.
Includes index.
1. BASIC (Computer program language)   I. Title.
QA76.73.B3S555 1986   005.26   85-27484
ISBN 0-8306-0350-6
ISBN 0-8306-2650-6 (pbk.)

Contents

Acknowledgments

Special thanks to Dave Wiesner for his creative work in writing the assembly-language subroutines for the Commodore 64 presented in Appendix B and for inventing the C-64 program chaining technique shown in Chapter 7. Thanks to Mike Hatlak for providing the Ctrl + Reset deactivation code for the Apple II shown in Chapter 3. Thanks to Bobbi Gold and Dana Clark for raising my consciousness about program design requirements, and to the many unnamed authors whose articles and books influenced the content of the present one. Finally, thanks to Barbara Gates, who performed the word processing on this book with her usual skill and speed.

Preface

This is a book about BASIC programming. BASIC is the most popular and widely-used programming language in history. In its early days, BASIC was generally regarded as beginner's language (the letters in the BASIC acronym stand for *B*eginner's *A*ll-purpose *S*ymbolic *I*nstruction *C*ode), but nowadays most people take it more seriously. It may not be as elegant as Pascal or as efficient as C or Forth, but it is easy to learn and can do powerful things. Moreover, microcomputer users have voted with their purchases of it, making it the standard microcomputer language.

This book focuses on the development of serious BASIC programs. I hope that the subject does not sound dull. "Serious," after all, does not mean "humorless" so much as "to be taken seriously." In the realm of software development, "serious" translates to mean something like "professional." This book, then, provides guidelines and specific techniques for developing serious programs that reflect some degree of professionalism.

What makes a serious program? In the recipe include user-friendliness—that is, making the pro-gram safe for users, and fairly easy to learn and use. Another ingredient is designing the program so that it is friendly to programmers—understandable, well-documented, and maintainable. The serious program makes full use of the resources available to it—the BASIC language, DOS (disk operating system), assembly-language routines—and whatever other tricks the programmer can invent, discover, or steal from others. Finally, such a pro-gram is usually developed systematically, not while the programmer is expressing momentary inspirations when seated before a video display in the hours after midnight.

The most important thing about a serious program is that its author has serious ambitions—a desire to perform a useful task in a professional manner. When you have this ambition, you discover that there is more to creating such a program than wishing. It takes specific knowledge and specific skills. Some programmers pick up what is needed through experience and training and, sad to say, some programmers never learn the tricks at all.

This book is my attempt to share what I have

learned about BASIC program development. It is full of general guidelines, specific techniques, subroutines, programs fragments, and everything else that I could contrive to get my message across. I have assembled this information from innumerable books and magazine articles, the mental recesses of programming experts, and from several years of designing, developing, and evaluating software for a variety of microcomputers. I think that some of these learning experiences may be helpful to others, and herewith I share them, dear reader, with you.

Introduction

This book was written for people who want to develop serious application programs in BASIC. It was written for programmers, by a programmer. Though it deals with the BASIC language, most of what it covers goes well beyond that language and will be useful to programmers who develop programs in any computer language.

This book has four themes. The first theme is that programs that people such as yourself design should be "friendly" to their users. To write a friendly program, you must understand your users and their needs. You must then consciously take these needs into account as you design and develop your program. This book shows you how to do these things.

The second theme is that the programs you design should be friendly to programmers. By this is meant that your program should be logically organized, readable, well documented, and maintainable. To write a program that allows this, you must make a special effort and do certain things. The payoff is that your program will not be a mystery to you six months after you write it, and

that it will be understandable to others. These things are important if you want to fix a bug or modify the program.

The third theme is that it is important for you to be in control of your computer. You should be able to make it do what you want it to. If, for example, you want to generate a menu or read a text file, you should be able to do it. There are two parts to this. First, the computer's software—DOS and BASIC—must permit you to do these things. Second, you must know what incantations to invoke, lines of code to type, and buttons to push to make the magic happen. Some dialects of BASIC make this easy, others more difficult. However, to realize the potential of your particular machine, you must study and learn some tricks besides. Unfortunately, no amount of study can make you a good programmer, any more than memorizing a Swahili-English language dictionary can make you conversant in Swahili. There is more to using either language than knowing what its linguistic atoms stand for. The big ideas concern the philosophy of and guidelines for program design. The little ideas are the programming tricks—workable techniques for performing certain common tasks within a program (such as generating a menu or reading a text file). This book offers a sampling of both.

The fourth theme is that programs should be developed systematically and according to a strategy. Software engineering is not a very exciting subject to most people, and we will try not to bore you too much with it in this book, but there are some important ideas here that bear emphasis. Among these ideas, to mention them briefly, is the "top-down" programming technique, developing a program as a set of modules (that is, building blocks), and systematic testing and evaluation. While most of these ideas are abstract, once you understand them, they can become very real to you and have an important effect on the way you design and develop a program. Programs that are properly engineered are better—simpler, easier to understand, and less likely to have bugs.

For whom was the book written? The short answer is that it was written for people who want to develop better programs. A more complete answer is that it was written for people who already possess some programming skill, who wish to develop serious application programs, and who would like to refine their skills as program developers. The book assumes a familiarity with at least one dialect of Microsoft™ BASIC. It does not stop to explain such things as how to connect your disk drive to your computer or what a FOR-NEXT loop is. It is assumed you already know these things, and the other elementary facts about your computer. This is not really a book for the beginning programmer. If you are one, then you would be well advised to set this book aside and improve your programming skills before picking it up again. You do not have to be a programming expert to use this book, but you must know the fundamentals. If you are not quite sure whether you are ready, then forge ahead with this book anyway. A strong effort has been made to explain everything fully and to illustrate points with examples to aid your understanding.

This book was written as if to a programmer whose system consists of a microcomputer with monochrome or color monitor, a 40- or 80-column display, at least one disk drive, and printer. If your hardware and software do not exactly match, do not despair. You will find that the majority of program code will work just fine, although you may have to make a few simple modifications. For most of the examples, it does not matter whether you have monochrome or color monitor, 40- or 80-column display, or one or two disk drives. (A disk drive is, however, required. In the unlikely event that you do not have one, either get one or return this book and get your money back.) Very little of this book deals with printed output, but any serious programmer needs a printer for the more fundamental reasons that are given in Chapter 2.

While BASIC is the standard microcomputer language, it is not a standardized language. There is no single version of BASIC that works on every microcomputer. This makes it difficult to write a book on BASIC programming. One option is to talk about the language at such a general level that it encompasses all versions of BASIC; usually such discussions are short on specific examples and leave much to the reader's imagination. Another option is to focus on one particular version of the language; such a discussion can be very concrete, but will be of limited value to the reader whose version of BASIC differs greatly from that being discussed.

A third option—the one chosen in this book—is to deal with a number of specific, representative versions of the language, and to focus on them. This makes the discussion both comprehensive and concrete. This book will discuss three versions of Microsoft™ BASIC: BASICA for the IBM PC, Applesoft™ BASIC for Apple II-series computers, and BASIC 2.0 for the Commodore 64 (C-64). The most powerful of these is IBM BASIC, which is very similar to the BASIC used in IBM-compatible computers, the TRS-80 Model 4, and many other machines. Applesoft BASIC is used only in Apples and Apple-compatible computers such as the Franklin Ace; this is fairly powerful, but not in the same league as IBM's. C-64 BASIC 2.0 is a limited version that takes considerable ingenuity to use effectively.

If you have one of these three computers, then

you can use the code examples in this book directly. If you have another type of computer, then you can select the BASIC most like yours and work from there. If your computer has a weird or esoteric version of BASIC—such as Hong Kong BASIC or Ernie's Deluxe BASIC—then your translation job may be somewhat more difficult.

The book contains examples of BASIC code in all three dialects—IBM, Apple, and C-64. Many of the code examples consist of subroutines and short programs. Where the code is similar among the three, a single code example is given. Where it differs greatly, separate examples are shown. To keep the text from becoming unwieldy, some of the Apple and C-64 code examples are explained in Appendix A (Apple Addendum) and Appendix B (Commodore 64 Addendum). Most of the text is illustrated with IBM PC BASIC, which is generally regarded as the most "standard" of the current versions of the Microsoft™ language.

The general approach to presenting information in this book is to support each principle with one or more practical examples that you can type into your own computer. Most of the chapters in this book contain several segments of BASIC code—code fragments, subroutines, or short programs—which you can try out for yourself. This is something you should do. Not only will you learn more this way, but learning will be more interesting and fun. In addition, if you save the subroutines that appear in each chapter, when you finish the book you will have a subroutine library that is very useful for developing programs of your own.

In general, this book follows the "less is more" philosophy. It may not always seem this way, but I have attempted to keep things as simple and straightforward as possible. From my own attempts to learn how to program, I have discovered that most of the time the problem was deciding which information would be useful and which I could safely ignore. Unfortunately, I could only make this judgment after learning (or attempting to learn) everything. Then I would throw away about 90 percent of all that stuff I had struggled so hard to master.

This book does not work that way. Rather than offer you a lot of choices about how to do this thing or that—center a character string on the display, create a data file, design a menu—it gives you one simple, straightforward way that works. Hopefully, this will make things easier since you will have less to wade through and discard.

This book is organized in nine chapters and two appendices. Chapters 1 through 3 are introductory, and cover subjects you should master before you sit down and start coding a program. Chapter 1, User-Oriented Program Design, discusses techniques for making your program friendly to users and to other programmers, describes some programmer's tools, and sketches a strategy for program development. Chapter 2, Getting Started, offers advice and suggestions on the materials you should acquire before attempting a serious programming project: hardware, software, publications. Chapter 3, Programming Tips, offers exactly what the title says.

Chapters 4 through 8 cover various programming subjects: 4—Output and Screen Design; 5—Data Entry, Error-Testing, and Validation; 6—Program Control; 7—Program Modularization and Chaining; and 8—File Handling. Each of these chapters discusses how to get control of a different aspect of your computer. Each also offers advice on how to do this in such a way that your program will be friendly to users.

Chapter 9 introduces Fred, a world-traveling novice programmer in search of certain ultimate (more or less) truths about systems documentation, and reports what he learns from the High Guru of Programming. Fred's adventures continue, telling what he learns about program user's guides and help screens.

As for reading this book, I suggest you start with Chapter 1 and read straight through to the end, trying out the things shown in each chapter. Later on, you may want to go back to Chapters 4–8, which contain the basic reference information in the book.

Chapter 1

User-Oriented Program Design

T his chapter introduces the four themes of the book: (1) making your program friendly to users, (2) making your program friendly to programmers, (3) getting control of your computer, and (4) developing your program according to a strategy. This chapter tells what the themes mean, why they are important, and attempts to raise your consciousness about them. The four themes flow through the rest of the book, in various ways, and pop up again and again.

How important are the ideas underlying these themes? This depends on your programming goals.

If you write programs strictly for your own use, then you probably do not care how "friendly" you make them to yourself in your role as program user or programmer (themes 1 and 2). You probably do care about what we call "getting control of your computer" (theme 3), and improving your strategy for program development (theme 4).

On the other hand, if you work with other programmers—in a user's group, for example, or on program-development projects—then you probably care very much about making your programs friendly both to users and programmers. You may also feel that you have less to learn about programming or program development.

Whatever your programming goals, this book offers techniques that will make you a better programmer. And this chapter lays the groundwork for the rest of the book. The chapter defines and describes each of the themes and explains its importance. The themes are discussed in the order listed above.

If this does not sound exciting, take heart. In this chapter you will discover, among other things, the basic formula for making programs user-friendly, a catalogue of programmer's sins, and—well, read on, and you will soon find out for yourself.

MAKING YOUR PROGRAM FRIENDLY TO USERS

User-friendliness is something we hear much about these days, although no one has yet given a satisfactory definition of what it is. It is generally regarded as a good thing, like the flag or motherhood, even by those who have only the vaguest notions about it. This makes a handy combination for advertisers: What this product is, is not very clear, but it is good.

It rings like a political slogan. Picture a brightly lighted auditorium, banners waving, and a politician (this one looks like a computer nerd), standing on a platform before a large audience, proclaiming something such as this:

"In the past, this nation has paid too little attention to the program user! We have not been friendly to users! We have promised, but not delivered. In our administration, we will see that users get what is coming to them! We will appoint a blue-ribbon panel to investigate past abuses of users, and make recommendations. We will then act, in a fair and deliberate manner. Our goal is to eliminate user abuse within this generation."
And so on . . .

A bit fanciful, perhaps, but no less so than the typical ad for a user-friendly program. You know. You have seen it. The ad proclaims that a program offers the ultimate in user-friendliness because it uses a mouse, can be mastered in 5 minutes, and can be used by an eight-year-old.

What, if anything, do such claims have to do with reality?

Consider this: Since the idea of user-friendliness has never been adequately defined, people have diverse, fragmented, and sometimes strange ideas about what it means.

For example, one programmer has the idea that user-friendliness means protecting the user against all possible data-entry errors. To assure that errors are prevented, each time the user enters something and presses the Return key, the programmer has the computer come back with the following on-screen prompt:

Are you sure? (y/n):____

When the user types *y,* this prompt appears:

Are you really, *really* sure? (y/n):____

This is helpful if the user has made a mistake, but becomes maddening after the user masters the program.

Another programmer's idea of user-friendliness is menus. Menus, the programmer believes, are good things. There is something magic about them that makes programs friendly. There is an element of truth in this, as in the idea that users should be protected from data-entry errors, but both of these ideas are oversimplifications of what user-friendliness is. The menuphile attempts to use a menu everywhere, even in places where it is unnecessary and undesirable. Menus can be helpful for certain things, but they also can be slow, especially for experienced users. Thus, a fixation on them, as on any single thing in life, is unhealthy.

A third programmer is into color. This programmer uses color on every display. The resulting programs are a visual delight, although sometimes the color combinations used produce apparent shadows and afterimages, or the contrasts make it difficult to read things. Well, color can be useful, but using it properly is actually quite tricky, and requires some knowledge of human color perception.

Another programmer is into graphics, another into icons, another into windowing, and so on.

One could go on further along this line, but rather than dwelling on misconceptions and errors, it is more productive to present a more accurate picture of what user-friendliness truly means.

Start with the User

In designing anything that people will use, it is a good idea to find out as much about the users as possible. That way you can tailor your design to fit their needs.

You do this, often unconsciously, in many ways already.

When you talk to a small child, you use simple words and short sentences, and pause frequently to make sure that the child understands.

When you barbecue steaks, you ask your guests how they want theirs—well-done, medium, rare—to make sure that they get what they like. (If your cooking skills are similar to mine, your steaks are not always "user-friendly," but at least you attempt to make them that way.)

When you write a scholarly paper for presentation in a journal, you use the particular discipline's technical vocabulary and leave many things unstated, since your audience should already know them. Your paper will probably be incomprehensible to the uninitiated, but your intended audience should have no difficulty with it.

When you write a letter to your rich and straitlaced Uncle Oscar, you avoid strong language, complimentary references to liberals, or saying anything nice about the Russians, since you know from experience that he is sensitive about these subjects and may cut you out of his will.

These are examples of ways in which you take your audience into account in your daily life. Most of this is unconscious, but some of it is very deliberate. For example, in writing to Uncle Oscar, you may go through a sort of mental checklist just to make sure that you have censored your letter properly. Talking to the small child is done more casually, and you probably do not think about what you are doing very much. But in each of these cases, consciously or not, you recognize that your audience has a certain need and that you must tailor the information you provide to meet that need.

This, in fact, is the essence of user-friendliness.

It is not as easy to write a friendly program as it is to write a friendly letter. In fact, the whole process may seem a bit foreign.

Where do you start? Start with the user. Pin down your user as accurately as you can. Ask yourself questions such as the following:

- How much computer sophistication will the user have?
- How much will the user know about how computer programs operate?
- How much will the user know about the theory behind your program? If you are writing an accounting program, for example, how much accounting sophistication will the user have?
- How intelligent will the user be?
- Will the user have any handicaps or im-

pairments (such as color blindness) that influence the way the program can be used?

This list of questions is by no means complete, but will give you an idea of the kinds of questions you must ask before you start program design. Once you know who your users are, you can determine their needs and design your program in such a way that these needs will be met.

For example, if your users will be children or adults who lack computer sophistication, then you must provide a good deal of on-screen prompting in your program to ensure that things do not go amiss. With sophisticated users, you can do less hand-holding, and worry more about making your program fast and efficient. If your users will have handicaps or impairments, then you must design your program so that these factors do not interfere with their use of the program. For example, if your users will mainly be males, you should not design your program's displays such that they require color vision. Approximately 10 percent of the male population has the handicap of color blindness.

This is what is meant by taking the user into account. It is not difficult, but to many programmers it is new. Programmers often take the user for granted. They design a program for themselves and assume that everyone has the mental equipment and skills that they have. This shows about as much sensitivity to the user as attempting to explain macroeconomic theory to a small child, or writing a letter to rich Uncle Oscar about your respect for the accomplishments of Leon Trotsky. A programmer must have better sense.

The User Learning Curve

An interesting thing happens as people gain experience and skill at doing something. With practice, and a good teacher, they do things more rapidly and accurately as time goes on. Actions which once required careful thought and deliberate movements become automatic and rapid. Decisions are made quickly and with what seems to be little conscious thought.

You have seen this happen to yourself and to others. There is no mystery about it. The way in which performance improves with experience is sometimes referred to as the "user learning curve." This term derives from research in experimental psychology, where some measure of performance (such as accuracy or speed) is plotted against experience, and a characteristic curve is generated (Fig. 1-1). The form of this curve is similar for many different kinds of tasks, and so you can depend on it applying in most human learning. The shape of this curve has a very simple interpretation: As people gain skill, they become faster and make fewer errors.

The change in performance is often dramatic. For example, if you design a simple program for computing, say, the monthly payment to fully amortize a loan of a particular principal amount, interest rate, and term, the user may be slow at using it at first, but several times faster once the program is mastered. The more complex the program, the longer it takes the user to master it, and the more drawn out the learning curve will be. Some programs are so complex that the user never attempts to master them fully, but uses only the portions of

interest. In such cases, the learning curve never actually flattens.

Generally, when the user masters a program, he or she uses it differently than when first starting. In the early stages there is usually a lot of trial and error, caution, and anxiety. Later, the caution and anxiety disappear and the user looks for speed. Program features which aid the novice user—such as obligatory help screens—become obstacles that slow the program down. Some users may in fact decide at this point that the program is not as good as it seemed earlier, forgetting how the help screens brought them to their current level of skill! In a way, you cannot really design a program for a single user, even if that user is one person. This is because the user will change with increasing skill.

This leaves you in a quandary. If you design the program so that it is easy to learn—with a lot of prompting, help screens, and so forth—the user will at some point outgrow it and find parts of it tedious. If you take the opposite approach, and provide very little on-screen help, the program will be more difficult to learn. In short, a tradeoff is in-

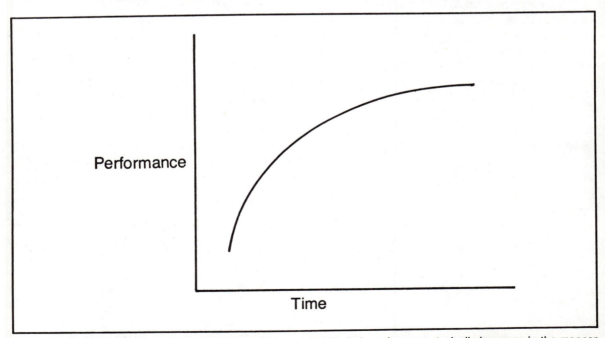

Fig. 1-1. User learning curve. As users gain experience and skill, their performance typically improves in the manner shown here. Performance improvement is greatest at the beginning, and levels off later.

volved between ease of learning and ease of use.

In some cases, it is best to make the tradeoff in favor of ease of learning. In other cases it is best to make it in favor of ease of use. The best way, of course, is to make is possible for the program to be both easy to learn and easy to use—that is, to change depending upon the user skill level. One way of doing this is to make help screens available, but optional. Another is to let the user select a program either with a menu (when inexperienced) or by typing in a program-calling code (when experienced). We'll discuss other techniques for taking the learning curve into account later in the book.

The main thing, for now, is to be aware that users learn, and change, and that you need to consider their changing needs in designing your program.

What to Expect from Program Users

Every programmer has anecdotes about the silly, stupid (or in some cases disastrous) things that have happened while using a computer program. For example, a program user calls the programmer and says that he or she followed the procedure in the program user's guide exactly, step by step, but could not get the program started. After a great deal of discussion, it dawns on the programmer that the user never pressed the Return key after typing in entries. "Why not?" the programmer asks. "The user's guide doesn't say anything about that," responds the frustrated user.

I once received a call from a user who was concerned that it was taking too long to compress a file, a procedure that should have taken a few minutes. The user was asked how long the program had been attempting to perform the compression. "About two days," came the reply. The user then asked if this was too long.

Have you ever seen someone get mayonnaise on a diskette? Fold one in half? Insert it into a disk drive sideways?

All of these things, and many more beside, have occurred. No doubt you can tell stranger tales than these—all of which brings the point: Expect *nothing* of users.

It is not their fault, nor is it up to them to know everything about computers or about your program. It is your responsibility as a programmer to minimize what they need to know, and to tell them everything that they *must* know. Above all, protect users from the consequences of their own ignorance.

Once you accept these ideas—and most experienced programmers eventually do—it changes the way you approach program design. You realize how important it is to error-test user data entries. You worry about what will happen to your program if the user presses the wrong keys at the wrong time—for example, pressing the Break or Reset keys while using your program. You then take action to prevent the anticipated disaster before it occurs.

Respect your users and protect them. Assume that they will do everything incorrectly. If you want to be safe, assume that they are out to get you, and will find ways to make your program crash or misbehave. It does not hurt to be a little paranoid when designing your program. Afterward, when people use it, you will discover whether you were paranoid enough.

Other Ways to Accommodate Users

User interaction with a program is a sort of conversation. The user makes entries, usually input via the keyboard. These entries may be data, or they may be commands that control what the computer does. The computer carries on its side of the conversation through its displays. In other words, the user talks to the computer by typing a command, the computer processes the command, and then it replies by presenting something on its video display or printer. The basic idea of a "user-computer conversation" is illustrated in Fig. 1-2.

The first part of the conversation, *user input*, is when the user enters information into the computer. Input may be entered through the keyboard or any other input device that is connected to the computer—joystick, light pen, mouse, trackball, voice input, or whatever. The user, as already noted, is imperfect and will make mistakes. Thus, the program must filter the user's inputs, and only accept those that are legal. This is done by error-

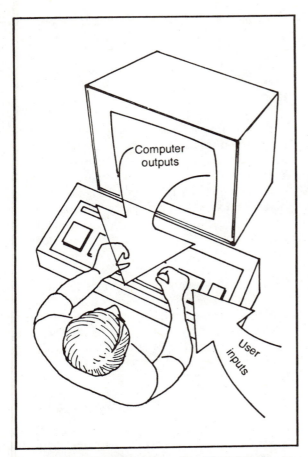

Fig. 1-2. User-computer conversation. The interaction between a user and a computer amounts to a conversation, with the user carrying on one side by making entries, usually through the keyboard, and the computer carrying on the other side with its outputs, usually through a video display.

testing. You must therefore design various input filters, or error tests, to sanitize the user's inputs.

The second part of the conversation is *output*—the information that the computer presents to the user. In most cases, output appears on the computer's video display. Output can, of course, be presented in various other ways, such as via a printer, speaker, or by controlling a servomechanism. Whatever the type of display, you must assure that it is clear and understandable. You must design displays that the user can understand and use effectively. There are good ways and bad ways to design displays, and you must know the dif-

ference. Fortunately, there are many design guidelines, especially for screen and hard copy displays.

User/computer conversation also occurs during *program control*. Program control is the way in which the user interacts with the program to make it do something. For example, one common method of control is to use program selection menus. In a menu-driven program, the user selects one of several displayed menu options by using the keyboard or a pointing device such as a light pen, and the computer then executes the program that the user selected (Fig. 1-3). Menu selection is but one of many possible methods of program control. It has advantages and disadvantages, just as all methods of control do. As a programmer, you need to know about the different control methods and their advantages and disadvantages, both from the user's point of view and in terms of program efficiency. Many people automatically think that all microcomputer programs should use menus. Not so. It is a big world out there, and menus are but one of the possibilities open to you.

In these three areas—input, output, program control—there are friendly and unfriendly ways to design your program. During design, it is difficult to separate the writing of code from the business of making your program friendly. Because of this, you need to learn the rules of friendliness and then follow them as you code. Subsequent chapters of this book will give you the rules. Key chapters are Chapter 4 (output and screen design), Chapter 5 (input, error-testing, and validation), and Chapter 6 (program control).

Debugging Your Program

No program with bugs in it is friendly. If the program crashes under certain conditions, loses data, presents messy displays, or does other things that it should not do, then it is not yet ready for users. The program that goes to a user should be bug-free and impeccable.

It is popular these days to talk about two basic styles of program development. In the quick style, a program is sort of slapped together and then debugged afterward. In the deliberate style, a good

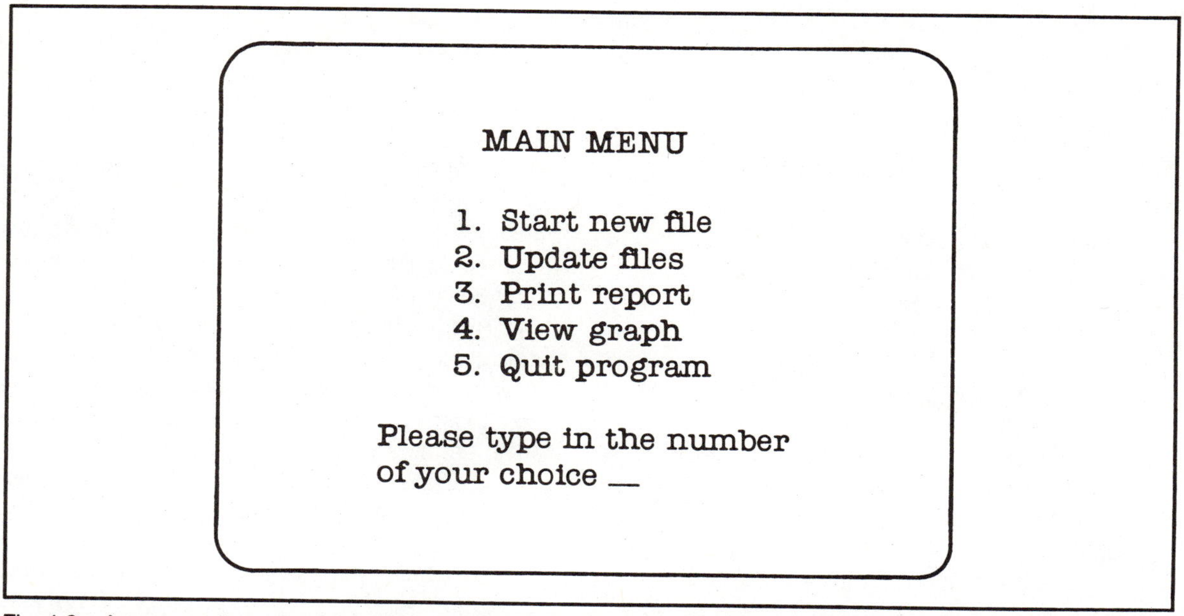

```
          MAIN MENU

      1.  Start new file
      2.  Update files
      3.  Print report
      4.  View graph
      5.  Quit program


      Please type in the number
      of your choice __
```

Fig. 1-3. A menu such as this is often used to provide the user with a method to control the functions performed by a computer program. The user selects the desired menu option, and the program then performs the chosen function.

deal of advanced planning goes on in an attempt to structure the program so that bugs in the final code are minimized.

The second style is the best because it prevents many errors from finding their way into a program in the first place. There is more front-end work because of the planning that is required, but it actually saves work in the end. A strategy for program development is described later in this chapter. Subsequent chapters in the book—particularly Chapters 4 through 8—correspond to steps in the strategy, and fill in the details.

User Documentation

User documentation is information that tells the user about your program. This may come in the form of a user's guide, as help screens or other informative information within the program, or as a combination of both.

As someone who has experience with microcomputers, you know that much of the user documentation provided with programs is inadequate. Often it is incomplete, confusing, inaccurate, or all three. To make matters worse, much user documentation is badly formatted and does not even look good. How many programs do you have whose documentation consists of a semi-readable photocopy with a staple in one corner? If you are sensitive to grammatical and spelling errors, you may wonder whom the publishers hire to write their manuals.

As in most things, there are good ways and bad ways to prepare user documentation and, again, as in most things, the bad ways far outnumber the good. Since there is no standard specification for what to put in user documentation, diversity and inadequacy are the rule rather than the exception.

There is hope.

There are ways to decide what combination of written and on-line (within-program) documentation your program should have. It is also possible to prepare a general outline that tells what a user's guide should contain. By following a few simple rules, you can devise a user documentation package that is adequate, if not exemplary. And it is certainly possible to do better than many program publishers have done.

How important user documentation is to you depends, of course, on who will use your program. If you are the only one, then it is not very important, since you already have this documentation in your head. If your program will be used by others, then user documentation is very important. No matter how great your program is by itself, without adequate documentation to explain it to others, it is like some alien spaceship that just landed in your yard.

You know, you open the hatch, walk in, and observe translucent rods, flashing displays, and hear a strange humming sound. You decide to fly it downtown to pick up a pizza at Mama Grimaldi's.

But how do you get it off the ground? How do you steer it to your destination? And how do you get safely home? You'd never know unless the aliens had thoughtfully left you a user's manual (preferably in English, and with lots of nice illustrations), or had a little screen that said, "Touch me for help."

User documentation is discussed in greater detail in Chapter 9. (It may or may not help you prepare user's manuals for spaceships!)

MAKING YOUR PROGRAM FRIENDLY TO PROGRAMMERS

Programmers are usually concerned with debugging their programs, maintaining (that is, making minor modifications or customizing) their programs, and sometimes with overhauling them or developing completely new programs based on pieces of the old. Several factors affect how easily these things can be done.

One of the factors is program size. If a program is small, figuring out what it does, debugging it, or upgrading it is usually easy. However, as a program gets bigger, at some point it becomes too complex for your mind to encompass. There is no formal way to decide when this point has been reached, although experienced programmers have a good idea. Anyone who had developed a BASIC program that is more than, say, 50 lines long, knows that it can be difficult unraveling what each line does.

A second factor that affects a programmer's understanding of a program is how it was designed, and what principles, if any, the original programmer followed during design. For example, it is usually easier to understand a program that is structured into modules that are identified with remarks in the code than one that is unmodularized and without remarks.

If you believe in writing programs that are friendly to other programmers, then you must make your programs easy for other programmers to understand. Of course, you may be the only programmer who ever looks at your code. Is there any point in worrying about friendliness then? If you have total recall, the answer is no. Because most of us suffer from imperfect memories, however, it is a good idea to design all of our programs as if they had to be understandable by other programmers.

A third factor that affects how friendly your program will be to programmers is how well you document it. Documentation written by programmers to explain how a program works is called *system documentation*. This consists of remarks within the code and various items of written documentation: written explanations of the subprograms; tables of functions, arrays, and variables; descriptions of subroutines; file descriptions with record layouts; and so forth. All of this documentation is intended to explain how the program works in enough detail that a programmer can make sense of it. Based on this understanding, the programmer can then correct an error, modify the program, or do something else that requires changes to program code.

It is a simple fact that without adequate system documentation, a BASIC program that is more than a few lines long is usually incomprehensible to another programmer. Actually, with time, incomprehensibility becomes a problem even for the program's original author. As our memories are faulty, we forget things. If we do not document our programs, in time our own creations become mysteries to us.

Some programmers do not see the point of writing system documentation. This may be due to their desire to keep their programs a bit mysterious. That way no one else can understand them, modify them, or threaten anyone's job. We have all heard or read about some programmer who was the only person in the world who knew how a particular program worked and was still called on, years later, to keep it running. When this happens, it is not always the programmer's fault, of course, but often it is. If you like to keep secrets, then ignoring system documentation may be your métier. However, since you are no doubt more enlightened than this, you can surely see the value of such documentation.

You must decide whether or not you need such documentation and, if so, how much you need. If you write a short program, you can often safely forget about it. With longer ones, you need it. Also, if you are the only person who ever analyzes your code, system documentation is less important than if others also do.

Whatever your decision, it is a good idea to design your programs so that they are readable. Techniques for doing this are described in this book. The last section of this chapter, for example, describes how to modularize a program, and Chapter 3 provides a model of a modularized program. The later chapters in the book provide many concrete examples of program modules.

System documentation is something you should understand well before you develop a program. Ideally, you should prepare this documentation as you code. The subject is covered in greater detail in Chapter 9.

GETTING CONTROL OF YOUR COMPUTER

You know that you are in control of your computer when you have effective and reliable ways (usually subroutines) to do such things as:

- Display information on your video display or printer.
- Collect data entries through the keyboard.
- Select and design the method of program control.
- Chain (that is, link) separate subprograms together.
- Design and use disk files.

The key to this is *modularization*. A module may be of any size, but usually it is a few lines long.

Subroutines are modules. Some modules include several subroutines, and some modules are even larger.

One of the most important ways to gain control of your computer is to tailor how you think about what a program is. Experienced programmers tend to think of programs as collections of modules, rather than as collections of BASIC statements. They do not usually write programs line by line, but rather, build as much of a program as they can from modules in their module and subroutine library. This is faster, easier, and more efficient than slogging through the business of building a program line by line. Program modularization is discussed later in this chapter and in Chapters 3 and 7.

The topics listed above are covered in Chapters 4 through 8. To give you an idea of what is coming, let us briefly preview some of the subjects covered in those chapters. Each of these chapters contains several examples of BASIC code to illustrate the discussion.

Chapter 4, "Output and Screen Design," covers screen (and printer) design principles, planning, and content. It presents techniques for cursor control, partial clearing of the screen, screen layout, screen formatting, and other aspects of information display.

Chapter 5, "Data Entry, Error-Testing, and Validation," tells how to handle the process of taking user data entries. This includes error-testing, error messages, and user verification and editing of entries.

Chapter 6, "Program Control," describes program control methods and gives guidelines for deciding what type of control technique—such as menu, two-way choice, or typing in a program name—to use in a program. It also shows how to combine different control techniques.

Chapter 7, "Program Modularization and Chaining," tells how to create a program consisting of separate modules, and how to link these modules together using the chaining technique.

Chapter 8, "File Handling," tells what you need to know to use text files. It covers file planning, sequential and random access files, and how to develop file write/read subroutines that you can use in your programs.

The other chapters in this book are also important, but in a different way. Chapters 1 through 3 cover preliminaries—things you should know before starting program design. Chapter 9 covers system and user documentation. Chapters 4 through 8 cover the very practical and down-to-earth business of writing program code. As such, these chapters have many examples of actual code, especially subroutines. They will give you a chance to exercise your fingers as well as your mind.

PROGRAM DEVELOPMENT STRATEGY

This section presents a strategy for developing microcomputer programs. We call it a *strategy* because it does not consist of a rigid set of steps, but a general approach. Engineers and others have written detailed program-development procedures in the past, but no single procedure works well for everyone. Programmers have different personalities, talents, and working styles—one size does not fit all.

This strategy consists of a mixture of procedures, requirements to meet, and warnings. It is admittedly a hodgepodge, and if you look at any single part of it too closely, you will find plenty to complain about. Actually, when you boil it all down, the resulting essence is a sort of program development philosophy. As you will see, this philosophy places heavy emphasis on making your program friendly to users and programmers, on planning, on complete documentation, and on careful testing of the final products.

The place to begin our discussion is with two key aspects of design philosophy—top-down design, and modular design.

Top-Down Design

Top-down design is rather like the concept of humanism: Most people seem to agree that it is a good thing, and many scholars make their livings writing about it, but it is difficult to find a simple explanation of what it means. Let us forego the technicalities here, and use a practical, common-sense way of thinking about it. Let us start by offering two case studies of design approaches. You guess which one is top-down design.

In Case A, the programmer sits down at his computer and types in the first line of code. When he finishes that, he types in the second line, the third, and so on, until he has typed in the last line of code. Then he runs the program to see if it will work. When bugs pop up, he fixes them. He continues in this way until the program works to his satisfaction.

In Case B, the programmer sits down and writes a design plan. First, she decides what her program's objectives are. Then she decides what functions her program must perform, and decides what modules are required to perform each function. She then goes to her subroutine library and looks for pieces of old programs to use in the new one. Then she sits down at her computer and develops the first module. She tests it, debugs it, and sets it aside. She then develops, tests, and debugs the next module. She then tests how well this module works with the first module. She continues in this way, module by module, until the whole program is developed.

It is not hard to guess which designer used top-down design: she was the systematic one. Her design approach was characterized by these features:

- She started by defining the program's high-level objectives.
- Next, she broke the program down into modules.
- She developed each module separately, thoroughly testing and debugging it before continuing.
- As she developed new modules, she tested their interface with old modules.

The top-down approach forces a program to be developed and debugged systematically in a series of logical steps (Fig. 1-4). This contrasts with the more haphazard approach of a programmer who

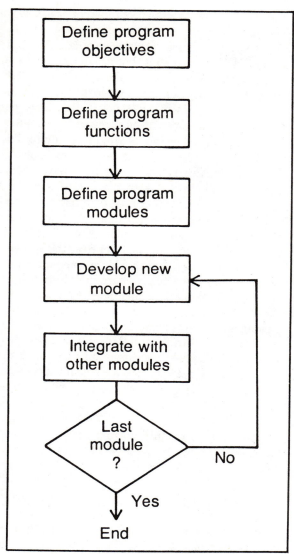

Fig. 1-4. Top-down design starts with a definition of a program's high-level objectives, and moves from there to a more detailed definition of the program's modules and their relationships.

sits down and simply starts writing program code.

Top-down design is increasingly important as a program grows in size and complexity. If you write very short and simple programs, then you can safely ignore it. But if you want to do something ambitious in a program, use top-down design. It in-

creases your power as a designer greatly.

Modular Design

A program module is a segment of code that performs a specific function. A subroutine is a module. Modules exist on higher levels, as well. Often a module includes several subroutines, and performs a high-level function such as creating a set of data files. In fact, there is no upper size limit to a module.

What is unique about a module is that it does something more sophisticated than a single statement of program code. In a sense, a program module is to a programming language what a high-level language such as BASIC is to the machine language of the computer. Just as programmers find it easier to work with high-level languages than with individual bits and bytes, most skilled programmers find it easier to work with program modules than with individual statements of code. Obviously, you cannot ignore the BASIC language or DOS, since your program is composed of it. But it is a good thing to start thinking of your program not as so many lines of code, but on a more global level—as modules.

The starting point in modular design is the programmer's subroutine library. One thing nice about having a good subroutine library is that it makes it easier for you to design a new program. You can take pieces of the old and put them into the new. A good subroutine library consists of subroutines that have been carefully tested and debugged. You can use them without testing them because you already have checked them out and you know that they work properly. A large part of a new program may consist of these subroutines. Creating the program becomes a matter of writing the *control structure* (that is, subroutine calls) and designing any unique input or display routines.

One other advantage of this approach is that your programs begin to look similar. Since they are all built of many of the same modules, you can go from one to another without a lot of reorientation. You also have a good idea of where problems are likely to occur, and find it easier to correct them.

Critics may argue that this approach to design is not very elegant. The reason is that it does not solve each design problem from scratch and look for the most efficient solution. Instead, it concentrates on ways in which the new problem is similar to ones that have already been solved and then uses pieces of the old solution in solving the new problem. However elegant or inelegant the approach, it has two enormous advantages: it allows rapid program development, and it minimizes errors.

Obviously, this approach is not for every programmer, or for every program. But in most cases, and with most programmers, it works very effectively.

Design Strategy

Now that you have a taste of design philosophy, it is time to look at the steps in the design strategy. These steps are illustrated in Fig. 1-5 and are discussed below. Remember, there is nothing rigid about this strategy, and you may modify the order of the steps, eliminate or add steps, or make other changes that you think necessary. If you do make such changes, however, be sure that you do not sacrifice the strategy⁰s emphasis on the user.

Step 1: Start with Users. The place to start any design is by knowing who will use your program. You must tailor your program to this audience. You must design displays they will understand, test for the types of errors they will make, and provide a method of program control they can use effectively. Later on, you must develop user documentation that will help them make the most of your program.

Know who these folks will be before you start. Do not wait until after you write your program. Then it will be too late or too expensive to make changes.

Step 2: Plan Your Displays. Decide what will go on your displays before you write your program. Displays are what the user will see. Since the main idea of most computer programs is for the user to interact with the computer through a display, the program should be designed backward from these displays. It is common but wrong to develop a program the other way around, by design-ing displays based on the program that has already been developed.

You do not have to plan every last detail of every display at the start, but design the displays as completely as you can. Make and show display mockups (on paper or on the video display) to your target audience, if you can. If you do this, then you are three or four rungs up on the poor programmer who completely develops a program, only to discover that users cannot make sense of its displays.

Step 3: Plan Your Data-Entry Routines. Your computer will talk to the user through its displays. The user will talk back to the computer through the keyboard or through some other input device. Together, computer output and user input comprise what some people refer to as the *human-computer interface*. This should be completely designed before you actually begin to code your program. Decide what data must be entered and then plan your input routines—the prompts, error messages, and verification and editing routines.

Step 4: Plan Your Program Modules. Decide what modules your program will consist of. Start at the highest level and work your way down. An example of a high-level program module is a data entry program that is used to collect data from the user.

Break each module down into submodules, until you get down to the level of the subroutine. Then go to your subroutine library and select subroutines to use in the submodules.

Overall, you will need subroutines to handle display (output), user input, program control, program linking, and file handling. (Conveniently and not exactly coincidentally, Chapters 4 through 8 contain many subroutines for these purposes.)

Step 5: Plan Your Data Structures and Files. Plan your data structures—the way you will represent data within the program using integer, real, and string variables and arrays. Plan your files and lay out the records that are required.

Step 6: Decide on a Method of Program Control. Decide how your user will interact with the program to control its operation. That is, decide whether the program will be menu-driven or use some other control method. Design the menus or

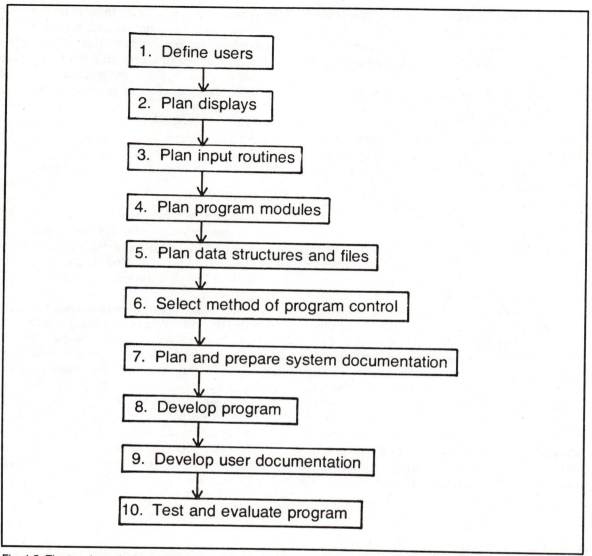

Fig. 1-5. The top-down design philosophy can be translated into a program development strategy, as shown here. The steps in this strategy place heavy emphasis on the user—starting by defining the user, the displays the user will view, and the program's input routines. The last two steps also stress the user—developing user documentation and having users test and evaluate both the program and its documentation.

other control screens.

Step 7: Prepare System Documentation. Begin developing system documentation as you plan the program. Planning program details such as data structures and record layouts is an important part of system documentation.

Prepare additional documentation as the pro-

gram evolves. As much as possible, develop system documentation concurrently with the program, not at the end.

Step 8: Develop Your Program. Start by developing the primary module in your program. In a program that manages a database, the primary module may be one to read or write files. In a program that uses extensive graphics, the primary module may be one to generate displays. Pick the module that is central to the operation of your program and develop it. Write system documentation for it.

Then develop the next logical module and its documentation.

When this module is done, link it to the first module and test the two together. Make the interface between the modules work the way it should.

Next, go the the third module, link it to other modules, test the interface, and document.

Continue in this manner until you have developed, integrated, debugged, and documented all program modules.

Step 9: Develop User Documentation. Develop a user's guide that tells your target audience how to use your program. Your user's guide should be comprehensive, and describe every essential aspect of your program, including information on system setup, a tutorial for the new user, and reference information for the experienced user.

In addition to written documentation, create the help screens and other internal documentation that your program requires. These should support the written documentation, and be optionally selectable by the user.

Step 10: Test and Evaluate Your Program. Testing goes on throughout program development. When the program is finished and user documentation has been prepared, try it out on its target audience. Train them in its use, give them the user documentation, and then have them use the program to perform specific tasks that you define. See how well users perform and how well they accept—that is, *like*—your program. Do not be surprised if they discover program bugs that your own tests missed.

Following these tests, revise your program to correct its shortcomings and maximize user acceptance.

A FINAL WORD

In reality, no programmer will ever follow this formula exactly in designing and developing a program. As noted, this is more of a design philosophy than a rigid formula. You should feel free to modify it to suit your working style and programming task.

Pay close attention to the essentials, however. Note that this is a very user-oriented approach, with the user being consulted during the early part of design and acting as the evaluator at the end. Also important is the approach's emphasis on modularity, and systematic, step-by-step program development.

The details will be filled in later in the book. Before continuing, it is suggested that you store this program development strategy up in your high memory area where you can gain ready access to it, without disrupting your normal flow of control.

Chapter 2

Getting Started

This chapter describes some ways to increase the power of your computer as a program development tool. It begins with a discussion of hardware—video monitors, printers, and disk drives. The discussion also covers the important subject of work station design, and tells what types of files (paper, not computer) you should use to keep track of your programs and listings.

The second section of the chapter covers software. It describes a number of program development utilities and related programs that come in handy to programmers such as yourself.

The third section identifies and describes several books and magazines that you should know about.

HARDWARE

This section discusses video and printed output, as well as other hardware issues.

Video Display

Most personal computers will drive either a video monitor or a TV set connected via a modulator. A modulator-driven TV set in fine for anyone who can get along with a 40-column display, who is not critical about picture quality, and who uses the display for less than, say, 30 minutes or so each day. Display quality is largely a function of how good the TV set it. If it is a cheap set, or an old cast-off that has lost its contrast, alignment, and resolution, then it will probably cause eyestrain. Some computer owners use black-and-white sets. The picture quality on these is slightly better than that of a color set, but without the advantage of color. If you must choose between a color TV and a black-and-white one, get color. The advantages of color outweigh the slightly poorer picture quality.

The overwhelming choice in video displays for most serious programmers is a video monitor. Many computers have built-in monitors, and so the decision has already been made for the user. But even where there is a choice to be made, most programmers require the superior picture quality of a video monitor.

Computer manufacturers generally market good quality monitors for their computers. Compatible monitors may also be purchased elsewhere, and it is often less expensive this way. There are several quality monochrome and color monitors available, and their main difference is price. Among the leading manufacturers of such monitors are Amdek, NEC (Nippon Electric Company), and Taxan. These monitors are widely available, often discounted, and of good quality. Their manufacturers sell both composite and RGB monitors.

For extended use, monochrome monitors generally cause less eyestrain than color monitors. If you intend to work long hours before the screen, and color is not essential, give serious consideration to a monochrome monitor. If you decide to get one, be aware that the size and quality of the monitor are more important than its phosphor color. The three most common phosphor colors available on monitors are white, amber (light yellow), and green. The eye is slightly more sensitive to green when there is low ambient lighting, and so if you intend to use your monitor in a semi-darkened area, green is best. If you will use the monitor in brighter surroundings, then white or amber are better.

Whatever display you decide on, get one that has a screen diagonal of at least 12 inches. A smaller screen than this is hard to read and not good for extended use. A larger screen is unnecessary and awkward to use if it is at a normal viewing distance (20-28 inches).

Printer

For serious programming, you need a printer. There are two reasons for this. First, a printer permits you to generate a hard-copy listing of the program you are writing. The listing is important during program development because you can usually find what you are looking for more quickly and easily with a hard-copy listing than by going through the program, screen by screen, on your video display. The listing is also a permanent record of your program that you cannot mistakenly erase, overwrite, or damage with a few careless keystrokes. While careful working practices reduce the likelihood of such accidents, occasionally they occur anyway. Many programmers have been saved by the hard-copy listing of the program that they kept on file.

Another reason you need a printer is to provide hard-copy output for the programs you develop. Not all programs generate reports, but most serious ones do. A word processor, database manager, or financial analysis program without hard-copy reports is unthinkable.

What type of printer should you get? For most programmers, the choice is between an impact dot-matrix printer and a letter-quality printer. Most letter-quality printers have a daisy wheel or thimble printing element that enables them to print fully formed characters. Print quality is superior to that of dot-matrix printers, but letter-quality printers are slower, noisier, more expensive, and generally less reliable than dot-matrix printers. In addition, they lack the graphics capabilities of dot-matrix printers. Anyone whose primary computer application is word processing probably needs a letter-quality printer, but this is not usually the main application of a programmer. If most of your computer's output will consist of program listings, graphics, or computer-generated reports, a dot-matrix printer is a better choice.

As you are probably aware, printer manufacturers often sell their products to computer companies which, in turn, market the same (or nearly the same) printer under their own label at a higher price. A careful shopper can save money by buying the printer under its own name. The computer companies seem to favor Epson and C.Itoh printers, and to a certain extent Okidatas. These brands are also very popular with computer owners.

Epson printers are very popular and are sold under the IBM label with the IBM PC. Epson printers have established a good reputation for product quality and reliability, but they tend to get paper jams, their controls are on the top instead of the front, and their covers make it difficult to monitor paper movement. In many ways, the Okidata and C.Itoh printers are superior, and should be carefully considered by any computer owner in the market for a good quality dot-matrix printer. For comparison purposes, the Okidata 92 printer costs about the same as the Epson FX-80 printer, but is faster, has its controls on the front, and is less likely to jam. Both Apple and Digital Equipment Corporation (DEC) are marketing C.Itoh printers under their brand names, and these printers have a proven history of product quality and reliability. (A C.Itoh printer is the hard-copy half of Apple's *IIc* and Macintosh computer systems.)

In addition to these, there are a number of other good quality dot-matrix printers on the market, not all of which have made the market penetration of the three brands just mentioned. Whatever you get, make sure that you can obtain maintenance support for it without sending it back to some factory in Tokyo, Taipei, or Seoul. In general, it is best to stick with major brand names.

Hardware Incidentals

A hard disk is a definite asset to a programmer such as yourself; it is much faster than a floppy disk drive and has much greater storage capacity. You need one if you spend a significant amount of time doing software development work, if your applications require a hard disk, or both. Hard disks and controllers are getting less expensive, and it is now possible to fit most major microcomputers with one for about $600.

If the history of the microcomputer industry gives any clues, it is probable that prices will continue to drop, and that by the time you read these words on a printed page, hard disks will be even less expensive. Again, noting the history of the industry, not only do prices drop, but so do companies. Moral: Buy only from well-known manufacturers.

If you live in an area where there are frequent power surges or drops, get a surge suppressor. If you live near a power station, this is not usually a problem. If you live on the outskirts—at the end of the power line—then you are likely to experience a greater amount of power variation. You know this is happening when the lights in your house dim momentarily, then brighten again, or you see other obvious signs of power fluctuations. These power variations can be very damaging to computer equip-

ment. They produce spikes that can destroy electronic circuitry.

If you decide to get a surge suppressor, find one with a line switch on it and enough outlets for your PC, printer, monitor, and other equipment. This allows you to use one power switch to turn everything on or off at once, instead of going through the numbers, component by component. It also saves the switches in your components. If you do not need a surge suppressor, get a power strip with a line switch on it so that you can turn all of your computer equipment on or off with one switch.

Surge suppressors cost about $50. You can make your own for much less than this. If you like to do this sort of thing, review "Ciarcia's Circuit Cellar," in *BYTE* magazine (December 1983) for directions on how to do it.

Your Work Station

Work station is the label that ergonomics experts attach to the arrangement of furniture and equipment in a person's work space. If you use a computer, you have a work station, but you probably call it something else. There are good ways and bad ways to design your work station, and the good ways are not always obvious to common sense. If your work station is poorly designed, and you use it for more than an hour or so each day, then you may suffer from such symptoms as eyestrain, backache, or pain in your arms or wrists. The solution is to redesign your work station. Here are a few suggestions:

- Get a good chair, one that is reasonably firm and that provides good lower back support. If your feet do not touch the floor, get a footrest or something else to set them on.
- Locate your keyboard at about the same height as your elbow (arms at side). You should not have to reach up to or across a desk to touch your keyboard. The keyboard should be a few inches lower than the height of the average desk. If you can raise your chair, this solves the problem, provided you

can still get your feet to touch something solid. You should be able to move up close to the desk or table, and be able to get your feet underneath it.

- Locate your video display about 2 feet away, at or slightly below your line of sight when looking straight ahead. Most PC users find it best to set their video display directly behind their keyboard.
- Adjust the lighting so that there are no reflections from the screen of the video display or other bright lights directly behind or in front of it. Your eyes should adapt to the brightness of the video display, not a competing light nearby.

Figure 2-1 summarizes the requirements for a good work station.

You do not have to go out and buy an expensive oak work station that has been hand crafted by a company with an organic-sounding name. Usually you can adapt inexpensive tables or office furniture to meet your requirements. But if you cannot meet the above recommendations with the furniture and lighting that you have, get a catalogue from a discount office furnishings outfit, take a trip to your local swap meet, make your own furniture, or look elsewhere to get what you need.

Files, Files, Files

Individual attitudes about filing cabinets and

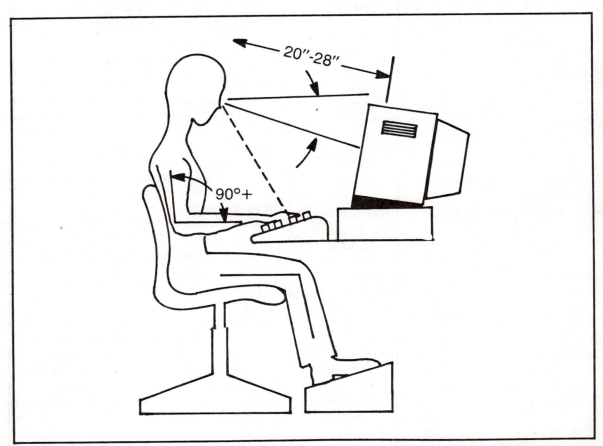

Fig. 2-1. Programmer's work station. It is important to have a chair with good back support, to locate the keyboard at about elbow height, and to locate the monitor about two feet away, at or slightly below the line of sight and positioned to be out of the way of interference from lighting.

files differ, and probably have a lot to do with one's early childhood. If you believe that neatness and orderliness are important things, then you probably see the wisdom of filing cabinets and files. If you have a more casual attitude about these matters, then you may regard files as a bother that you prefer to avoid.

I would like to avoid taking a position on this issue, since it has so much to do with personal working style. However, it is impossible to be even-handed about this since, in programming matters at least, I tend to be a bit compulsive about such things as neatness and orderliness. A programmer who keeps his or her working materials—program listings, documentation, disks, and so forth—in a well-organized file is much better off than one who relies on memory for where things are to locate them.

We all have friends whose desks look like dumping grounds for books, magazines, and debris, and often we regard them as brilliant eccentrics. Folklore holds that such folks know exactly where everything is, and can find whatever they want, when they want it. In some cases this is certainly true, but be skeptical about such claims. A programmer who treats working materials this way is courting disaster. In programming, there is too little margin for error. Programs mush be exact things, and the records and versions of them that we keep must be kept exactly. Much of what a programmer does today is based on what was done yesterday—using pieces of old programs, troubleshooting a particular program module, writing a user's manual. In any of these or other related activities, it is necessary to be able to locate quickly the working materials used previously. It is not good enough to be reasonably sure that what you have found is what you were after. You must be exactly sure, because you deal in an exacting discipline. Moreover, your time should not be spend rummaging through stacks of paper, looking through drawers or bookshelves, or performing other mindless drudgery.

What files do you need? Start with a flip file, one of those plastic boxes with a transparent cover that holds about 50 floppy disks. Put this on the table beside your computer and keep your frequently used programs in it. Separate it into sections for utility programs, original and backup disks of the program you are currently working on, blank disks, and the other logical categories of programs that are relevant to you in your program development work. The flip file is handy for ongoing work, and for keeping commonly used programs ready at hand.

Once you complete a programming project, remove the program disks from the flip file and keep them in plastic storage boxes. Get a half dozen or so of these to start, and use them for keeping the working copies of your programs. A plastic storage box costs less than $5—less, if you buy in quantity—and holds about 10 disks. Label the boxes, put them on a shelf, and then pull them down when you need them. Colored storage boxes can be helpful. Use different colored boxes to store different programs, or to separate the disks used in your different computers. You can also use the cardboard boxes which sometimes come with disks for this purpose.

If you do any significant amount of programming, get a file cabinet. Use this for keeping your program listings, archival disks, documentation, information on hardware and software purchases, copies of articles, and other important material. Get file dividers and index tabs. Spend some time organizing your file. The test of your success is how quickly you can find what you want. You should be able to open a file drawer, locate the file tab, and pull what you want out in no more than about 10 seconds. If it takes longer, than you need better organization.

Organizing files—flip files, storage boxes, filing cabinets—is extra work when you start. In the long run, however, it will save you work, confusion, and headaches.

Floppy Disks

What is there to say about disks? First, buy good ones, not cheap ones (no brand names, please). Bargain basement disks are available, but avoid them. They will lose data and bring you grief. You do not have to buy the most expensive disks, either. Just stay away from the cheapies. The best way to buy disks is by mail order. You can buy good quality disks this way at a discount. If you want to give your local computer store business, buy the big things from them—computers, disk drives, printers, and so forth. The amount of extra service they can offer you when they sell you a box of floppy disks is miniscule.

Every programmer knows that taking care of disks is important. It does not take much more than common sense: Keep them in a box when they are not in use so that they do not get dusty, do not handle them while you are eating french fries, keep your cat from walking on them. Also look out for the more subtle dangers. Pencil erasures are bad news, so do not spread them around where your disks are. Flea powder (if you have a pet), chalk (if you teach), diatomaceous earth (if you have a pool or aquarium), tobacco (if you smoke), and saliva (if you have a dog or a small child) all are dangerous.

How long do disks last? Nobody seems to know the answer to this question. Manufacturers are particularly cagey about it, and will not answer it directly. The answers I have received range from "about a year" to "forever." The conditions do not seem to matter. Along these lines, the best advice is not to use a disk for more than about a year. Keep a good supply of them on hand, and do not keep using the same ones over and over again.

Disks for a programmer are like typing paper for a writer. They are working materials, necessary to do the job, and should not be treated as if they were made of some precious material. A good test of how cheap you are is how many blank disks you have. If you have fewer than five new, blank disks, then you are not being fair to yourself. Go out—no, call up a trustworthy mail-order firm—and buy yourself another box. Better yet, buy two boxes. Get good ones.

SOFTWARE

Most microcomputers are shipped with several commands and utilities important for program development. In some cases these are resident in the BASIC language, are DOS commands, or are available when loaded from disk. Expensive computers such as IBM PC are equipped with a wonderful assortment of BASIC and DOS commands important in program development. Less expensive machines such as the Apple have fewer. Inexpensive machines such as the C-64 have very few. If your machine lacks essential commands and utilities, you can often acquire them separately on disk or ROM for use in programming.

More specifically, here are some utilities and commands that you should have:

- Renumber—Renumbers program lines. Preferably, this should allow you to renumber a specified range of lines, and not restrict you to the entire program.
- Merge—Allows the merging of two programs.
- Disk-Disk Copy Program—Allows the contents of one disk to be copied to another. The program should be fast, reliable, and verify the copy that it makes.
- Trace—Displays the number of the line currently being executed. This command comes in various forms, such as TRACE or TRON (remember the movie of that name?), and is deactivated with another command, such as NOTRACE or TROFF.
- Delete Line Range—A command that allows a range of lines to be deleted by typing in something such as DEL 40-100. Without this command, ridding a program of a range of lines must be done on a line-by-line basis, which is very tedious and time-consuming.
- Line Cross-Referencer—Tells which lines in a program are called from other lines with GOTO and GOSUB statements, and identifies any calls to nonexistent lines. This helps the programmer comprehend the control flow within a program, identify ways of increasing its efficiency, and avert jumps to nonexistent lines.
- Variable Lister—Displays all variables, functions, and arrays currently in use in a program. This is useful for documenting the program and while building the program, to

assure that variable, function, or array labels are not inadvertently duplicated.

- Global Search and Replace—Searches through a program to find a particular character string (which may consist of any combination of numbers, letters, and symbols) and change it to specified replacement string. This enables the programmer to make many modifications very quickly, and is also useful to locate a part of the program or to determine whether or not a specified character string exists within the program.
- Compactor—Removes remarks from a BASIC program and compresses the program further by fitting as many statements onto as few lines as possible. File compression reduces file size by as much as 50 percent and increases program execution speed dramatically. This permits the programmer to develop a program for maximum readability (with one statement per line, and many remarks in code), and then to optimize it with the compactor to maximize its speed and minimize its demand on disk and computer memory. Compacting also increases the security of a program, since it reduces program readability.
- Compiler—Converts high-level BASIC code, which must be interpreted as it is executed, into machine-level instructions that can be executed directly. The result is a program that operates at higher speed, but that usually requires a greater amount of space for disk storage and in computer memory. Additional benefits of compiling are greater security to the program, and being able to use the compiler as a code debugger—the compiler checks the syntax of program lines during compilation, and thereby helps the programmer identify syntax errors.
- Formatter—Converts a standard BASIC listing into a more readable format by separating and indenting FOR-NEXT, IF-THEN, and WHILE-WEND statements to show program structure; breaking multiple statements into single lines; and making pro-

gram remarks stand out.
- Line Editor—An editor is a utility program that simplifies line editing. Such editors usually enable a line to be entered without regard to the cursor's position, simplify insertions and deletions, and enable the cursor to be moved quickly around the line.
- Text File Editor—An editor for program and data files.

Which of these do you need? You must answer this question for yourself, but in my opinion, everything but the last four items is essential for any serious program development work. Some of the remaining utilities are essential for certain types of programming. A compiler is important if you develop programs that receive heavy usage, since the increased speed of a compiled program equates to a decrease in the amount of time the program requires to perform its task, a probable reduction in person-hours and costs, and greater overall efficiency. A BASIC formatter is important when it is critical for your programs to be readable—if you teach, if you work with other programmers on team programming projects, if you develop very large and complex programs of your own, and in similar circumstances. A line editor is essential if your computer's editor is inadequate. A text file editor is important if you do a lot of work with text files.

Many programmers have turned their talents to developing utility programs that perform one or more of the functions outlined above. No single utility package does everything, but you probably do not need everything anyway. What follows is a brief description of some typical products that are available. The catalog is not complete, but representative. Further, the fact that a product is listed here is not an endorsement, but indicates that the product performs the function indicated.

For the IBM PC, IBM markets a software package called the *BASIC Programming Development System*, whose utility programs include a BASIC cross-referencer, a BASIC formatter, a BASIC compactor, and a text file editor. Softool Systems produces the *BASIC Development System*, whose features include line cross-referencing, variable listing, BASIC compression (and uncompression), single-step trace, and line renumbering with line relocation. Compilers for IBM BASIC are manufactured by IBM Corporation, Microsoft, and Softech Microsystems.

For the Apple, Southwestern Data Systems markets *APPLE-DOC*, a program development utility that includes a variable lister, line cross-referencer, and variable replacer. Sensible Software markets *Basic Enhanced Software Tools*, which contains variable and line cross-referencers similar to those of *APPLE-DOC*; a variable optimizer, remark remover, and line compactor; and a renumbering and merging program. Beagle Brothers markets *Global Program Line Editor*, which enables rapid entry and editing of program lines, does global searching and replacement, and performs several other editing features. Compilers for Apple BASIC are sold by Microsoft, Alison Software, and other companies.

Machines such as the C-64 have a limited BASIC and DOS and need considerable enhancement to be made effective program development systems. One of the most effective ways to enhance such computers is with a plug-in ROM card. For the C-64 in particular, several of these are available. One such card is *Vic Tree*™ from Skyles Electric Works. Vic Tree enhances BASIC and DOS by adding 42 new commands—most for disk control, editing, and debugging—that simplify such things as reading the disk directory, reading and writing files, copying disks, loading and saving programs, initializing disks, renaming files, and deleting files. Richvale Telecommunications manufactures the *RTC BASIC Aid*, which adds 33 additional commands to C-64 BASIC to read the disk directory, and to initialize, rename, copy or delete disk files. Commodore's *Simon's BASIC* adds 114 programming commands to the C-64's language to enhance string handling, input, screen control, and graphics and music generation.

The above descriptions will give you a general idea of the types of utilities available. There are many more utilities besides these. Moreover, products change, and new products are constantly being introduced. In short, do not feel limited by this summary. Visit your computer dealer, check the magazine ads, and talk to your friends. See what the various utilities can do, how their features match your needs, and see what magazine reviewers, dealers, and other programmers recommend.

There are public domain (that is, non-copyrighted) programs for performing some utility functions, and user's group libraries often include such programs. In addition, a user's group is a good place to get additional information about program development utilities that may suit your needs. If you do not already belong to such a group, join one. Even if you are a recluse and antisocial by nature, the free programs and consulting you can get make it worth it.

BOOKS AND MAGAZINES

The best source of information about your computer, about programming, and about new hardware and software is books and magazines. The serious programmer probably subscribes to several magazines and has a shelf full of computer books. They fall into three general categories:

- Magazines—Provide programs, programming tips, and news about software and hardware developments.
- Computer-Specific Books—Provide information on your computer that is broader in scope than a magazine article.
- General Books—Provide information on topics of interest to the programmer such as programming techniques, hardware, writing, etc.

This section provides brief descriptions of publications that I've found particularly useful. Some of these are necessary, and others optional. The list is far from complete, but it is a good place to start.

To begin with, you must have your computer's BASIC and DOS manuals, and the technical reference manual if one is available. The quality of these manuals varies from computer to computer, and seems to be in proportion to the cost of the computer. Manuals for expensive computers such as

IBM and Hewlett-Packard are generally excellent. Those for the Apple are very good. Those for the inexpensive Commodore are—well, you have the formula for figuring it out.

If the computer's documentation is inadequate, you can usually go to your local computer store or bookstore and find books that provide help with BASIC, DOS, or specific application programs. If you have a rare or discontinued computer, you may have difficulty finding such books. (If you are in this fix, it may be a good idea to trade in your old IMSAI for a newer, more widely used computer.)

The following three books are recommended:

The Elements of Style, Strunk and White (Macmillan). This is a book about writing. It is a classic, though only 71 pages long. It offers 39 rules for effective written communication that you can actually understand and apply. This book has influenced not only writers, but also had a strong impact on programmers. The two classic works on programming technique, described below, were modeled after it.

The Elements of Programming Style, Kernighan and Plauger (McGraw-Hill). Kernighan and Plauger are to programming technique what Gilbert and Sullivan were to the operetta—the guys who set the standard and who everyone copied or acknowledged. (Brian Kernighan was one of the primary developers of the highly structured C language.) This book offers simple rules for writing solid programs and developing a good programming style.

BASIC with Style, Nagin and Ledgard (Hayden). This is a concise book on BASIC programming technique, close in spirit to Strunk and White's book on writing. All programmers in BASIC should read it.

Like books, magazines come in both general and machine-specific varieties. The number of good machine-specific magazines depends upon the popularity of the particular computer. Thus, you may find many on such computers as IBM PC, Apple, TRS-80, and Commodore 64, but very few on ATARI, Osborne, or ADAM computers. The content of a machine-specific magazine depends upon its editor's concept of the perceived needs of readers. Most of these magazines are aimed at users, not programmers, and emphasize application programs rather than programming. If you are not already subscribing to the magazines relating to your computer, check them out, see what they have to offer, and subscribe to the ones that appear worthwhile.

There are several useful non-system-specific magazines. The best of these, and granddaddy of them all, is *BYTE*. *Microcomputing* recently bit the dust, which is unfortunate, for it was one of the earliest magazines, and consistently published articles of interest to programmers. Another useful magazine is *InfoWorld*, a weekly that consistently prints the most up-to-date information you can get. Unlike most magazines, which usually have a three-month or greater delay between creating editorial content and publishing, *InfoWorld* works on a weekly deadline.

Chapter 3

Programming Tips

This chapter moves beyond the introductory material in Chapters 1 and 2 and gets into actual programming. It contains a series of tips designed to make your life as a programmer easier. Most of the information offered is based on my experience as a programmer, or the experience of other programmers I know.

This chapter also shows you a good way to structure a typical program. It describes the content and organization of the model program that is used throughout the rest of the book. This chapter presents the program framework; later chapters fill in the details.

Regard what is presented in this chapter as a set of recommendations, rather than a prescription that you must follow rigidly. How you design a program is very much a matter of style and personal preference. No one can write a rulebook that works for everyone. In defense of what is presented here, these techniques have worked well for me, and for others I know. They were not developed sitting behind a desk, but through a good deal of struggle and experience. They should help you as well. And by following them, you may be spared some of those unpleasant occurrences that are afterward referred to philosophically as "learning experiences."

This section presents a potpourri (a fancy name for a disorganized list) of programming tips. These include obvious things like backing up your files, and more complex things like making your program readable. There are 10 tips, and each is numbered. They were not handed down on stone tablets, nor are they numbered with Roman numerals. Still, they are commandments of a sort: Each begins with a predicate, and tells you something that you should or should not do. You get the idea.

1. BACK UP YOUR FILES

Ever lost a program or data file? If not, you are the first programmer in history who hasn't. It happens to everyone, even experienced programmers. The disk may become physically damaged. You know, you get frustrated, late at night, and attempt to jam the disk into the drive, or some other physical misfortune befalls it. The disk may wear out. This is rare, but sometimes occurs.

The most likely problem, however, is that some sort of human error occurs. You may overwrite a file, or otherwise make it useless. In a moment of carelessness, you may leave the disk lying on top of your 1954 Philco TV set, where the yoke of the picture tube scrambles the disk's magnetic medium.

Your disk directory may, for known or unknown reasons, suffer a stroke and make it impossible to access your files via the normal route. A solution to some such problems is to use a specific utility program to get at a file via the back door. But no utility program can save the day if the file is overwritten.

The only solution to such calamities is to avert them by backing up your disks with a sort of single-minded compulsiveness. You must back up any disk that is written to regularly. This includes both program and data disks, and also any utility disks that are written to.

Back up your data disks on some systematic basis, such as once a week or after each update is made to a set of data files. Backing up files this way is straightforward: Decide how often the disk needs to be backed up, and then get in the habit of doing it.

Backing up program disks is different from backing up data disks because—for a programmer

at least—a program disk is in a constant state of flux. During program development, the program constantly changes as newer versions replace older versions. What is the best way to handle backups in this situation?

One common way is to use two disks, labeled "Disk 1" and "Disk 2." The programmer works mainly with Disk 1, saving the developing program to it frequently. At intervals, Disk 1 is copied to Disk 2. How often? This usually depends on the programmer's paranoia and the number of recent bad experiences in losing program files. Basically, a trade-off is involved among the probability of Disk 1 becoming bad, the probability that Disk 1 already is bad, and the work involved in backing up Disk 1.

Another way of looking at it is that you do disk backup for insurance. Disk 2 is the insurance policy. But if what you copy to it from Disk 1 is bad, then your policy does not pay off. There is always the chance that Disk 1 may go bad in some way that you do not detect. For this reason, I suggest a somewhat more cautious approach to doing disk backups. It involves three disks instead of two. The recommended procedure is illustrated in Fig. 3-1, and works like this:

- Use three disks. Label these "Disk 1," "Disk 2," and "Disk 3."

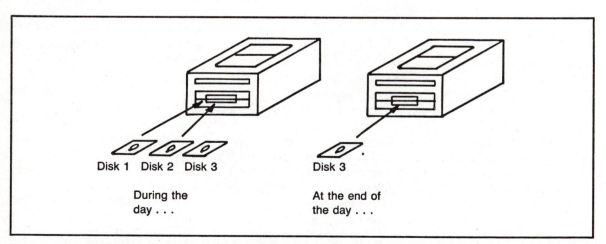

Disk 1   Disk 2   Disk 3   Disk 3

During the   At the end of
day . . .   the day . . .

Fig. 3-1. A three-disk backup procedure provides extra insurance against the loss of program files during program development. Disks 1 and 2 are periodically switched throughout the working session, and Disk 3 is copied only at the end of the session. Disk 3 thereby provides backup in case both Disks 1 and 2 lose an important file.

- Make Disk 1 your master. Work with it and keep the most current versions of all programs on it.
- As you make program changes, periodically switch between Disk 1 and Disk 2. Finish your working session with Disk 1 in the drive.
- At the end of the session, transfer your work to Disk 3. Disk 3 is your *archive copy*. It is what you fall back on if you lose useful copies of your work on both Disk 1 and Disk 2 during a working session. Do not transfer information to Disk 3 with a disk-disk copy program, such as IBM's DISKCOPY. Save your work with the SAVE command.

Disk 3 is your fallback insurance policy. It is updated once per working session, it contains draft versions of the program, and it is not meant to be a perfect copy of Disk 1. Rather, it contains snapshots of the program across time. If something should go wrong with both Disk 1 and Disk 2, you can pull Disk 3 out of your file and use it for a fresh start.

Never transfer all of Disk 1 to Disk 2 until you are sure that every file on Disk 1 is sound. The only way you can test this is to run the programs that Disk 1 contains or load each program separately and go through its listings to check it.

2. SAVE PROGRAMS CAREFULLY

As you develop a program, you must save it to disk countless times. Each time you issue a SAVE command you take the risk that you may save the program you are currently working on with the name of another program. The consequences may or may not be serious. They are not serious if you recognize the error and have a backup copy of the program just overwritten. They are serious if you overwrite a program that lacks a backup; whether or not you recognize the error at the moment is immaterial, for it will soon become apparent.

Minor mischief can also occur if you rely on your memory for the name of the program you save to disk. You may not recall the program's name exactly, and be forced to make your best guess as you save. You begin to recognize the limits of your memory when you examine the disk directory and discover that you have programs named BUDGET1.BAS, BUDG.BAS, BUDGT.BAS, and BUDGT1.BAS, or some other assortment of similar yet different names.

If your computer's line editor allows a line to be entered without regard to the position of the cursor on the line—most modern line editors do—make line 1 of your program a remark statement followed by the appropriate SAVE command. For example, with the IBM PC, use a line such as this:

```
1 REM SAVE"PROGNAME.BAS",A
```

Substitute your program's name for PROGNAME.BAS. To save the program, list line 1, space over or delete the line number and REM statement, and press the Return key. Your program will then be saved.

If your line editor requires the cursor to be at the end of the line to enter it—as with the Apple—then a different technique must be used. Here, the easiest way is to add a line containing the appropriate SAVE command, like this:

```
40000   PRINT CHR$(4);
        "SAVEPROGNAME.BAS,D1"
        :END
```

Then, to save the program type in GOTO 40000 from the keyboard and press the Return key. This line should be preceded by a line with an END or STOP statement to prevent your program from being unintentionally saved if control of the program happens to run past the last line.

Using such techniques makes it unnecessary for you to remember the program name, but it also serves another purpose, which is equally important: it acts as the program's identification. Every program should have its name prominently displayed somewhere. This is necessary because program files sometimes do get mixed up, despite the programmer's most careful efforts, and there should be some quick and convenient way to look at a program to tell what it is. In addition, it is quite easy for a programmer to lose track of the name of the program being worked on. This is unlikely if you work on one large program whose name is something short and simple like BUDGET, but very likely if your program consists of several subprograms with obscure or similar names, such as H3E, H4E, and H2I; or BUD0, BUD1, and BUD2. In short, it is good practice to identify the program internally, and the SAVE REM is a good place to do it.

3. PLAN YOUR VARIABLE ASSIGNMENTS

Many programmers assign variables as they develop a program, sort of pulling them out of the air. Some new part of the program must be written, and the programmer realizes that this requires a variable, an array, or whatever. The programmer then asks himself or herself what variable to use. The assignment cannot be made carelessly, or confusion with other variables may occur. The programmer tries to recall what variables are already in use, and makes up one that is not. In large programs this is difficult, as there may be scores or even hundreds of variables. One solution is to pick some really improbable variable name and use that. The alternative is to look at the program's listing and check every variable in use. Sound familiar?

We all do this, and get away with it to a certain extent. If the program is small, then we really can keep track of all the variables (and functions and arrays) inside of our heads. Beyond a certain point, however, we are only kidding ourselves, and risking some nasty variable confusions.

The best way to prevent variable confusion is to be systematic about making and keeping track of variable assignments. Make as many assignments as you can before you start coding. Decide what local and global variables you will need and assign as many of them as you can at the beginning. Local variables are the workhorses in most programs—they are used again and again, on a temporary basis, in many parts of a program. They are the faceless ones whose identities are constantly changing. Global variables have greater integrity—they are used to represent one thing.

After you have decided what variables you need, make a record that lists each one. For global

variables, list each variable and what it represents. Local variables usually have many different identities, often very briefly, so it does not always make sense to tell what they stand for. However, make a list of them. Examples of such documentation appear in Chapter 9.

You cannot possibly anticipate all variable assignments at the start, and so you must assign some new variables later on. When the time comes, check your records to see what variables are in use. By having a record, you can prevent making duplicate assignments. After you make the new assignment, document it. In short, keep a careful record as you go.

What should you name variables? The current thinking among people who study program documentation is that the more descriptive the label, the more readable the program. For example, if you want to store the value of a sale price in a variable, it would be a good idea to use something like SALEPRICE. Likewise, a good string variable for storing someone's name would be NAME$. It does not make much sense to follow this rule with local variables, since they do not represent a single thing. It makes sense for global variables, however.

One problem with long names is that they take up extra memory. How much extra depends upon the number of variables, but in most cases it will not have a serious overhead cost.

Many versions of BASIC allow you to represent a variable with more than two characters, but only pay attention to the first two characters. These versions do not discriminate, for example, between the two variables FARE and FACT. If you use long variable names, and your BASIC works this way, be very careful to avoid such confusions.

Variable names do not have to be complete words to be informative. An abbreviation that has a mnemonic relationship to the thing being represented is better than a name that has no relationship at all. For example, if you do not want to use SALEPRICE and NAME$, S and N$ are better than X1 and Q$. S and N$ bear a mnemonic relationship to *sale price* and *name*, but X1 and Q$ do not. The names that you assign—long, short, informative, uninformative—are much a matter of style and personal preference. Within this book, the tendency is not to use long variable names, but short ones that are meaningful mnemonics of what they represent. In some programs, long names may be better than the short ones used in these examples.

In making variable assignments, be careful to avoid reserved words. These words include all BASIC and DOS statements, commands, function names, and operator names. You are probably familiar with these terms already, but it is a good idea to locate them in your computer's manual and put a tab on the page so that you can find it quickly during programming.

Some versions of BASIC outlaw the use of reserved words as all or part of any variable name. Others, such as IBM PC BASIC, permit you to use a reserved word as part of a name. Thus, variable names such as ABSOLUTEMP#, INLET$, PECOS%, or AUTOPRICE are perfectly legal, but the reserved words they contain—ABS, LET, COS, AUTO—are not acceptable as variable names.

IBM PC BASIC has four DEFtype statements—DEFINT, DEFSNG, DEFDBL, and DEFSTR—which can be used for declaring variable types. Use of these statements is optional, but some programmers—especially those used to more structured languages such as Pascal, where such declarations are required—may be inclined to use them. If the DEF TYPE statements are used, they should be put at the beginning of the program, as they would be in a Pascal program, to document the variables in a formal way. While the notion underlying these statements is good (that a programmer should formally declare program variables before using them) there is a darker side to their use in BASIC programs that can sometimes cause problems. First, the DEF TYPE statements make weak rather than strong declarations, since a type statement occurring within a program always takes precedence over the original DEF TYPE statement. The following short program illustrates the problem:

```
10   DEFSNG E-G
20   E# = 1/3
30   PRINT E#
```

If you enter and run this program, the result printed is a long double-precision number. In other words, the declaration of all variables E through G as single-precision numbers on line 10 does not prevent you from redefining and using E as a double-precision number on lines 20 and 30. This ability gives you flexibility, but it also undercuts the restrictions that such declaration statements should impose on variable usage.

A second and in some way more serious problem is that declaration statements treat a variable without a type suffix (!, #, %, or $) according to the type defined in the DEF TYPE statement. This can sometimes produce peculiar results. This short program illustrates one of the problems that can occur.

```
10   DEFSTR A-D
20   C = 123.45
30   PRINT C
```

Running this program on an IBM PC produces a "Type mismatch error in 20" message. However, changing the program to read as follows makes everything work fine.

```
10   DEFSTR A-D
20   C = "123.45"
30   PRINT C
```

Since all variables from A through D were declared to be strings in line 10, any variable falling in that range without a suffix is treated as a string. Thus, the assignment statement on line 20 is perfectly legal, though not what most programmers are used to finding in a BASIC program. It would be far better, of course, to declare the variable's type each time it was used, since this makes its type explicit, and leaves no doubt. However, if you do this, then the bottom line is that DEFtype statements are not really necessary.

You may reach a point during coding where your records say that a particular variable is not in use, but you are not sure whether or not to believe them. At such times, it is very helpful to have a utility that will create a variable listing. You can do much the same thing by using a global search and replacement utility. When it comes time to make the assignment, it may occur to you that a particular variable would be logical on the basis of its mnemonic qualities. Use your global search and replacement utility to search your program to see if that variable is already in use. Either replace the variable with itself, or do not make any replacements. This will tell you if you can make the new assignment without conflicts.

4. MAKE YOUR PROGRAM READABLE

The BASIC programming language is widely criticized by computer scientists and others for its lack of readability. Some feel that the language itself, with its flexible control structure, ability to define data structures in the course of a program, and its mischievous GOTO statement, have cursed it with a sort of Original Sin that renders any program written in it unreadable.

However, the problem is not entirely in the BASIC language. Much of it lies in bad examples and bad advice about how to use it. The BASIC program examples printed in popular magazines tend to support the academicians' contentions, usually being incomprehensible without a written explanation. You can make a BASIC program very readable if you organize it logically, use remarks, and put only one program statement on each line. How many programs have you seen that were coded this way? Probably very few.

To add to the confusion, many authoritative sources offer programmers advice that, if followed, will tend to make their programs less readable. For example, the IBM PC BASIC manual, Appendix I, advises that you can improve program performance by minimizing the use of remarks and putting as many statements of code on each line as possible. This information is accurate, of course, but given without qualifications. Program speed is a good thing, and so is making a minimum demand on computer memory. However, leaving out remarks and bunching up program statements makes it much more difficult to read a program and understand what is going on in it. Actually, you can have it both ways (have a program that is both readable and fast) by creating two different versions of it. Code the program first for readability, and then optimize it

with a program compression or compilation utility. A compression utility of the sort described in Chapter 2 will remove remarks, and compress program statements onto as few lines as possible. Utilities are much better at doing this sort of thing than people. They do not mind working with long lines of code, and are indifferent to remarks. A programmer, on the other hand, finds it much easier to figure out that he or she is working on the Analysis Display Generator if there is a line of code containing a remark that says "Analysis Display Generator." Likewise, it is easier to change code if each statement is on a separate line.

Many of us have gotten the idea that using remarks is wasteful, a sign of amateurishness, or something we should avoid. We may have similar ideas about using only one program statement per line. These ideas are wrong. Forget what some programming manuals say, what bad code examples you have seen in magazines or books, or what your favorite computer genius does. Instead, write your program for clarity. Write it so that others will understand it. In doing this, you will make it much easier for you to understand, make it easier to modify, and reduce the chances of errors. Here are two simple rules for making a program readable:

- Use remarks liberally. Use them to identify the program modules and submodules within your program, to tell what is going on. Use enough remarks to tell the story.
- Use one program statement per line. This will make your program easier to read and to modify. After you see code written this way for a while, you may begin to like it. There is a sort of elegant simplicity in this style. It suggests an ordered mind, good work habits, solid character, and respect for one's fellow human beings. (Feel free to add other virtues to the list.)

These simple rules can make a world of difference in the readability of your programs. To illustrate, compare Figs. 3-2 and 3-3. The program listing in Fig. 3-2 follows these rules. The listing in Fig. 3-3 does not. Decide which one you would find the easiest to work with.

```
  0 REM Program with Sufficient Remarks for Readability
  1 REM SAVE"FIG3-2",A
12000 REM--Get Data Disk I.D.--
12010 INPUT"Type in data disk identification number: ";ID$
12020 IF LEN(ID$)=0 OR LEN (ID$))12 THEN BEEP: GOTO 12010
12030 GOSUB 8000:REM write data disk id to file
12040 GOSUB 8250:REM read array dimensioning parameters
12050 REM--dim new arrays--
12060 A=A%(0):REM array 1 dimension
12070 DIM O$(A),O(A),O1(A),O1%(A),O2%(A):REM name, acct bal, mo pmt, day of mo d
ue, term (months)
12080 A=A%(1)
12090 DIM P$(A),P(A),P1%(A),P2%(A):REM checkbook entry, amount, check#, day
12100 REM--Initialize Record--
12110 REM-Clear Data Files of Old Values-
12120 REM-Loan Data-
12130 FOR A=0 TO A%(0)
12140 O$(A)=""
12150 O(A)=0
12160 O1(A)=0
12170 O1%(A)=0
12180 O2%(A)=0
12190 NEXT
12200 REM-Payment Data-
12210 FOR A=0 TO A%(1)
12220 P$(A)=""
12230 P(A)=0
12240 P1%(A)=0
12250 P2%(A)=0
12260 NEXT
12270 REM--Collect User Data--
12280 GOSUB 20000:REM access data-entry module
12290 GOSUB 24000:REM sort file
12300 GOSUB 8500:REM write data file
12310 GOTO 10000:REM return to main menu
```

Fig. 3-2. Listing of a portion of program with sufficient remarks to make it readable.

You can make your listing even more readable by using a BASIC formatting utility of the type described in Chapter 2. Such a utility will usually separate and indent FOR-NEXT, IF-THEN, and WHILE-WEND statements to show program structure, break multiple statements into single lines, make remarks stand out, and perform other magic to make the listing easier to understand. To illustrate, Fig. 3-4 shows a formatted version of the listing shown in Figs. 3-2.

Some BASIC versions permit you to insert remarks into a program by placing them after either a REM statement or a single quotation mark or other character. Some programmers use two techniques within the same program, but it is better practice to use one technique consistently. Using REM is preferable, since it is more visible and easier to spot when searching through a listing. It also helps to make the content of the remark look different from the program to make it conspicuous. One way of doing this is to place some readily-recognizable characters (such as dashes or asterisks) at the start and end of the remark. Another is to use mixed- or lowercase characters in the remark to make it differ from the active statements of the program, most of which will normally appear in all uppercase characters. Clearly, these are not weighty matters, but you should consider them and make some rules for yourself to follow.

There are a few additional points about program compression or compilation that you should consider. When you compress or compile a program, save an uncompressed source code version of your program. You will need the source code version for making program changes later on. A compression utility will often pack the lines so tightly

```
0 REM Program without Sufficient Remarks for Readability
1 REM SAVE"FIG3-3",A
12010 INPUT"Type in data disk identification number: ";ID$
12020 IF LEN(ID$)=0 OR LEN (ID$))12 THEN BEEP: GOTO 12010
12030 GOSUB 8000
12040 GOSUB 8250
12060 A=AX(0)
12070 DIM O$(A),O(A),O1(A),O1X(A),O2X(A)
12080 A=AX(A)
12090 DIM P$(A),P(A),P1X(A),P2X(A)
12130 FOR A=0 TO AX(0)
12140 O$(A)=""
12150 O(A)=0
12160 O1(A)=0
12170 O1X(A)=0
12180 O2X(A)=0
12190 NEXT
12210 FOR A=0 TO AX(1)
12220 P$(A)=""
12230 P(A)=0
12240 P1X(A)=0
12250 P2X(A)=0
12260 NEXT
12280 GOSUB 20000
12290 GOSUB 24000
12300 GOSUB 8500
12310 GOTO 10000
```

Fig. 3-3. Listing of the same portion of the program shown in Fig. 3-2, but without any remarks. Although the BASIC statements are recognizable, the purpose of this program and what is going on in it are impossible to determine based on the listing alone.

```
0     REM Program with Sufficient Remarks for Readability

1     REM SAVE"FIG3-2",A

12000   REM--GET Data Disk I.D.--

12010   INPUT"Type in data disk identification number: ";ID$
12020   IF
          LEN(ID$)=0 OR LEN (ID$))12
            THEN
              BEEP:
              GOTO 12010
12030   GOSUB 8000:

        REM write data disk id to file

12040   GOSUB 8250:

        REM read array dimensioning parameters


12050   REM--DIM new arrays--

12060   A=AX(0):
```

Fig. 3-4. Listing of the program shown in Fig. 3-2, but formatted with a formatting utility that increases its readability.

```
         REM array 1 dimension

12070    DIM
            O$(A),
            O(A),
            O1(A),
            O1%(A),
            O2%(A):

         REM name, acct bal, mo pmt, day of mo due, term (months)

12080    A=A%(A)
12090    DIM
            P$(A),
            P(A),
            P1%(A),
            P2%(A):

         REM checkbook entry, amount, check#, day


12100    REM--INITIALIZE Record--

12110    REM-CLEAR Data Files of Old Values-

12120    REM-LOAN Data-

12130    FOR A=0 TO A%(0)
12140    |   O$(A)=""
12150    |   O(A)=0
12160    |   O1(A)=0
12170    |   O1%(A)=0
12180    |   O2%(A)=0
12190    NEXT

12200    REM-PAYMENT Data-

12210    FOR A=0 TO A%(1)
12220    |   P$(A)=""
12230    |   P(A)=0
12240    |   P1%(A)=0
12250    |   P2%(A)=0
12260    NEXT

12270    REM--COLLECT User Data--

12280    GOSUB 20000:

         REM access data-entry module

12290    GOSUB 24000:

         REM sort file

12300    GOSUB 8500:

         REM write data file

12310    GOTO 10000:

         REM return to main menu
```

that insertions are impossible. Thus, to make changes, you must go back to the source code version, modify it, and then recompress it. Maintain source code versions of programs on different disks from compressed versions. The source code is important. Treat it with great care. Put it safely away in a file with the program listing, rather than keeping it out among disks you actively work with.

Always make a listing of the source code version of your program. Making a listing of a compressed version is optional. It may help you troubleshoot a problem in the program, but it is fairly easy to relate a compressed program to the source code listing by following GOTO and GOSUB statements and variable names. If some problem does exist in the compressed version, attempt to produce the same problem in the source code version, and then work with it to correct the problem. Generally, it is not advisable to attempt to make changes to a compressed program because the statements are packed too closely.

5. PLAN AND ORGANIZE YOUR PROGRAMS CONSISTENTLY

Among creative people—and programmers usually are creative—consistency is not always a popular idea. The creative person does not like to be hemmed in by rules that hinder freedom of action. However, there is a powerful argument for consistency in programming: It reduces the amount that you must learn and remember, and thereby reduces the likelihood of errors. If you do things consistently, then there is less to learn, less to remember, and a smaller chance of misrecalling something and making a mistake.

If every one of your programs looks different from every other one, then the mysteries of each one must be fathomed separately. Each new program is a new adventure, planned from scratch, executed, and then put into use. Later on, when you go back to it, you must figure it out all over again.

A more sensible approach is to build all programs on the same basic model. Obviously, there is a limit to how completely you can do this. Different programs will do different things, and require different building blocks. However, a surprising amount of what you do from program to program remains the same. Usually a program requires you to do some or all of the following:

- Generate displays.
- Take user inputs.
- Control your program.
- Read and write data files.

Often, you can use the same (or very similar) subroutines for doing these things in many different programs. If you do this, then your programs begin to look similar, and this makes each one easier to understand and work on. Though such consistency is obviously not for everyone or for every program, it is a good ideal to keep in mind. If your programming style and application permit, you may find that it works very well for you. If you have not been programming this way in the past, it may take some getting used to.

To get started in this direction, you must first devise a plan (or *architecture*, to use the fancy word) that you can use as the framework for designing many of your programs. As you develop programs, start with this framework. Modify it to suit the specific application. If you do this, you will find that developing a new program becomes less a matter of spinning cloth from thin air and more a matter of taking parts of what you have done before, adapting them, and adding the new pieces that are necessary. All programmers do this to some degree, but some are more systematic about it than others. Try to be very systematic, if your personality and programming style permit it.

To illustrate one way of building a program framework, let us consider a model program. Different parts of this program contain different things. Later in this book, details will be added by showing subroutines and other elements of code that fit in each part of the model. The model is illustrated in Fig. 3-5, and is divided into three parts:

1. Setup Routines (lines 0 – 999)
2. Subroutines (lines 1000 – 9999)
3. Main Part of program (lines 10000 – 63999)

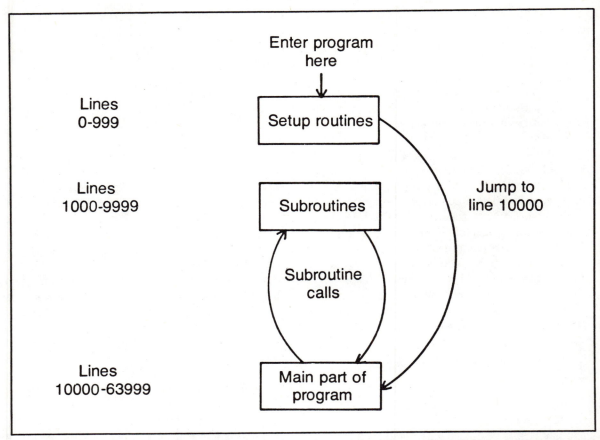

Fig. 3-5. A common way to build a program is to break it into three main parts, as shown here. Setup routines are placed first, followed by subroutines, which are given low line numbers to increase their speed of access. The main part of the program begins at line 10000.

When the program first starts, the setup routines are executed. These prepare the display, dimension arrays, define functions, and so forth.

The last line in the setup routines is the statement GOTO 10000, which jumps over the subroutines to the main part of the program. Subroutines are placed early in the program to increase the program's speed of execution. The lower their line numbers, the more quickly the computer can access and execute them.

The real action in the program is in its Main Part. The program's control structure and subroutine calls originate from there, and this is where the program's actual intelligence lies. The Setup Routines lay the program's foundation, and the Subroutines are workers called on to do different jobs. But what makes the program unique is what lies in its Main Part. In fact, most of what is transferable from program to program is what exists in the Setup Routines and Subroutines.

Most experienced programmers place frequently accessed subroutines early in their program. Some programmers prefer to place them ahead of everything else, and use the program organization shown in Fig. 3-6. The difference between this organization and that shown in Fig. 3-5 is that the locations of Setup Routines and Subroutines are reversed. This organization is satisfactory, but that shown in Fig. 3-5 will be used as the model in this book.

Returning to Fig. 3-5, let us consider what goes on inside each of the three main blocks of the program.

Setup Routines (Lines 0 – 999). When a program begins to execute, it must usually perform several functions to initialize the program. These functions generally include some or all of the following:

- Set up an error-handling routine.
- Clear the display screen.
- Display the program's title page.
- Deactivate certain keys (such as Break or Reset) to prevent the program from interrupting if the keys are touched by mistake during the program.
- If color is used, set the colors of the display border, background, and foreground.
- Assign constants with assignment statements and by reading DATA statements.
- Dimension arrays.

- Define functions.
- Obtain required inputs from the operator.
- Read the files necessary to initialize the program.

Most of these functions are optional, and some programs require additional functions to be performed during initialization. However, these are typical of many programs. The order in which they are performed is arbitrary, although some things must be done before others. In general, it is best to clear the display screen early, set the colors, and present the title page, if one is used. This keeps the user occupied, and averts the the impression that something is wrong as the computer sits there with a blank screen. Dangerous key combinations should be disabled before taking operator inputs.

Arrays must be dimensioned before assigning values to them with READ statements or reading files that use the arrays. And so on.

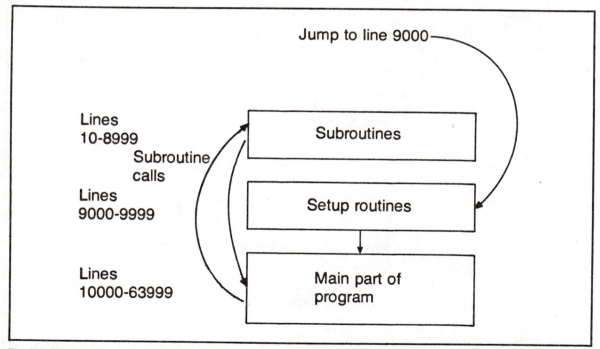

Fig. 3-6. An alternative to the program organization shown in Fig. 3-5. Here, subroutines are placed at the very beginning of the program, and setup routines afterward. This organization may result in slightly faster access to frequently used subroutines.

Figure 3-7 contains the listing of the setup routines in a hypothetical program for the IBM PC. This code performs all of the functions described earlier, and also includes a remark line that can be used to save the program (line 1), a copyright notice (lines 10–20), and a date (line 30).

Line 1 contains a remark statement which both identifies the program and can be used to save it. Line 2 sets up an error-handling routine (see Tip 10). Line 5 clears the screen. Lines 10 and 20 contain a copyright notice. Line 30 is the date the program was last updated. Line 40 calls a subroutine to deactivate "dangerous" keys such as the Ctrl + Break combination (see Tip 8).

Line 110 sets the colors of the screen, background and characters (see Chapter 4). Lines 200–240 assign constants. Lines 300–310 dimension arrays. Lines 400–410 define functions. Lines 500–540 assign constants by reading DATA statements. Lines 600–620 collect operator input.

Line 700 calls a subroutine that reads the program's setup file. Line 990 contains a GOTO statement that jumps program control to line 10000.

Subroutines (Lines 1000–9999). In locating your program's subroutines, you must take three main factors into account. First, you must divide the subroutine line range into different categories, depending upon the types of subroutines your program uses. This model uses four categories (Output, Input, Control, Files) plus a catch-all category of Miscellaneous. Second, you must allot enough lines to each category to include all of the subroutines it needs. Third, give the lowest line numbers to the subroutines that will be called most frequently.

The subroutine categories and line ranges assigned in the model program are as follows:

- Output (lines 1000–2999)
- Input (3000–3999)

```
0 REM Hypothetical Setup Routines
1 REM SAVE "FIG3-7.BAS",A
2 ON ERROR GOTO 9800:REM set up error-handling routine
5 CLS:REM clear screen
10 REM Copyright 1984 by Henry Simpson
20 REM All Rights Reserved
30 REM 6/15/84
40 GOSUB 9010:REM deactivate "dangerous" keys
100 REM--Set up Display--
110 COLOR 7,0:REM set display colors
200 REM--Assign Constants--
210 C1%=10
220 C2=.5
230 C3#=.333333432674408#
240 C$="sea string"
300 REM--Dimension Arrays--
310 DIM MONTH$(12):REM months of year
400 REM--Define Functions--
410 DEF FNPLUS(A,B)=A+B
500 REM--Read Months of Year--
510 DATA Jan,Feb,Mar,Apr,May,Jun,Jul,Aug,Sep,Oct,Nov,Dec
520 FOR A=1 TO 12
530 READ MONTH$(A)
540 NEXT
600 REM--Operator Input--
610 INPUT"Please type in your name: ";NAMES$
620 IF NAMES$="" GOTO 610
700 GOSUB 6200:REM read setup file
990 GOTO 10000:REM jump to main part of program
```

Fig. 3-7. Setup routines typical of those used early in a program to initialize the display, disable certain keys, dimension arrays, and perform other program start-up activities.

- Control (4000 – 5999)
- Files (6000 – 8999)
- Miscellaneous (9000 – 9999)

The subroutines presented later in this book are allocated line numbers according to this plan.

Main Part of Program (Lines 10000 – 63999). This part of the program comes at the end, and occupies the greatest range of lines. It is impossible to create a general model of its content, for it will differ from program to program. It will call on subroutines to perform their functions, and use built-in rules or operator input to control the flow of events. But beyond these simple things, little more can be said.

The way this model program is organized is but one of many. The important thing in this model is not so much what line numbers are assigned to different parts of the program, or even what parts of the program are included. Rather, it is that the program has a plan that is easy to describe and understand. The rest of this book will fill in the details of the plan, mainly by creating a set of model subroutines to go in the subroutine section of the model program.

6. CREATE A SUBROUTINE LIBRARY

If you tend to write programs that perform similar functions, subroutines can simplify your life a lot. Once you develop a good subroutine for reading a sequential file, clearing a portion of your display screen, or generating a menu, the problem is more or less solved. The next time you must perform that function, you can go to that subroutine, use it directly or modify it, and your problem is solved. Not only does this speed things up, but it reduces errors. Perfect and debug a subroutine once, and you never need do it again.

7. PROCEDURALIZE WHAT YOU DO

Proceduralization can be done in a variety of ways. The following are four specific examples of the general principle.

Example 1: Use of Subroutines. One important reason to use subroutines (see Tip 6) is that they reduce the amount of thinking that you must do. You take some complex function, package it in the form of a subroutine, and from that point on, all you need to perform the function is to set the arguments and call the subroutine with a GOSUB statement. What is inside the subroutine is transparent, and not really important to you as you write your program. By writing and then using that subroutine, you have proceduralized a complex function.

This use of subroutines is a specific example of the more general principle of proceduralization. The basic idea is that you should try to find ways to package the various functions that must be performed during programming to make them simpler. This applies to other areas of program development as well. Earlier in this chapter, this simple, one-line routine was presented for saving a program to disk:

```
1 REM SAVE "PROGNAME.BAS",A
```

This is an example of proceduralization. This routine saves time, reduces work, and reduces the demand on memory and the likelihood of error.

Example 2: Program Disk Preparaton. Prepare your program disks so that they are formatted properly and include the program and other files needed to be useful during program development. If your disks are ready to use, then you do not have to take time out during programming to transfer support programs or files to them, or to start over on a new disk that has DOS on it.

Some types of DOS give you the option of including or not including DOS on your disks. Including DOS requires additional disk space, but it is generally a good idea to include it since this makes the disk competent on its own to start your system and get your program running. It also saves you the trouble of swapping between a disk with DOS and the one you want to work on.

If your BASIC language is stored on disk and not on ROM, include your BASIC file on the disk. If you consistently use a utility program, such as a separate line editor or renumbering program, include this program on disk. You may also want to add a start-up program that will automatically activate these utilities when you boot the disk. If your program has function keys, and you find it useful to redefine them for use during programming, then you should write and include a BASIC program (called something logical, like KEYS) that will make the key assignments for you quickly and conveniently (see below).

Including DOS and other files on your program disk does take up space, and in some cases this may pose problems. Obviously, if you lack sufficient room for everything, then the support programs, DOS, or both, must go. The place to start, however, is with them there, the logic being that they will save you time during the development process.

Example 3: Use of Function Keys. Some computers are equipped with function keys that can be defined to perform a specific function when pressed. True function keys are continuously "alive," and do not require a particular line of a program to be executed to have an effect. The function keys of the IBM PC, for example, work this way. Many less expensive computers have keys labeled function keys which (except for labeling) are like the letter and number keys on the keyboard. These are not true function keys because they are active only when the particular lines of code being executed are able to sense them. The keys on the C-64, for example, work this way.

True function keys are obviously more powerful, and can come in quite handy during programming. If your computer has such keys, make full use of them during programming. For example, use them to store certain frequently repeated sequences of keystrokes in order to save work, time, and effort during programming. Word processing programs usually assign text-editing functions to these keys. A program used for displaying graphics usually assigns common graphic manipulation functions to the keys. And, for programing, common program development functions should be assigned to the keys. For example, with the IBM PC, the following functions are assigned to the 10 function keys:

F1	LIST
F2	RUN + Enter key
F3	Load"
F4	SAVE"
F5	CONT + Enter key
F6	,"LPT1:"
F7	TRON + Enter key
F8	TROFF + Enter key
F9	KEY
F10	SCREEN 0,0,0 + Enter key

For program development purposes, you may want to modify such assignments. The best assignments for function keys depend upon what types of programming tasks you are performing, your personal working style, and the stage of program development. There is probably no ideal set of function key assignments for all programmers and all programming tasks, but it is a fair bet that you can improve on the assignments of the manufacturer.

Here are my personal preferences for the assignment of the keys on the IBM PC. I seldom use any of the functions called with IBM's assignments, except for F2 through F4, but there are several missing ones that I do use.

F1—I tend to clear the screen before listing a program, and so I change the assignment of F1 to clear the screen and then list the program.

F2 through F4—These assignments are left unchanged.

F5—EDIT. Handy for displaying a line prior to editing it.

F6—FILES + Enter key. Useful for finding out what programs are on the disk in the default drive.

F7—DELETE. Useful during editing, to remove one or more lines from the program.

F8—REM. Consistent with the emphasis in this book on using remarks in programs, I tend to use a lot of REM statements.

F9—LIST 1 + Enter key + two Cursor up keys + five spaces. Press this key and line 1 of your program as listed, and the cursor moves up and spaces over the line number and REM, enabling you to save the program simply by pressing the Enter key—provided, of course, that line 1 of your program contains a remark with a SAVE statement, as described above.

F10—CLS + Enter key. This simply clears the screen.

Figure 3-8 is the listing of a program that can be used to make the Function key assignments described above. No one in their right mind would type in the assignments of all these keys through the keyboard each time because it is too much trouble. It is much easier, therefore, to write a little program such as this to do the work for you. Line 1 is a SAVE REM of the type described earlier. Lines 10, 20, and 30 assign appropriate character strings to ENTER$ (Enter key), QUOTE$ (single quotation mark), and UP$ (Cursor up key), respectively. Lines 40 – 130 then make the key assignments.

The purposes of lines 140 – 170 are not as obvious. Line 140 turns the key assignments on row 25 of the display on. This is necessary if this program is called from an AUTOEXEC.BAT file when the system is initialized, because IBM DOS 2.1 will not automatically turn row 25 on. Line 150 clears the screen. Line 160 causes the disk directory to be displayed. And line 170 erases the key assignment program from memory, thereby paving the way for the next program. (This line does the same thing to the program that the time traveler did to himself when he accidentally killed his great-great grandfather, thereby making himself nonexistent.)

If you create this type of program, make sure that you save it before running it.

After this lengthy discussion of how to save programs, prepare disks, and use function keys, it is just possible that some readers may have lost track of the more fundamental point that all of these specific examples illustrate: *proceduralization*. Keep in mind that this is a general principle that applies throughout most aspects of programming, and that you should be on the lookout for ways to apply it. The objective, as always, is to make things simpler for you and to reduce errors.

8. BEWARE THE DANGEROUS KEYS

"Dangerous" keys are keys which, if activated alone or in combination with other keys, may interrupt a BASIC program. These vary from computer to computer, and have different effects depending upon the situation. Examples of such keys on the IBM PC are Ctrl + Alt + Del, which restarts the system, and Ctrl + C and Ctrl + Break, which may interrupt the program. Analogous keys on the Apples are Ctrl + C and Ctrl + Reset, and on the C-64 are RUN/STOP and RESTORE. These keys were provided for a purpose: namely, to give the program user the power to stop the program that is currently running in order to do something else. Moreover, since most are key combinations

```
0   REM SAVE "FIG3-8.BAS",A
1   REM SAVE "KEYS.BAS",A
10  ENTER$=CHR$(13):REM Enter key
20  QUOTE$=CHR$(34):REM "
30  UP$=CHR$(30):REM Cursor up key
40  KEY 1,"CLS:LIST "
50  KEY 2,"RUN"+ENTER$
60  KEY 3,"LOAD"+QUOTE$
70  KEY 4,"SAVE"+QUOTE$
80  KEY 5,"EDIT "
90  KEY 6,"FILES"+ENTER$
100 KEY 7,"DELETE "
110 KEY 8,"REM "
120 KEY 9,"LIST 1"+ENTER$+UP$+UP$+"        "
130 KEY 10,"CLS"+ENTER$
140 KEY ON
150 CLS
160 FILES
170 NEW
```

Fig. 3-8. IBM PC function key definition program.

that require more than one key to be pressed, there is a built-in safety factor. That is, the user is unlikely to press two keys simultaneously by accident.

However, in some cases it is a good idea to deactivate one or more of these keys in order to prevent them from being pressed for either accidental or intentional reasons. For example, you do not want the program user to interrupt the program while a file is being written, if interruption will cause data to be lost, or in a host of other situations. What keys to deactivate, when to deactivate them, and when to reactivate them (if done) depend upon the particular program, and you must be the judge of these matters.

How do you deactivate such keys? The answer depends very much on the particular computer. It would be nice if all versions of BASIC had a statement (such as DEACTIVATE *keyname*) that could be executed early in the program to lock out certain keys. To my knowledge, no such statement exists in any dialect of BASIC, although it is badly needed. The key deactivation techniques are generally of the back door type, not well documented, and only come to light in occasional magazine articles or through furtive phone calls to friends who are professional programmers and whose employers usually regard such tricks as trade secrets.

To illustrate key deactivation, what follows are descriptions of ways to deactivate the dangerous keys of the IBM PC, Apple, and C-64. The IBM technique works on the IBM PC, PCjr, PC XT, and PC AT. The Apple technique works on all Apple II-series computers. The C-64 trick works strictly on the C-64. As you read on, you will discover that the keys on each machine are deactivated in entirely different ways. With the IBM PC, function keys are defined to trap the unwanted keys; with the Apple, a series of values is poked into memory locations to redirect the Reset vector; and with the C-64, two values are poked into memory to turn off the keys.

IBM PC Key Deactivation. It is more difficult to trap (that is, intercept) some IBM PC keys than others. For example, you can easily trap any

key that has an ASCII code by simply using an IF-THEN statement. If you want to prevent someone from using an ampersand (&) in what they type, you can do it by using a statement such as the following:

```
10000   A$ = INKEY$:IF A$ = " " THEN 10000
10010   IF A$ = "&" GOTO 10000
```

Line 10010 looks for the unwanted character and, discovering it, sends control back to the previous line, thus keeping the program in a loop until some other key is pressed.

Unfortunately, you cannot use this technique for the three key combinations of concern, and certain others, since they do not display recognizable characters or have standard ASCII codes (try, for example, to find the ASCII code for a Ctrl + Break in your BASIC manual). However, there is another approach to key trapping, and it involves using the KEY, KEY (n) ON, and ON KEY (n) statements to trap the unwanted keys. The technique requires advanced BASIC (BASICA or PCjr Cartridge BASIC) and will not work with standard disk BASIC. This technique was not documented in the first edition of IBM's BASIC manual, although it is documented, interestingly, in the BASIC manual for the PCjr, and the PC manual may be updated by the time you read these words.

In order to trap the keys, you must use *scan codes* instead of ASCII codes or characters. The scan codes for the IBM PC are shown in Fig. 3-9 to the left of the keys. For example, the scan code for the Scroll Lock/Break key is 70, for the C key is 46, and for the Delete key is 83. A scan code is the code your keyboard generates internally and sends to its system unit. The system unit then interprets this code, converting it into the appropriate ASCII value, or into a code that indicates that the key requires special handling. The three key combinations of concern require special handling because they send an interrupt through the PC.

By using the scan codes, however, you can intercept the key signals before they have a chance to interrupt your PC. Here is what is involved in setting and activating the traps:

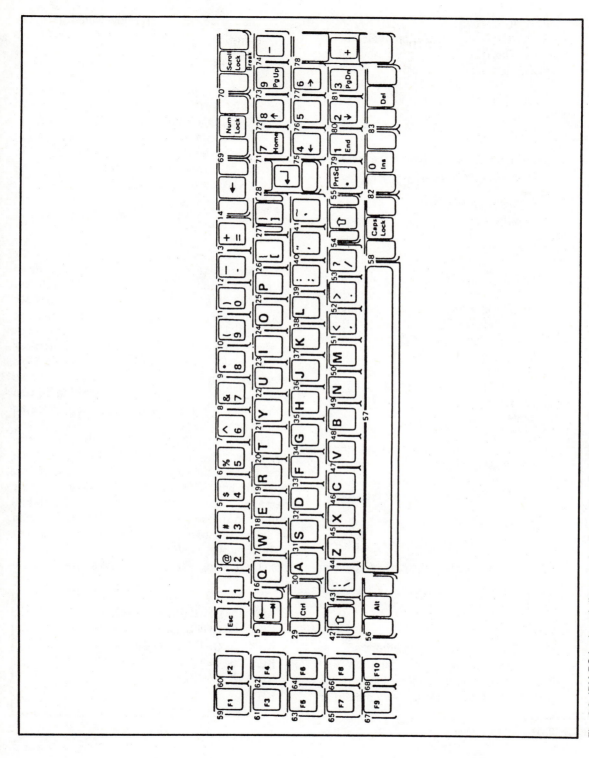

Fig. 3-9. IBM PC keyboard diagram showing scan codes of keys. (Courtesy of IBM Corporation.)

1. Activate BASICA.
2. Select the key combinations you want to trap. The three key combinations under discussion are:

   Ctrl + Alt + Del (3 keys)
   Ctrl + C (2 keys)
   Ctrl + Scroll Lock/Break (2 keys)

3. Determine the Shift Code of the combination. Shift codes are as follows:

   Unshifted key: 0
   Shifted key: 1
   Ctrl: 4
   Alt: 8

   If shift combinations are used (such as Ctrl + Alt) the shift code is the sum of the individual codes. For example, the shift code for the Ctrl and Alt keys used together is 12, and for the Shift and Ctrl keys used together is 5.
4. Determine the scan code of the final key that is to be pressed. The scan codes of the three keys of interest are 70, 46, and 83, as noted earlier.
5. Use key numbers 15 through 20 to create one or more routines to trap the key combinations. Use the KEY statement to define the key combinations to trap. The format of the KEY statement is as follows:

   Key n, CHR$(Shift Code) + CHR$ (Scan Code)

   For example, to trap the Ctrl + C key com-

bination, the expression would look like this:

   KEY 15, CHR$(4) + CHR$(46)

Some additional examples are shown in Fig. 3-10.

6. Add ON KEY(n) and KEY(n) ON statements to activate the traps. For example, to activate the trap for the "A" key, include these two statements after the KEY statement itself:

   ON KEY (15) GOSUB line number
   KEY (15) ON

Figure 3-11 is the listing of a subroutine that deactivates the three dangerous keys according to the procedure outlined above. Lines 9010, 9020, and 9030 are the KEY statements. Lines 9040, 9050, and 9060 contain the ON KEY(n) and KEY(n) ON statements to activate key trapping. These latter three lines each contain a GOSUB statement that accesses a subroutine at line 9080. This subroutine does nothing more than beep the speaker, but you can have the subroutine do less or more than this, depending upon the requirements of your program.

For example, you can make your program simply ignore the trapped keys by having the subroutine consist only of the RETURN statement. You can have the subroutine display an error message. You can also use the RETURN line number format (for example, RETURN 10000) in the subroutine to direct control to a particular part of the program, such as the main menu. If you do this, then using the trapped keys works as an

Trap for "a" key	KEY 15, CHR$(0) + CHR$(30)
Trap for "A" key	KEY 15, CHR$(1) + CHR$(30)
Trap for Alt + A combination	KEY 15, CHR$(8) + CHR$(30)
Trap for Ctrl + A combination	KEY 15, CHR$(4) + CHR$(30)
Trap for Ctrl + C combination	KEY 15, CHR$(4) + CHR$(46)
Trap for Ctrl + Alt + Del combintion	KEY 15, CHR$(12) + CHR$(83)

Fig. 3-10. Trapping for various keys and key combinations.

```
Ø REM "Dangerous" Key Deactivation Subroutine
1 REM SAVE"FIG3-10.BAS",A
9000 REM--Deactivate "Dangerous" Keys--
9010 KEY 15,CHR$(12)+CHR$(83):REM Ctrl Alt Del
9020 KEY 16,CHR$(4)+CHR$(46):REM Ctrl C
9030 KEY 17,CHR$(4)+CHR$(70):REM Ctrl Break
9040 ON KEY (15) GOSUB 9080:KEY(15) ON
9050 ON KEY (16) GOSUB 9080:KEY(16) ON
9060 ON KEY (17) GOSUB 9080:KEY(17) ON
9070 RETURN
9080 BEEP
9090 RETURN
```

Fig. 3-11. IBM PC subroutine to deactivate "dangerous" key combinations.

escape mechanism for the operator. However, you must be cautious about having the program execute such a nonstandard RETURN, since pending GOSUBs, FORs, or WHILEs remain active and may, like unpaid bills, cause problems later.

Once you have created a key-trapping routine such as described above, you may want to deactivate it within the program. It is much easier to do this than it is to activate the subroutine, and only requires the KEY (n) OFF statement. Figure 3-12 is the listing of a subroutine that cancels the three key traps created by the subroutine shown in Fig. 3-11.Once the deactivation subroutine has been activated, the keys operate normally.

It is a good idea to try these routines out before using them in an actual program. You can do this by creating a short program that includes both subroutines, an INKEY$ loop, and a way to call either subroutine selectively. The following lines, combined with the two subroutines, will do the trick:

```
10   REM—Key Test Subroutine—
30   A$ = INKEY$
```

```
40   IF A$ = "D" THEN GOSUB 9000:REM deac-
     tivate dangerous keys
50   IF A$ = "A" THEN GOSUB 9100:REM ac-
     tivate dangerous keys
60   GOTO 30
```

When you run this program, typing in D deactivates the dangerous keys and typing in A activates them. Save the program to disk before running it, since using the Ctrl + Alt + Del combination when these keys are active will restart the system and cause the program to disappear from memory

Apple Key Deactivation. There are a number of ways to deactivate the Ctrl + Reset key combination. These generally involve poking a series of values into memory to change the routing of the reset vector so that, instead of interrupting the program, control is sent to a designated program line. Figure 3-13 contains the listing of a routine that will poke in the required values and send program control to the line designated by the variable A in line 9020, that is, line 10000. Once the keys are deactivated, the Ctrl + Reset key combination will no longer interrupt the program, but will simply send

```
Ø REM "Dangerous" Key Reactivation Subroutine
1 REM SAVE"FIG3-11.BAS",A
9100 REM--Activate "Dangerous" Keys--
9110 KEY (15) OFF
9120 KEY (16) OFF
9130 KEY (17) OFF
9140 RETURN
```

Fig. 3-12. IBM PC subroutine to reactivate dangerous keys deactivated by subroutine shown in Fig. 3-11.

```
0    REM    FIG 3-12
1    REM    CTRL-RESET DEACTIVATION ROUTINE
9010   REM --RESET TRAP--
9020 A = 10000
9030   FOR B = 768 TO 787
9040   READ C
9050   POKE B,C
9060   NEXT
9070   DATA 32,234,3,32,251,218,169,0,133,81,169,100,133,
       80,32,65,217,76,210,215
9080   POKE 1010,0
9090   POKE 1011,3
9100   POKE 1012,166
9110   POKE 775,A / 256
9120   POKE 779,A -   PEEK (775) * 256
9130   RETURN
```

Fig. 3-13. Apple II subroutine to deactivate Ctrl+Reset key.

control to line 10000. Line 10000 can contain anything, but normally it should be some central point in the program, such as the main menu.

The Ctrl+C key combination is trapped with an error-handling routine based on the ONERR GOTO statement. Error-handling routines are discussed in greater detail under Tip 10, below.

C-64 Key Deactivation. You can deactivate the RUN/STOP and RESTORE keys with this statement:

POKE 808,225

After this statement has been executed, the user can press either of these keys, or both together, and the C-64 remains unimpressed. It is as deaf to these keys then as if the user tapped on the tabletop or scratched a toe. You can reactivate both keys with this statement:

POKE 808,237

If you decide to use key deactivation code in your program, test it but keep it from functioning during program development. If you deactivate all of your interrupt key combinations, then you will be unable to stop your program when you want to. The easiest way to have the routine both in and out is to incorporate it in a subroutine (such as Fig. 3-11

or 3-13) and then convert the subroutine call to a remark statement such as this:

40   REM GOSUB 9010:REM deactivate "dangerous" keys

Leave the REM there while you develop the program, and delete it when the program is finished in order to make the subroutine call functional.

9. BUILD A "TURNKEY" SYSTEM

A turnkey system is one that works properly with a minimum of operator intervention. For example, a turnkey system for nonprogrammers is usually designed in such a way that the user does not have to interact with the program at the level of DOS or BASIC, but can work with something that is simpler to grasp and less prone to error.

One of the most common features of a turnkey system is that the operator is required to do nothing more to get the system going than to turn on (or execute a restart of) the computer. Once the computer comes to life, it automatically loads DOS, then BASIC, and then runs the program. The operator is not required to know or to type in any DOS or BASIC commands. The system also allows the user to move between subprograms easily, by linking them together in a single package, instead of requiring the user to exit one subprogram, return to BASIC, and then load and run the next. Disk insertions and removals are minimized, and those that are required are fully prompted. The objective is to have the system do as much as possible in order to minimize the user's decision-making and work.

While turnkey systems are generally thought of as being aimed at unsophisticated program users, it is sometimes useful to apply this technique to sophisticated users, such as yourself. For example, as discussed in Tip 7, it is often helpful to the programmer to prepare working program disks with a function-key definition program that executes automatically when the computer is turned on. The program described earlier actually does three things: defines function keys, clears the screen, and displays the disk directory.

With most BASIC dialects, it is relatively easy to create a start-up file. For example, with IBM PC BASIC, the most straightforward method is to create an AUTOEXEC.BAT file containing the command BASIC or BASICA followed by the name of the program you want to have executed when the computer is turned on. When the computer starts up, it will look for this file and, if it is present, will execute the commands it contains. If the file contains BASIC and a file name, then BASIC will be put into memory, and the program will then be loaded and executed.

With the Apple, a similar technique is used, although the approach differs depending upon whether DOS 3.3 or ProDOS is used. With DOS 3.3 the simplest way is to initialize a disk (with the INIT command), using the name of the program that is to begin execution when the disk is booted. For example, if you want the program MENU to execute, simply initialize the disk with the command INIT MENU. Then create or transfer the files to that disk. From that point on, whenever the disk is booted, or an appropriate PR# or IN# command is given, the program called MENU will be executed. With ProDOS, self-starting is a bit more involved. ProDOS does not have an INIT command. Instead, disks are initialized with the ProDOS Filer utility program. Once the disk has been created, Filer is used to transfer the ProDOS and BASIC.SYSTEM files to the formatted disk. When such a disk is booted, it will activate, in turn,

ProDOS, BASIC.SYSTEM, and then go looking for a file named STARTUP to run. The STARTUP file will be executed in the same manner as a greeting program on a DOS 3.3 disk. You can put whatever you want in STARTUP—it can be the program you want to run, or another program that calls the program you want to run.

The C-64 (and certain other computers with limited DOSs), lacks the resident DOS commands required to enable automatic start-up of programs.

10. HANDLE ERRORS

A variety of errors can occur during a program's operation. These errors can be divided into three categories, based on who is responsible:

- Computer—For example, an internal malfunction occurs in BASIC.
- Programmer—For example, the programmer left a syntax error in the code.
- Operator—For example, the operator attempts to print a report but cannot because the printer is out of paper.

The first type of error is rare and can, for most purposes, be safely ignored. It may sound computer chauvinistic, but the fact is that the microcomputer, unlike its human programmers and operators, seldom makes errors.

The second type of error is more common. In developing any program, errors are inevitable, and the programmer learns to deal with them. Dealing with them does not mean living with them (tolerating their continued existence) but it does mean expecting them and working systematically to get rid of them. Before a program is put into use by operators, the programmer should be confident that its code is free of errors. The probability that a program actually is free of errors is a function of many factors; the three most important are programmer skill, program complexity, and the amount of time devoted to program testing. Since no programmer can guarantee that a program is completely free of errors, these types of errors can and do occur.

The third type of error—operator error—is

usually the most common. Even skilled operators make such mistakes as leaving a disk drive door open, putting the wrong disk into the drive, and leaving their printer turned off when it should be on.

Error conditions in BASIC or DOS usually cause the program to crash. This can be very irritating to operators, especially if they have spent time entering data or doing other work that the crash kills. Programmers sometimes face the same problem during program development. Trying out a program at this stage can be a little like walking through a mine field. You may want to clear a particular part of the mine field without getting blown up on the terrain you must cross to get there. That is, you may want to ignore certain errors temporarily in order to work on fixing others.

For these reasons, you should include an error-handling routine in your programs. An error-handling routine informs the operator that an error condition exists, describes the condition, and may do more (such as give the programmer's telephone number). More importantly, it prevents the program from crashing, and thereby allows pending business—using the program or debugging it—to be finished without interruption.

The key to error-handling is the BASIC statement ON ERROR GOTO or its equivalent. This statement, followed by the line number at which the error-handling routine starts, is typically placed very early in the program. For example, this statement, located at line 2, will handle errors with a routine that starts at line 9800:

```
2  ON ERROR GOTO 9800
```

In simple BASIC dialects such as that of the Apple, the error-handling routine is not required (by BASIC or DOS) to contain anything special, and may simply be a safe line to send control to when the error occurs. More sophisticated versions, such as that of the IBM PC, require that an error-handling routine contain at least a RESUME statement. In either case, after an error occurs and control has been sent to the line, something more than merely continuing the program should happen. The operator needs to be alerted to the existence of the error condition, its nature, and perhaps given a corrective action. Doing less than this is like sweeping dust under a rug. It may hide the problem, but will not help anyone identify or get rid of it. The routine should also identify the error so that corrective action can be taken.

When an error condition occurs, BASIC usually returns error data in some form. In the IBM PC it assigns the data to the variables ERR (error code of last error) and ERL (line number at which error occurred). With the Apple, BASIC sends error data to memory locations 222, 218, and 219. Error code number can be determined by peeking at memory location 222, like this:

```
CODE = PEEK (222)
```

CODE can be translated to error type by referring to BASIC and DOS error codes. For example, 0 corresponds to a "NEXT without FOR" error, error 16 a BASIC syntax error, and so on.

The line number at which the error occurred can be determined by peeking at memory locations 218 and 219, like this:

```
LINE = PEEK (218) + PEEK (219)*256
```

Once the error data have been obtained, you can easily construct a statement to print out the relevant error information. For example, this will work for the IBM PC:

```
9800  REM—Error-Handling Routine—
9810  PRINT "Error code #";ERR;"in program
      line #";ERL
9820  RESUME
```

A simple routine such as this will print the error information on the screen wherever the cursor happens to be, and then resume the program immediately. While this routine will do the job, and may be fine for programmers, it has two shortcomings: It does not identify the error, but gives an error code that must be looked up in a manual; and it does not cause a pause in the program. An error-handling routine should, generally, include both of these features.

In order to identify errors, your error-handling

routine must relate the error code, ERR, to a relevant error message. Thus, you can have your routine test for certain ERR codes and print out the appropriate error message. The following code illustrates the technique.

```
9912  IF ERR=53 THEN PRINT "File not
      found"
9914  IF ERR=58 THEN PRINT "File already
      exists"
   •
   •
   •
```

One problem is that there are usually many error codes and many possible error messages—too many to include in an error-handling routine. A strategy is needed to reduce the list to a more practical size. The basis for this reduction is the three categories of errors that were given earlier; namely, computer, programmer, and operator errors. As noted, computer errors are rare, and program errors should be rare, but operator errors are fairly common. The strategy, therefore, is to have the error-handling routine provide detailed information on operator errors, but more generalized information on other types of errors. Fortunately, this is a workable strategy because there are usually only a few error codes that concern operator errors. These codes relate mainly to disk operations, the printer, and other hardware devices for whose proper functioning the operator can generally be held accountable.

Let us now see how these ingredients can be put together into a more sophisticated error-handling routine. Figure 3-14 is the listing of a routine for the IBM PC that performs the following tasks:

1. Clears the screen.
2. Alerts the operator.
3. Displays the error code number and line number.
4. Displays an error message.
5. Inserts a temporary pause, until the space bar is pressed.
6. Resumes program operation at line 10000.

The subroutine consisting of lines 4010 – 4080

```
0 REM Error-Handling Routine (full screen)
1 REM SAVE"FIG3-13.BAS",A
4010 REM--Temporary Pause Subroutine--
4020 LOCATE 23,WIDE%/2-13
4030 COLOR 16,7:REM inverse flash
4040 PRINT"[Press Space Bar to Continue]";
4050 COLOR 7,0:REM normal video
4060 A$=INKEY$:IF A$()" " GOTO 4060
4070 PRINT
4080 RETURN
9800 REM--Error-Handling Routine (full screen)--
9804 REM NOTE:
9805 REM if using 40-column display, subtract 20 from
9806 REM second argument of all LOCATE statements
9810 BEEP
9820 CLS
9830 LOCATE 6,33
9840 COLOR 0,7:REM inverse
9850 PRINT "ERROR CONDITION"
9860 COLOR 7,0:REM normal video
9870 LOCATE 10,30
9880 PRINT"ERROR CODE #:    ";ERR
9890 LOCATE 12,30
9900 PRINT"PROGRAM LINE #: ";ERL
9910 E$="Program or file error"
9912 IF ERR=53 THEN E$="File not found"
```

Fig. 3-14. IBM PC full-screen error-handling routine.

```
9914 IF ERR=58 THEN E$="File already exists"
9916 IF ERR=61 THEN E$="Disk is full"
9918 IF ERR=70 THEN E$="Disk is write-protected"
9920 IF ERR=71 THEN E$="Disk is not ready"
9922 IF ERR=72 THEN E$="Disk media error"
9924 IF ERR=73 THEN E$="Advanced BASIC needed"
9926 IF ERR=24 OR ERR=25 OR ERR=57 THEN E$="Device or I/O error"
9928 IF ERR=7 OR ERR=14 THEN E$="Out of memory"
9930 LOCATE 14,30
9940 COLOR 1,0:REM underline
9950 PRINT E$
9960 COLOR 7,0:REM normal video
9970 E$=""
9980 GOSUB 4010:REM temporary pause
9990 RESUME 10000
```

is not part of the error-handling routine, but is used by it. This subroutine inserts a temporary pause in the program, until the space bar is pressed. Line 4020 moves the cursor to row 24 and column 26 (the bottom of the screen). Line 4030 converts to inverse flashing print mode. Line 4040 prints the message "Press Space Bar to Continue", centered and at row 24 of the screen. Line 4050 converts back to normal video. And line 4060 is an INKEY$ loop that cycles until the space bar is pressed.

The error-handling routine consists of lines 9800–9990. Lines 9800–9950 alert the operator

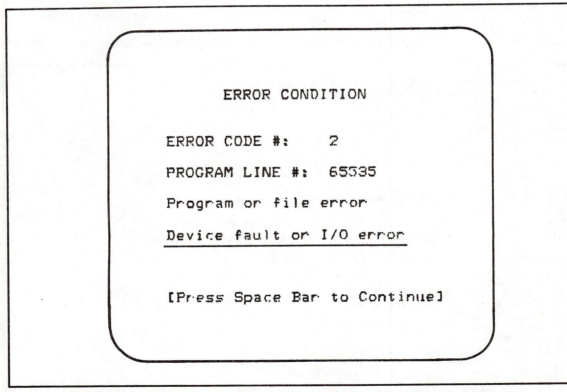

ERROR CONDITION

ERROR CODE #:   2

PROGRAM LINE #: 65535

Program or file error

Device fault or I/O error

[Press Space Bar to Continue]

Fig. 3-15. Appearance of display screen when error-handling routine (Fig. 3-14) encounters an error.

by clearing the screen, causing a speaker beep, and printing the message "ERROR CONDITION" centered and at row 6 of the screen. Lines 9870 – 9900 display the error code and error line number. Lines 9910 – 9928 then determine the appropriate error message. The default message is set at line 9910—"Program or file error". Most nonoperator errors fit in this category, or at least come close. Lines 9912 – 9928 then perform IF-THEN tests to assign an error message string to the string variable E$ based on the error codes of the most common operator errors. Lines 9930 – 9950 then print the error message, underlined. Line 9970 sets E$ to the null string, line 9980 calls the temporary pause subroutine, and line

9990 tells the program to RESUME at line 10000. Note that the error-handling message assignment code (lines 9910 – 9928) could be made faster by including GOTO 9930 statements at the end of each line, but a few bytes of memory can be saved by omitting this code, and with luck this routine will not be executed often enough for the loss of speed to matter.

The actual appearance of the screen when an error condition occurs is shown in Fig. 3-15. Figure 3-16 contains an equivalent error-handling routine for the Apple.

In some programs, you may not want to disrupt the entire screen to display the error information, but rather, to display the message on a single line.

```
1   REM   ERROR-HANDLING ROUTINE (FULL SCREEN)
4010   REM --TEMPORARY PAUSE SUBROUTINE--
4020   VTAB 23: HTAB 6: REM  USE HTAB 26 FOR 80-COLUMN DISPLAY
4030   FLASH : REM  USE INVERSE IF USING 80-COLUMN CARD
4040   PRINT "(PRESS SPACE BAR TO CONTINUE)";
4050   NORMAL
4060   GET A$: IF A$ < > " " GOTO 4060
4070   PRINT
4080   RETURN
9800   REM  --ERROR-HANDLING ROUTINE (FULL SCREEN)--
9804   CALL  - 198
9808 CODE =  PEEK (222)
9812   IF CODE = 255 THEN 9900: REM     CTRL-C
9816 LINE =  PEEK (218) + 256 *  PEEK (219)
9820   REM   IF USING AN 80-COLUMN DISPLAY
9824   REM   ADD 20 TO ALL HTAB ARGUMENTS
9828   HOME
9832   VTAB 6: HTAB 13
9836   INVERSE
9840   PRINT "ERROR CONDITION"
9844   NORMAL
9848   VTAB 10: HTAB 10
9852   PRINT "ERROR CODE #:    ";CODE
9856   VTAB 12: HTAB 10
9860   PRINT "PROGRAM LINE #: ";LINE
9864   PRINT : PRINT
9868   IF B = 4 OR B = 6 OR B = 8 OR B = 9 GOTO 9880
9872   PRINT "PROGRAM OR FILE ERROR"
9876   GOTO 9896
9880   IF B = 4 THEN  PRINT "DISK IS WRITE PROTECTED"
9884   IF B = 6 THEN  PRINT "FILE NOT FOUND ON DISKETTE:": PRINT "INSERT CO
       RRECT DISKETTE INTO DRIVE"
9888   IF B = 8 THEN  PRINT "INPUT/OUTPUT ERROR:": PRINT "ASSURE THAT DISKE
       TTE IS PROPERLY": PRINT "INSERTED AND DRIVE DOOR IS SHUT"
9892   IF B = 9 THEN  PRINT "DISK FULL:": PRINT "TOO MANY FILES OR RECORDS
       ON DISK"
9896   GOSUB 4010
9900   REM  END OF ROUTINE
```

Fig. 3-16. Apple full-screen error-handling routine.

```
0 REM Error-Handling Routine (single line)
9800 REM--Error-Handling Routine (single line)--
9805 REM NOTE: requires 80-column display
9806 REM reformat as two rows if using 40 columns
9810 BEEP
9830 LOCATE 23,1
9840 COLOR 0,7:REM inverse
9850 PRINT "ERROR CONDITION:";
9860 COLOR 7,0:REM normal video
9870 LOCATE 23,18
9880 PRINT"Error code #";ERR;"in program line #"ERL;" ";
9910 E$="Program or file error"
9912 IF ERR=53 THEN E$="File not found"
9914 IF ERR=58 THEN E$="File already exists"
9916 IF ERR=61 THEN E$="Disk is full"
9918 IF ERR=70 THEN E$="Disk is write-protected"
9920 IF ERR=71 THEN E$="Disk is not ready"
9922 IF ERR=72 THEN E$="Disk media error"
9924 IF ERR=73 THEN E$="Advanced BASIC needed"
9926 IF ERR=24 OR ERR=25 OR ERR=57 THEN E$="Device or I/O error"
9928 IF ERR=7 OR ERR=14 THEN E$="Out of memory"
9940 COLOR 1,0:REM underline
9950 PRINT E$
9960 COLOR 7,0:REM normal video
9970 E$=""
9990 RESUME NEXT
```

Fig. 3-17. IBM PC single-row error-handling routine.

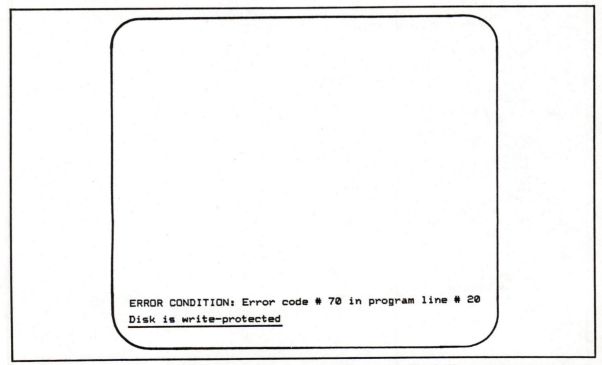

```
ERROR CONDITION: Error code # 70 in program line # 20
Disk is write-protected
```

Fig. 3-18. Appearance of display screen when single-row error-handling routine (Fig. 3-17) encounters an error.

The routine just described (Fig. 3-14) can be easily modified to do this. The revised routine is shown in Fig. 3-17. Since this simple code is based on code already described, you can figure it out. Do, however, note that line 9990 of this routine tells the program to RESUME NEXT, rather than to RESUME 10000 as in the previous routine. RESUME NEXT is used here based on the assumption that the programmer wants the error-handling routine to alert and inform the operator, but not to disrupt the program by sending control to a different part of the program than where the error occurred. When an error occurs, this routine will print error information out on row 23 of the screen in the form shown in Fig. 3-18. (You can change the display row by modifying the LOCATE statement on line 9870.)

Error-handling routines such as these, while useful, are certainly no substitute for systematic testing of a program to prevent the errors for which the programmer is responsible. You can also help reduce operator errors by providing the necessary on-screen prompts and by providing good program documentation. (More on this latter point later in the book.)

If your computer's BASIC lacks an ON ERROR GOTO statement, then you must, in effect, make your program perfect and immune to operator errors. This is, of course, impossible, and the sort of realization that gives programmers ulcers or the desire to seek out a better BASIC than the one they are using.

Chapter 4

Output and Screen Design

This chapter covers the fundamentals of program output and display screen design. The computer's display screen (a monitor or television set) is its window onto the world. Through this window the computer presents various types of information to users: English (or other) language statements, numbers, graphics, warnings, requests, directions, and whatever else the clever minds of programmers can invent. The programmer's goal is to design screens that both convey information and are attractive to look at. Since both considerations are important, designing display screens is something of an art.

However, it is also a science—or at least a technology—in that there are a number of practical rules to help you during design. One such rule is to center information on the screen. the idea is simple enough, but it is surprising how many programmers either have not thought about it or simply do not bother.

The main goal of any display screen is to communicate information to the program user. Many factors influence communication:

- The amount of information presented.
- How the information is presented—using numbers, words, or graphics.
- How fast the information comes.
- The colors used.
- Screen layout.

Beside these factors, other less tangible things influence communication, such as how pleasing to the eye the screen appears. Is it possible to design an ugly screen, one so bad that it turns users off? Certainly it is, as many misguided programmers have demonstrated. So, along with providing some of the technical details on screen design, we will work in a few of the aesthetics.

This chapter consists of a series of discussion points. Most of the points are illustrated with examples of BASIC code. As you read the chapter, and go through the examples, try the techniques out on your own computer. You will learn more this way, and it will also make the chapter more interesting. Discussion points covered in this chapter are:

- Design Principles
- Using Color
- Use of Special Video Modes
- Cursor Control
- Clearing a Line or Range of Lines
- Screen Access
- How to Lay Out a Screen
- How to Display Text
- How to Display Numbers
- Designing Printed Reports

DESIGN PRINCIPLES

The two most important principles for screen design are *simplicity* and *consistency*. They are universal principles which apply not only to screen design, but also to how you collect user inputs, control the program, and deal with a host of other design issues.

Keep your screens simple, uncluttered, focused on a single idea. You will not win any prizes for how much you can fit onto one screen. You will just confuse the person who is using your program. Design the screen so that it has some open space. Present information in bite-sized chunks.

Display information consistently from screen to screen. This makes it easier for users to learn and remember how you present information to them. For example, if you display prompts at the bottom of one of your screens, the user will naturally expect them to appear there on other screens. Make it easier for them by fulfilling their expectations. The same idea applies to the other things you present on your screens—display titles, menus, warning messages, and the information content of the screen itself. In short, do it the same way from screen to screen.

USING COLOR

Many programmers use color displays with their computers, and for this reason the subject of color must be covered. Still, most probably use monochrome displays, and the discussion of color is brief. Its main purpose is to acquaint those of you with color displays with a few simple rules for using color. This section is the only point in the book at which color is covered, and the code examples that appear elsewhere assume a monochrome display. (If you have a monochrome display, you may want to skip this section and move on to the next.)

Though the use of color in serious programming is increasingly common, most serious programs do not really need it. Still, color cannot be ignored because it is so easy to misuse. Color is misused when it is put in for flash or appearance, rather than to serve a useful purpose. It is often misused when the designer relies on instinct or personal preference for the color combinations used. Misuse of color often makes a display less, rather than more legible, and may cause eyestrain as well.

The use of color on video displays is complex. It involves human color perception—a difficult subject in itself—as well as the characteristics of the hardware and software necessary to generate the displays. The discussion in this section offers practical guidelines for using color and avoiding certain common errors. It focuses on the use of color to convey information in serious programs. When color is used in this way, the main concern is to pick an appropriate color combination for use on the video display.

At least two colors are required to present information on any display. Any two colors may be used, but they must differ, and the program user must be able to discriminate between them. One of these colors is the background, or field, against which the information is presented in a second, contrasting color.

You can do a lot more with color than this section covers. For example, you can use many different colors, and use color-coding so that different colors represent different concepts. However, color coding is beyond the scope of this book. While color can also be used to add flash and excitement to a program, this is rarely done in serious programs. At any rate, deciding how to use colors this way is more a matter of fine arts than computer programming.

This section begins by describing how to control color on your PC. It then discusses color contrast, selection, and recommended colors for use on displays.

Color Control

Color control varies from BASIC to BASIC. Some (such as Applesoft) restrict the use of color to graphics modes. Others (such as IBM PC BASIC) permit the use of color in both text and graphics modes. And some computers, (such as C-64 BASIC) make no distinction between text and graphics modes, and permit the use of color at any time.

In text mode, it is generally possible to set the color of the screen characters, background, and border with simple BASIC statements. For example, IBM PC BASIC has a COLOR statement with this format:

COLOR character, background, border

The three arguments are numbers between 0 and 15 (see Table 4-1) which define the corresponding color on the screen. C-64 BASIC lacks a COLOR statement, but allows the same three colors to be set by poking color codes into memory and printing selected CHR$ codes. The discussion that follows is illustrated with examples of IBM PC BASIC. However, the techniques shown can be applied (with appropriate changes) to any BASIC that allows you to set the color of characters, background, and border.

The IBM PC is capable of presenting 16 different colors. In text mode, the color combinations possible include 16 character colors, 8 background colors, and 16 border colors. In graphics mode, the combinations are more limited; this discussion refers only to text mode. The colors that can be displayed on the IBM PC are given in Table 4-1.

Color is set by selecting the appropriate color codes from Table 4-1 and then using them as the arguments of the COLOR statement. For example,

Table 4-1. IBM PC Color Codes.

Color	Code
Black	0
Blue (dark)	1
Green (dark)	2
Cyan (dark)	3
Red (dark)	4
Magenta (dark)	5
Brown	6
White	7
Gray	8
Blue (light)	9
Green (light)	10
Cyan (light)	11
Red (light)	12
Magenta (light)	13
Yellow	14
White (high-intensity)	15

to set character color to white, background to black, and border to brown, use a statement of this form:

COLOR   15,0,6

Figure 4-1 shows the listing of a subroutine for setting the colors. Subroutine arguments are:

CHAR: Character color code (0-15)
BACK: Background color code (0-8)
BORD: Border color code (0-16)

To use this subroutine, set the values of CHAR, BACK, and BORD early in the program and then use a GOSUB 1020 statement to set the color initially and reset it from time to time during the program.

You can also use this subroutine to change colors during the program. This comes in handy under certain circumstances. For example, you might use different color combinations in different parts of your program to help the user remain oriented. You might use a particular color combination to issue a warning, to alert the operator to an error condition, or to attract the user's attention to a situation that requires action.

You can use the subroutine to change any one or all of the color parameters. For example, after setting the character, border, and background

```
0 REM Color-Setting Subroutine
1 REM SAVE"FIG4-1",A
1020 REM--Set Display Colors--
1030 COLOR CHAR,BACK,BORD
1040 RETURN
```

Fig. 4-1. IBM PC display color-setting subroutine.

colors initially, a subsequent subroutine call need only set one of these parameters, such as character color. This makes the subroutine somewhat handier than using COLOR statements directly in your program code. However, since the subroutine is so simple—it consists of nothing more than the COLOR statement with the variable arguments—some programmers may prefer to use the COLOR statement directly, rather than this subroutine.

Note that, if you intend always to use the same background and border colors, you should make the background and border arguments identical. That is, modify line 1030 of the subroutine to look like this:

1030   COLOR CHAR,BACK,BACK

In serious programs, be conservative in your use of color. You can do very eye-catching things with it, but that alone does not justify its use. Color for its own sake is fine in game or entertainment programs, but not in serious programs. It can only be justified if it serves a useful purpose. Color is useful as a search aid and as an information code. It can be used for both purposes on some displays. Color is also useful in separating different areas of a display screen. To use it this way, divide the screen area up into different blocks, paint each block a different color, and then fill in the information content of the screen in appropriate character colors. This is a very effective way to separate different areas of the screen, but it must be done with care to avoid border interference between colors, and wide contrast differences between colors. These two problems must also be avoided in selecting appropriate character and background color combinations, as described below.

Contrast

To display information on a screen, characters must be presented against a background. For example, a screen might contain white characters against a black background. The contrast could be reversed by presenting black characters against a white background.

Which is best—light characters on a dark background, or dark characters on a light background? This depends mainly on the surrounding lighting where the screen is viewed. If viewed in a bright area, then it is best to present dark characters on a light background. If viewed in a dark area, then light characters on a dark background are best. The reason is that the eye tends to adapt to the surrounding light level, and if the screen brightness is similar, the eye will see better when viewing the screen.

Generally, high contrast between characters and background makes displayed information more legible. Using a wide contrast range, such as white on black, is more legible than using a narrow range, such as light blue against dark blue. A wide range, however can strain the eyes.

It is becoming increasingly common to use dark characters against a light background, although the majority of programs still use light against dark. Which is best depends upon the situation, as noted earlier. In addition, most users have a preference, one way or another, and these preferences should be taken into account.

Color Selection

The colors that can be displayed depend upon the computer and its dialect of BASIC. Some computers can display only a few colors, and others dozens or more. Yet, in a typical program it comes down to deciding on just 2 colors: one for characters, the other for background.

To illustrate how the decision may be made, let us consider a specific example: color selection for the IBM PC. Although your computer may differ, you can use the same analytical technique in deciding on the colors to use with it.

The IBM PC can present 16 different character

colors and eight different background colors, and this means that there are 120 different color combinations in which background and character colors differ. That sounds like a lot of possibilities. It is, in a certain sense. However, when you start eliminating various colors, the numbers drop quickly.

First, consider background colors. Of these, it is suggested only white and black be considered. There is no reason to use a color background, other than that it may look pretty. The background is used only to contrast with the characters. In addition, some of the colors—such as red, magenta, yellow, blue, and orange—conflict with colors that might be used for presenting information. For example, when you put red and blue together, or yellow and green, you get interference at the border that looks like shadows. Okay, so now we are down to two background colors. These colors, and their brightness levels, are:

Black   Dark
White   Bright

Now consider the character colors. The background colors can also be used as character colors in certain combinations, such as black and white. Some colors are seldom used for presenting information. these include blue, cyan, red, magenta, and brown. There is nothing wrong with these colors, although the eye is less sensitive to most of them than to the remaining colors.

The colors left over are green and yellow. There are two greens, light and dark. There is one yellow. Interestingly, the remaining color combinations approximate those of the phosphors of three most popular monochrome monitors: white, green, and amber.

Recommended Colors

Table 4-2 summarizes the recommended background and character color combinations for the IBM PC. Two background colors are shown: black and white.

Before actually selecting colors for your display, try out several different combinations. Fig-

Table 4-2. Recommended Background and Character Color Combinations.

Background Color	Character Colors
Black	White, Yellow, Green (Light)
White	Black, Gray

ure 4-2 is the listing of a short program that can be used on the IBM PC to generate different background and character colors to test their appearance. When the program starts, it requests the background color (a number between 0 and 15 from Table 4-1). The next prompt requests the character color. When the Enter key is pressed, screen background turns to the background color and the screen fills with characters of the character color. The character color selection prompt then reappears, enabling the definition of a new screen. Modify the program shown in Fig. 4-2 for your computer and save it on disk for use in the future.

It may seem a shame to limit programs to only a few colors. Why not be more adventurous and use red characters against a blue background, or magenta against black? While such color combinations may be pretty to look at, they are very hard for users to work with, and you must be very careful what colors you put on a display. If you have any doubts about the matter, be conservative.

Using Special Video Modes

Most BASIC versions allow you to display characters in both normal video—light characters against a dark background—and one or more special video modes, such as:

- Inverse—Dark character against light background
- Flashing (normal)—Light character flashes against dark background
- Flashing (inverse)—dark character flashes against light background
- Underlined
- High intensity

```
0 REM Color-Setting Program
1 REM SAVE "FIG4-2",A
10 INPUT "Background: ";BACK
20 INPUT "Characters: ";CHAR
30 COLOR CHAR,BACK,BACK
40 CLS
50 FOR X=1 TO 40
60 PRINT"ABCDEFGHIJKLMNOPQRSTUVWXYZ01234567890";
70 NEXT
80 PRINT
90 PRINT
100 GOTO 20
```

Fig. 4-2. IBM PC program for generating display background and character color combinations.

These modes are engaged differently, depending upon the particular BASIC. IBM PC BASIC, for example, allows all of these modes to be set with the COLOR statement. Applesoft BASIC enables inverse and flashing (normal) video with the INVERSE and FLASH statements, respectively. The C-64 enables inverse video with printed CHR$ characters, and will flash with a POKE 204,0.

What are these special video modes good for, and when should they be used? Though the answer to this question is somewhat a matter of style and preference, there are usage conventions and guidelines to follow.

Obviously, normal mode should be used for most things. It provides the backdrop against which the special modes contrast. Since these modes differ from normal mode, they do (or should) attract attention or emphasize something on the display. The most effective way to attract attention is to use flashing video. Inverse, underlining, and high-intensity video also attract attention, but not as much as flashing. For this reason, flashing has traditionally been used in error messages or other messages that require the program user's immediate attention.

The remaining three video modes—inverse, underlining, high intensity—are typically used for emphasis. Inverse has no common analog in written text, but underlining and high intensity correspond to italics. In computer displays, inverse video is often used in the labels on a display to distinguish them from the information content of the display. In short, here are the recommendations for using special video modes:

- Use flashing for alerting messages.
- Use inverse video in display labels and headings.
- Use underlining or high intensity to give special emphasis.

Note that some versions of BASIC permit special video modes to be combined in various ways. IBM PC BASIC permits not only inverse video, underlining, and flashing, but all three at once. Bear in mind that each of these combinations is an information code, that is, a way of telling something through how the message is presented. Operators have difficulty keeping track of the various codes if there are more than about a half dozen. It is best, therefore, not to get carried away by the possibilities. You do not want your operator, after a long day, to be scratching his or her head and trying to recall the difference between a regular flashing message, a flashing message that is underlined, a flashing message that is underlined and in high intensity, and—well, you get the idea. Keep it simple.

Note that you can use inverse video mode to produce a negative image; that is, a screen with dark characters against a light background. While the use of negative images is sometimes desirable, you should not use inverse video screens with green or yellow phosphor monitors. Use inverse video sparingly, and only to make something stand out on a display that is in normal video mode.

CURSOR CONTROL

It is important for you to have complete control over the location of the cursor. You must be able to move it where you want it quickly, easily, and with minimum complications. Having this control gives you freedom in how you generate display screens within a program.

It is possible to create a screen without giving much thought to where the cursor is located. For example, you can clear the display, print its top row, then print its next row, and so on, until you get down to the bottom (Fig. 4-3). Creating a display this way is not always convenient. It works well enough with simple displays, but not with complex ones.

Often, it is more convenient to print certain parts of the display (such as headings) first, and then to go back later and print other information (Fig. 4-4). To create a screen this way, you must be able to move the cursor to any location very readily. This frees you from the tyranny of line-by-line display generation. New vistas open.

Most BASIC dialects have statements for absolute cursor positioning to specified horizontal and vertical coordinates of the screen. The most common statement is LOCATE V,H, whose arguments V and H specify screen row and column, respectively. Applesoft BASIC has VTAB V and HTAB H (or POKE 36,H), which are equivalent to LOCATE. Some machines, such as the C-64, lack such statements, and require the programmer to use some other technique for cursor positioning.

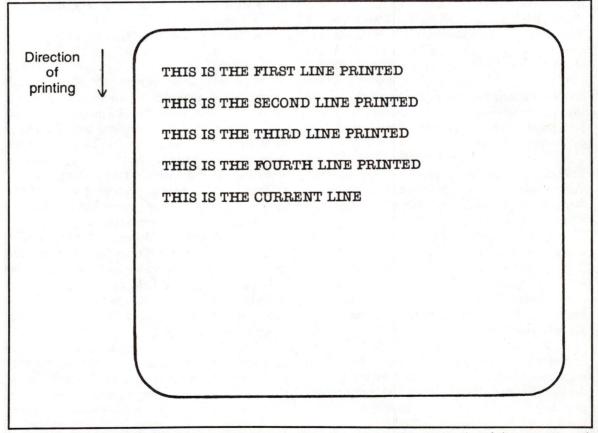

Direction of printing

THIS IS THE FIRST LINE PRINTED

THIS IS THE SECOND LINE PRINTED

THIS IS THE THIRD LINE PRINTED

THIS IS THE FOURTH LINE PRINTED

THIS IS THE CURRENT LINE

Fig. 4-3. If the screen is cleared and then data entries are taken without controlling the location of the prompts, each successive prompt will appear one row further down the screen.

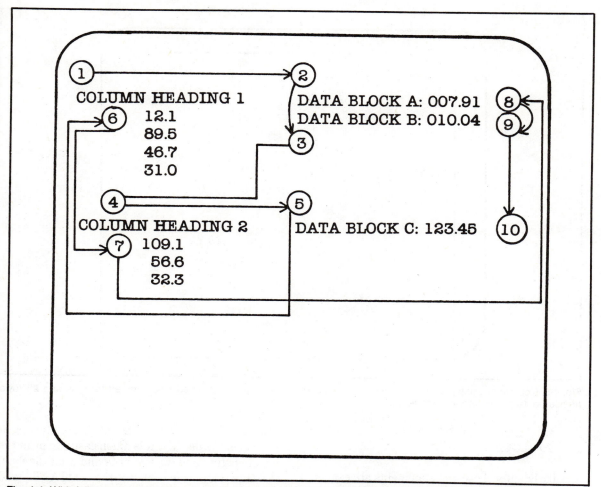

Fig. 4-4. With full cursor control, it is possible to print the different parts of the display in whatever order is convenient, as shown here by the circled numbers, which represent the order in which the item was printed.

(C-64 owners should refer to Appendix B for a discussion of the possibilities.) The following discussion is illustrated with the LOCATE statement, but applies equally to other BASIC statements (such as VTAB and HTAB) that allow absolute cursor positioning.

The LOCATE statement can be used to position the cursor to any vertical and horizontal coordinates on the screen. The coordinates are measured as shown in Fig. 4-5. Row number ranges from 1 to 25 and column number from 1 to 80 (or 40, if a 40-column display is used). The syntax of the LOCATE statement is as follows:

LOCATE V,H

Arguments are V (row numbr, 1-25) and H (column number, 1-80). For example, to position the cursor to row 10 and column 56, this statement is used:

LOCATE 10,56

Only one argument is required, not both. If one of the arguments is left out, then the statement uses the previous value of the argument. For example, after these two statements are executed, the cursor will be in row 20, column 40.

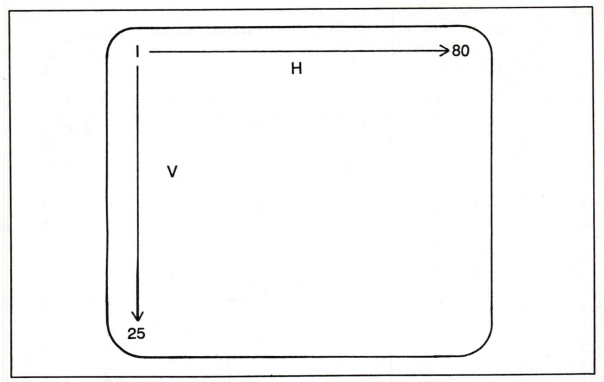

Fig. 4-5. Coordinates of typical screen display, consisting of 80 columns, measured 1-80 from left to right; and 25 rows, measured 1-25 from top to bottom.

```
10   LOCATE 20,10
20   LOCATE ,40
```

Similarly, after these two statements are executed, the cursor will be in row 12, column 36.

```
10   LOCATE 1,36
20   LOCATE 12
```

To illustrate how the LOCATE statement may be used to generate a screen, suppose that you have laid out the screen shown in Fig. 4-6, and want to write a little program that will generate the screen by first printing the headings, and then going back and printing the data.

Figure 4-7 shows code for the IBM PC that will generate the screen in these two stages. The headings are printed starting at line 11000, and the data are printed starting a line 12000.

Consider what would be involved in generating a screen like this on a line-by-line basis, starting at the top of the display. It is much easier to print the headings first and then go back and print the data.

One nice thing about the LOCATE (and equivalent) statements is that they give you good control of the cursor for horizontal tabbing. The TAB statement allows you to print information at a particular horizontal tab position, but it does not always follow orders. To illustrate, type in and run the following program:

```
10   PRINT TAB (10) "AAAA";
20   PRINT TAB (12) "BBBB"
```

Most BASIC versions will display the output on two separate rows, like this:

AAAA

BBBB

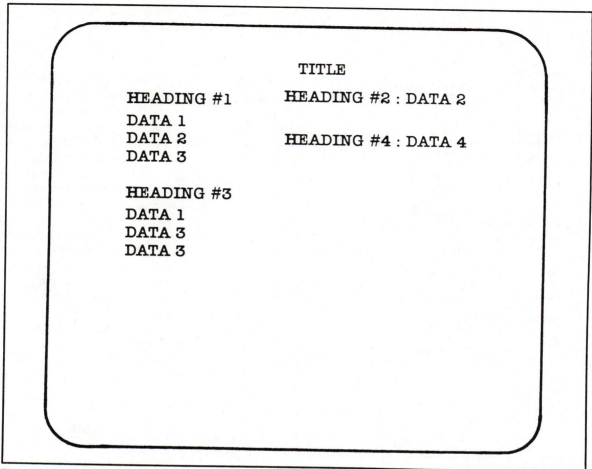

```
                              TITLE
         HEADING #1          HEADING #2 : DATA 2
         DATA 1
         DATA 2              HEADING #4 : DATA 4
         DATA 3

         HEADING #3
         DATA 1
         DATA 3
         DATA 3
```

Fig. 4-6. Hypothetical screen design.

The program told the computer to print **AAAA** at tab position 10 and **BBBB** at tab position 12. The second string should have overwritten the first, but BASIC retained the integrity of the two strings by printing them on separate rows instead of overprinting them. It helped out, even though such help was not asked for. One should not anthropomorphize this too much, but can imagine BASIC saying something to itself such as, "That poor ninny couldn't possibly mean for those two strings to print on top of each other! I'll fix things by moving the second one to the next row." But assume that you knew what you were doing (a reasonable assumption) and wanted to overprint them? Too bad. You cannot do it with the TAB statement.

Another thing that TAB does not usually permit is to print the columns in a row from right to left instead of from left to right. For example, if the program is modified to look like this:

```
10   PRINT TAB (30) "AAAA";
20   PRINT TAB (10) "BBBB"
```

the two strings are printed on separate rows. BASIC does not usually permit you to move the cursor backward with TAB (it will with Apple's HTAB, however).

You do not have these problems with LOCATE

61

```
0 REM Screen-Generation Program
1 REM SAVE"FIG4-7",A
10000 REM----Generate Display----
10010 REM--Print Title--
10020 CLS
10025 COLOR 0,7:REM inverse
10030 LOCATE 1,38
10040 PRINT"TITLE"
11000 REM--Print Headings--
11010 LOCATE 3,20
11020 PRINT"HEADING #1"
11030 LOCATE 3,50
11040 PRINT"HEADING #2:"
11050 LOCATE 12,20
11060 PRINT"HEADING #3"
11070 LOCATE 6,50
11080 PRINT"HEADING #4:"
11090 COLOR 7,0:REM normal video
12000 REM--PRINT DATA--
12010 REM-Data 1-
12020 FOR V=4 TO 7
12030 LOCATE V,20
12040 PRINT"data 1"
12050 NEXT
12060 REM-Data 2-
12070 LOCATE 3,62
12080 PRINT"data 2"
12090 REM-data 3-
12100 FOR V=13 TO 16
12110 LOCATE V,20
12120 PRINT"data 3"
12130 NEXT
12140 REM-Data 4-
12150 LOCATE 6,62
12160 PRINT"data 4"
12170 LOCATE 23,1
12180 END
```

Fig. 4-7. IBM PC code for generating screen shown in Fig. 4-6 by first printing headings and later printing the data.

(or VTAB/HTAB). To illustrate, this program

```
10   LOCATE 10,10
20   PRINT"AAAA";
30   LOCATE 10,12
40   PRINT"BBBB".
```

will produce **AABBBB**, starting at column 10. This routine does not second-guess you, and permits you to overwrite if you've a mind to.

You can also print backwards. To illustrate, changing lines 10 and 30 as follows:

```
10   LOCATE 10,30
30   LOCATE 10,10
```

produces **AAAA** starting at column 30 and **BBBB** starting at column 10—printing backwards!

CLEARING A LINE OR RANGE OF LINES

In generating screens, it is often necessary to clear part of the display. Most versions of BASIC permit you to clear the entire display with a CLS statement or its equivalent (such as Applesoft's HOME or in C-64 BASIC by PRINTing CHR$ (147)), but usually there is no simple way to clear part of the display. Applesoft BASIC is an exception to this rule, with CALL to clear from the cursor position to the end of the row (CALL-868) or end of the screen (CALL-958). Where such CALLs or equivalent statements are unavailable, you are at a disadvantage in generating and rewriting screens. It is awkward to erase and rewrite the entire screen when you only want to change one or two parts of it. Not only is this extra work, but it is irritating to the user, whose displays periodically disappear and then return. It is much better to be able to clear only the part of the display that you are interested in. In general, it is useful to be able to perform three types of display clearing operations:

- single line
- to end of screen
- range of lines

You may want to clear a single line for several reasons. For example, you may want to erase displayed information, erase so that you can display other information, or erase so you can print a prompt and collect input from the user.

You may want to clear to end of screen for similar reasons. Often this comes in handy if you want to erase the lower part of the screen so that you can print new data there or perhaps a menu at the bottom of the screen.

Being able to clear a range of lines is most useful for erasing written messages or tabular data that appear in the middle rows of the screen.

While it is possible to perform these clearing operations on the spot in program code, these three clearing functions are needed often enough that it

```
0 REM Clear One Line Subroutine
1 REM SAVE"FIG4-8",A
1300 REM--Clear One Line--
1310 LOCATE V,H:REM position cursor
1320 PRINT SPACE$(WIDE%+1-H);:REM clear to end of line
1330 LOCATE V,H:REM reposition cursor
1340 RETURN
```

Fig. 4-8. IBM PC subroutine to clear to the end of a line.

makes good sense to write the code in the form of subroutines that can be used anywhere in a program. It is fairly easy to construct BASIC subroutines that will do the job, as described below.

Clearing a Single Line

Figure 4-8 is the listing of a subroutine for the IBM PC that can be used to clear a single line. The arguments of this subroutine are WIDE% (number of display columns, 80 or 40), V (row number) and H (column number). The subroutine erases everything on row V to the right of column H and then returns the cursor to position V,H. This enables a single subroutine call to clear the line and locate the cursor appropriately for printing something in the space that was cleared.

The inner workings of the subroutine are simple. Line 1310 positions the cursor initially. Line 1320 uses the SPACE$ function to print WIDE%+1−H spaces—the number of spaces needed to erase the line from the cursor position to the right edge of the display. Line 1330 then repositions the cursor to coordinates V,H. Since display width will not ordinarily change during a program, WIDE% should be set equal to 80 or 40 very early in the program so that it does not have to be set with each subroutine call.

To use the subroutine, program code must set the arguments and then make a subroutine call with the GOSUB statement. For example, to clear row 15 to the right of column 24, code such as this would be used:

```
1100 V = 15
11010 H = 24
11020 GOSUB 1300
```

Figure 4-9 shows an Apple subroutine equivalent to Fig. 4-8. Figure 4-10 shows an equivalent C-64 subroutine, which uses an assembly-language SYScall based on code presented in Appendix B; refer to Appendix B for details.

It is a good idea to try this subroutine out to get the feeling of it. The short program shown in Fig. 4-11 will fill the screen with characters and let you set the subroutine arguments to see what happens when the subroutine is called. Enter this program, and also include the subroutine shown in Fig. 4-8.

Clearing to End of Screen

With the IBM PC, you can clear from the cursor position to the end of the screen by using the

```
0    REM   FIG 4-9
1    REM    CLEAR ONE LINE SUBROUTINE
1300   REM --CLEAR ONE LINE--
1310   VTAB V: HTAB H: REM   POSITION CURSOR
1320   CALL   - 868
1330   VTAB V: HTAB H: REM   REPOSITION CURSOR
1340   RETURN
```

Fig. 4-9. Apple subroutine to clear to the end of a line.

```
1300 REM--CLEAR ONE LINE--
1310 SYS C0,1,V,H
1320 RETURN
```

Fig. 4-10. C-64 subroutine to clear to the end of a line. (Requires assembly-language subroutine loader; see Appendix B.)

subroutine shown in Fig. 4-12. Equivalent Apple and C-64 subroutines are shown in Figs. 4-13 and 4-14, respectively. Arguments of this subroutine are again WIDE% (number of columns), V (row number), and H (column number).

This subroutine, like Fig. 4-8, is simple. Line 1360 positions the cursor initially. Line 1370 clears the top line. Lines 1380-1390 then clear the lines

```
0 REM Demonstration Program
1 REM SAVE"FIG4-11.BAS",A
10 REM--Demonstration Program--
20 CLS
30 INPUT "V ";V
40 INPUT "H ";H
50 CLS
60 FOR A=1 TO 44
70 PRINT "ABCDEFGHIJKLMNOPQRSTUVWXYZ1234567890!@#$";
80 NEXT
90 PRINT
100 GOSUB 1300
110 COLOR 0,7
120 INPUT"THIS IS THE PROMPT!",X$
130 COLOR 7,0
140 END
```

Fig. 4-11. IBM PC program for use in demonstrating screen-clearing subroutines shown in Fig. 4-8,. 4-12, and 4-15.

```
0 REM Clear to End of Screen Subroutine
1 REM SAVE"FIG4-12",A
1350 REM--Clear to End of Screen--
1360 LOCATE V,H:REM position cursor
1370 PRINT SPACE$(WIDE%+1-H);:REM clear to end of top line
1380 FOR A=1 TO 23-V:REM clear all lines below
1390 PRINT SPACE$(WIDE%);
1400 NEXT
1410 LOCATE V,H:REM reposition cursor
1420 RETURN
```

Fig. 4-12. IBM PC subroutine to clear to the end of the screen.

```
0   REM  FIG 4-13
1   REM   CLEAR TO END OF SCREEN SUBROUTINE
1350  REM --CLEAR TO END OF SCREEN
1360  VTAB V: HTAB H: REM  POSITION CURSOR
1370  CALL  - 958
1380  VTAB V: HTAB H
1390  RETURN
```

Fig. 4-13. Apple subroutine to clear to the end of the screen.

```
1350 REM--CLEAR TO END OF SCREEN--
1360 SYS C0,3,V,H
1370 RETURN
```

Fig. 4-14. C-64 subroutine to clear to the end of the screen. (Requires assembly-language subroutine loader; see Appendix B.)

below. Note that this subroutine will clear down to line 24. If you want it to clear to line 25, change the 23 in line 1380 to 24. (Try this subroutine out by adding it to the program shown in Fig. 4-11. Change the subroutine call in line 100 to read GOSUB 1350.)

Clearing a Range of Lines

You can clear a range of lines by using the subroutine shown in Fig. 4-15. Arguments of this subroutine are WIDE% (number of columns), V1 (top row), and V2 (bottom row). Equivalent Apple and C-64 subroutines are shown in Figs. 4-16 and 4-17, respectively.

When the subroutine is called, it will erase all rows between and including V1 and V2. For example, to clear rows 15 – 17, use code like this:

```
11000 V1 = 15
11010 V2 = 17
11020 GOSUB 1430
```

Line 1430 positions the cursor to the first column of row V1. Lines 1450 – 1470 then print WIDE% blank spaces across the rows from V1 through V2. Line 1480 then repositions the cursor to coordinates V1,1. (Try this subroutine out by adding it to the program shown in Fig. 4-11. Change the INPUT statements on lines 30 and 40 to collect both V1 and V2, and change the subroutine call in line 100 to read GOSUB 1430.)

SCREEN ACCESS

Have you ever worked on a time-sharing computer system? If you have, then most of what the computer displayed to you came scrolling off the bottom of the display. Walk into a computer science laboratory sometime and watch the displays as the students work with their terminals. The screens are

```
0 REM Clear Range of Lines Subroutine
1 REM SAVE"FIG4-15",A
1430 REM--Clear Range of Lines--
1440 LOCATE V1,1
1450 FOR A=1 TO V2-V1+1
1460 PRINT SPACE$(WIDE%);
1470 NEXT
1480 LOCATE V1,1
1490 RETURN
```

Fig. 4-15. IBM PC subroutine to clear a range of lines.

```
0   REM   FIG 4-16
1   REM   CLEAR RANGE OF LINES SUBROUTNE
1400  REM --CLEAR RANGE OF LINES--
1410  FOR V = V1 TO V2
1420  VTAB V: HTAB 1
1430  CALL  - 868
1440  NEXT
1450  VTAB V1: HTAB 1
1460  RETURN
```

Fig. 4-16. Apple subroutine to clear a range of lines.

```
1400 REM--CLEAR RANGE OF LINES--
1410 SYS C0,4,V1,0,V2
1420 RETURN
```

Fig. 4-17. C-64 subroutine to clear a range of lines. (Requires assembly-language subroutine loader; see Appendix B.)

generated line-by-line, and go scrolling up. If you watch long enough, it can make you dizzy. If you have vertigo, you may be in trouble.

Screen Paging

People who started their computer experience with time-sharing systems, large mainframe computers, or the venerable Teletype are used to scrolling screens, and often take them for granted. If you started your computer experience with a microcomputer, you may have an altogether different perspective. Most well-written programs avoid scrolling screens and use the *paging* technique first clearing the screen, and then generating the entire screen at once, from top to bottom. Paging makes a clear break between the old display and the new. It also causes less eyestrain.

Scrolling causes eyestrain, shows a fixation on the single line (rather than a more healthy, holistic orientation toward the entire screen), and, for all we know, may be a sign of poor character (add anything else that fits!).

Well, perhaps it is not that bad, but it is not a good thing.

It is easy to page. Just clear the display with a CLS or equivalent statement at the beginning of your screen-generating code. Once you have cleared the display, create the screen by printing its contents.

Temporary Pauses between Screens

Most display screens require some overt action from the operator before they are replaced. Some programs—of the demonstration variety—display a screen for a fixed amount of time, such as 30 seconds, before erasing it and displaying the next screen. It is usually necessary to introduce a pause into the program after displaying the screen. This may be done in several ways. One common way is to require user input, as discussed in Chapter 5.

Another common way is to introduce a temporary pause that requires the user to press the space bar or a key. Figure 4-18 is the listing of a simple subroutine for the IBM PC that prints the following statement in reverse video, centered and at row 23 of the display, awaiting a space bar press:

[Press Space Bar to Continue]

This subroutine was used by one of the error-handling subroutines described in the last chapter (see Fig. 3-13). You can modify the subroutine to look for some other keypress by changing what you put between the quotation marks in line 4060.

Using this subroutine is simple. It has no arguments. Just insert a GOSUB 4010 wherever you want a temporary pause in your program. When the subroutine executes, it displays the

```
0 REM Temporary Pause Subroutine
1 REM SAVE"FIG4-18.BAS",A
4010 REM--Temporary Pause--
4020 LOCATE 23,WIDE%/2-13
4030 COLOR 16,7:REM inverse flash
4040 PRINT"[Press Space Bar to Continue]";
4050 COLOR 7,0:REM normal video
4060 A$=INKEY$:IF A$<>" " GOTO 4060
4070 PRINT
4080 RETURN
```

Fig. 4-18. IBM PC subroutine to print the prompt ''[Press Space Bar to Continue]'' and halt the program until the space bar is pressed.

```
Ø   REM   FIG 4-19
1   REM    TEMPORARY PAUSE SUBROUTINE
4010   REM --TEMPORARY PAUSE--
4020   VTAB 23: HTAB 6: REM  USE HTAB 26 FOR 80-COLUMN DISPLAY
4030   FLASH : REM  USE INVERSE IF USING 80-COLUMN CARD
4040   PRINT "<PRESS SPACE BAR TO CONTINUE>";
4050   NORMAL
4060   GET A$: IF A$ < > " " GOTO 4060
4070   PRINT
4080   RETURN
```

Fig. 4-19. Apple subroutine to print the prompt "<PRESS SPACE BAR TO CONTINUE>" and halt the program until the space bar is pressed.

```
4010 REM--TEMPORARY PAUSE--
4020 SYS C0,0,24,6
4030 PRINT CHR$(18);:REM REVERSE VIDEO
4040 PRINT "[PRESS SPACE BAR TO CONTINUE]";
4050 GET A$
4060 IF A$<>" " GOTO 4050
4070 PRINT
4080 RETURN
```

Fig. 4-20. C-64 subroutine to print the prompt "[PRESS SPACE BAR TO CONTINUE]" and halt the program until the space bar is pressed. (Requires assembly-language subroutine loader; see Appendix B.)

```
Ø REM TX-Second Delay Subroutine
1 REM SAVE"FIG4-21.BAS",A
4100 REM--TX-Second Delay--
4110 FOR A=1 TO TX*987
4120 NEXT
4130 RETURN
```

Fig. 4-21. IBM PC subroutine to introduce a delay of TX seconds.

```
Ø   REM   FIG 4-22
1   REM    TX-SECOND DELAY SUBROUTINE
4100   REM --TX-SECOND DELAY--
4110   FOR A = 1 TO TX * 960
4120   NEXT
4130   RETURN
```

Fig. 4-22. Apple subroutine to introduce a delay of TX seconds.

message and awaits the appropriate key press before continuing.

Equivalent subroutines for the Apple and C-64 are shown in Figs. 4-19 and 4-20, respectively.

Timed Pauses between Screens

Another way to pause is to insert a time delay of a particular number of seconds. Figure 4-21 is the listing of a subroutine for the IBM PC that introduces a delay of TX seconds (more or less). You might use a delay such as this in a series of screens

```
4100 REM--TX SECOND DELAY--
4110 FOR A=1 TO TX*870
4120 NEXT
4130 RETURN
```

Fig. 4-23. C-64 subroutine to introduce a delay of TX seconds.

that are presenting instructions or a demonstration to the user. Adjust the display time to suit the subject. (If the information is difficult, let the user control how long it is displayed.) Usually 60 seconds is long enough (often too long!) to digest an 80 × 25 screen. To introduce a delay this long, insert in your program the statements TX = 60 and GOSUB 4100. When the subroutine executes, the FOR-NEXT loop in lines 4110 – 4120 will start counting and distract your computer's attention for about 60 seconds.

Equivalent subroutines for the Apple and C-64 are shown in Figs. 4-22 and 4-23, respectively.

HOW TO LAY OUT A SCREEN

Display screens can be well or poorly designed. Knowing a few simple rules can improve your design a great deal. This section offers some of these rules, along with several examples.

Rules are relative, of course. You are an in-

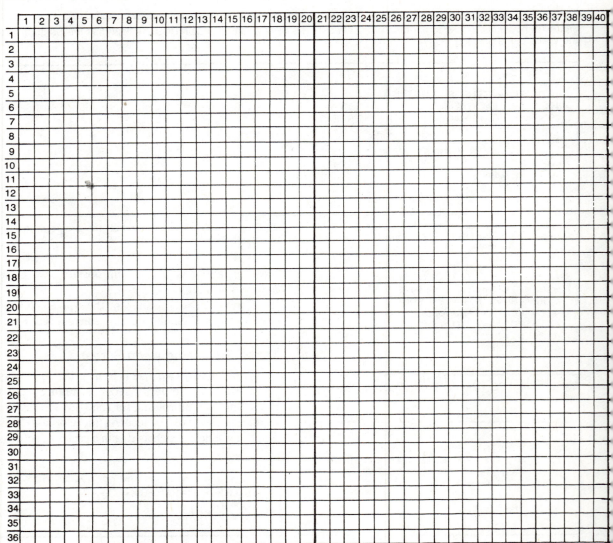

Fig. 4-24. 80-column display design matrix.

telligent, thinking being, or you would not be interested in computers or reading this book. Breaking these rules will not land you in jail, but will make your screens less understandable and attractive. It sometimes makes sense to break the rules, but before you break a rule, know what it is.

Use a Screen Design Matrix

Figure 4-24 is an 80 × 25 display design matrix. Figure 4-25 is a 40 × 25 matrix. These are wonderful things. You can use them to design a screen (or printed report) with paper and pencil before you sit down at your computer and start coding. Columns (1 – 80) are listed across the top and bottom, and rows (1 – 25) down the left and right sides.

Creating a screen is an act of planning and design. This should be done with paper and pen-

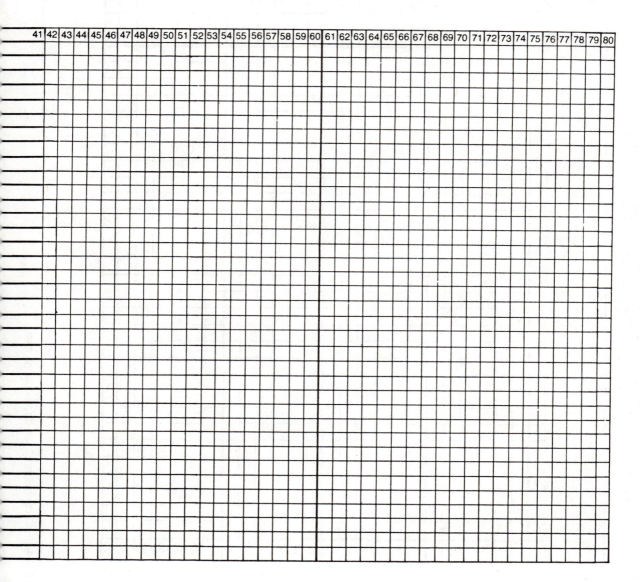

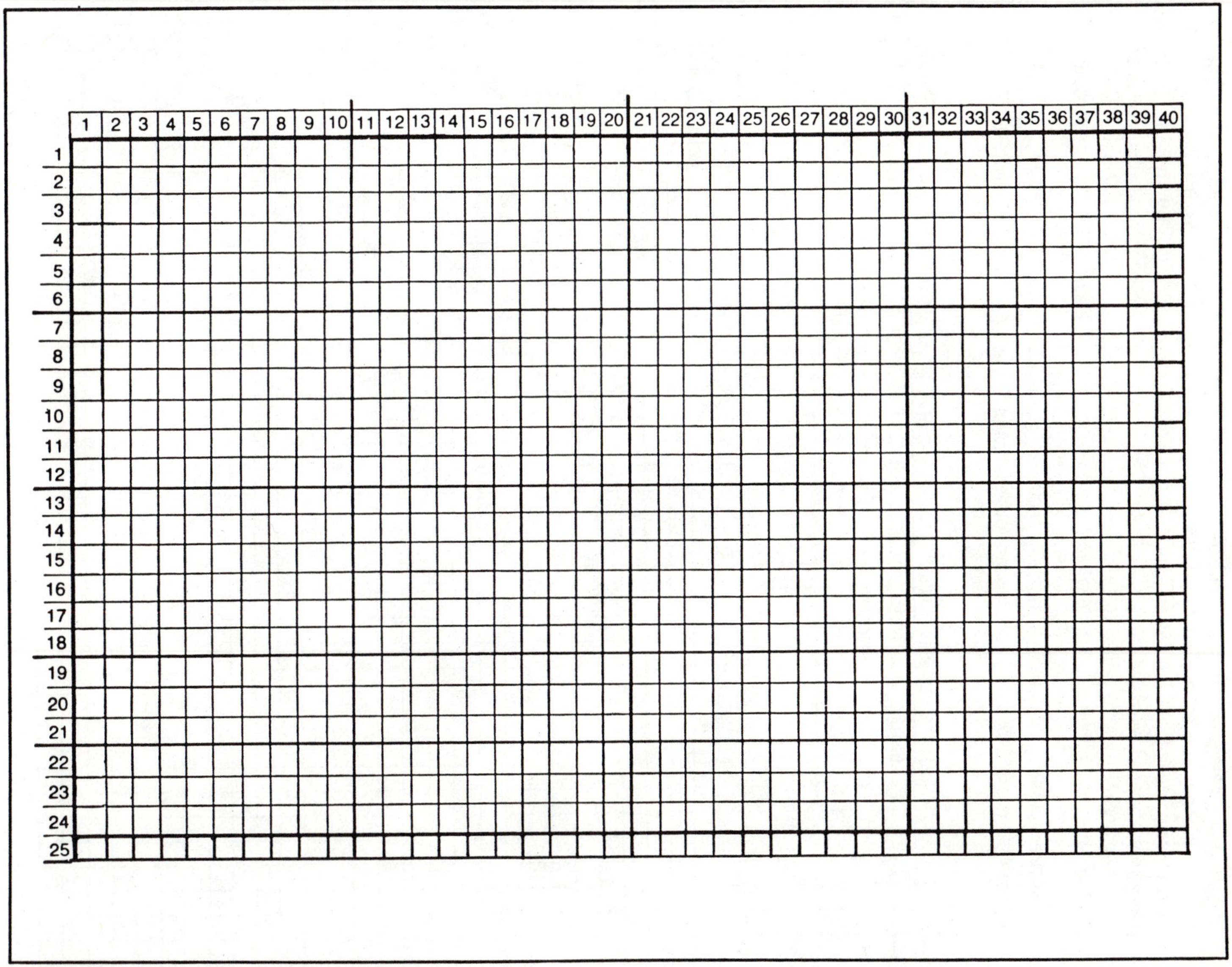

Fig. 4-25. 40-column by 25-row display design matrix.

70

```
0 REM Center & Print Title Subroutine
1 REM SAVE"FIG4-26.BAS",A
1500 REM--Center & Print Title--
1510 T=(WIDE%+1-LEN(T$))/2
1520 LOCATE ,T:REM position cursor horizontally
1530 COLOR 0,7:REM inverse
1540 PRINT T$
1550 COLOR 7,0:REM normal video
1560 RETURN
```

Fig. 4-26. IBM PC subroutine to center and print title on display screen.

cil, not while sitting at your computer attempting to get the display to come out right. Coding should be a mechanical act of translating the paper plan into cursor-positioning and PRINT statements.

Take Fig. 4-24 (or 4-25) to your copy shop and make several copies of it for use later.

Title Your Display

How would you feel if you walked into a bookstore whose books had blank front covers? How about going to a convention where all the folks had little paper signs on their pockets that said:

HI!

MY NAME IS _____

The problem is simple. People want to know what or whom they are dealing with. Tell them! Even if it is obvious to you, there are many to whom it is not obvious. And even experienced users sometimes become disoriented—you know, they get up from the computer, walk into the other room, look at a football game on TV or talk to someone—and when they return, they have lost track of what display they were looking at earlier.

Solution: Label each display by printing a title at the top of it. It is suggested that you put that title in all capital letters and inverse video.

Figure 4-26 is the listing of a subroutine for the IBM PC that centers and prints any title in reverse video. Arguments of this subroutine are WIDE% (number of columns) and T$ (title). Set T$ equal to the title and then call this subroutine. For example, you can center and print the word "TITLE" by including these lines in your program:

```
100   T$ = "TITLE"
110   GOSUB 1500
120   END
```

When these lines are executed, they center and print the title in inverse video.

Equivalent subroutines for the Apple and C-64 are shown in Figs. 4-27 and 4-28, respectively.

The subroutine does not clear the screen first, and so you can use it to center and print a title anywhere on the screen by first locating the cursor to the correct row. If you do want to print the title at the top, clear the screen before calling the subroutine.

```
0   REM   FIG 4-27
1   REM   TITLE CENTER & PRINT SUBROUTINE
1500   REM --CENTER & PRINT TITLE--
1510 T = (COLS + 1 -  LEN (T$)) / 2
1520   HTAB T
1530   INVERSE
1540   PRINT T$
1550   NORMAL
1560   RETURN
```

Fig. 4-27. Apple subroutine to center and print title on display screen.

```
1500 REM--CENTER & PRINT T$--
1510 T=(39-LEN(T$))/2
1520 PRINT CHR$(18);
1530 PRINT TAB(T) T$
1540 RETURN
```

Fig. 4-28. C-64 subroutine to center and print title on display screen.

Divide the Screen into Logical Areas

The display screens that you use in programs will probably contain certain classes of information. For example:

- Screen title—Centered at the top of the display.
- Data—Text, numbers, graphics, or some combination of all three. Data are usually printed on the center of the display.
- Data input area—Input prompts may appear at the top, center, or bottom of the display.
- Control area—A menu or control prompt may be printed anywhere on the display.
- Message area—Warnings, status information, or other messages may be printed anywhere on the display.

These are the most common categories of information that appear on display screens. The only thing fixed about where information should be displayed is that the title should appear at the top and data should appear below it. Other than this, you can design a screen display any way that makes sense to program users.

Most programs use several different display screens. These screens contain some or all of the above classes of information, as well as others not mentioned. The rule of consistency argues for presenting each class of information on a particular part of the display. To assure that your displays are

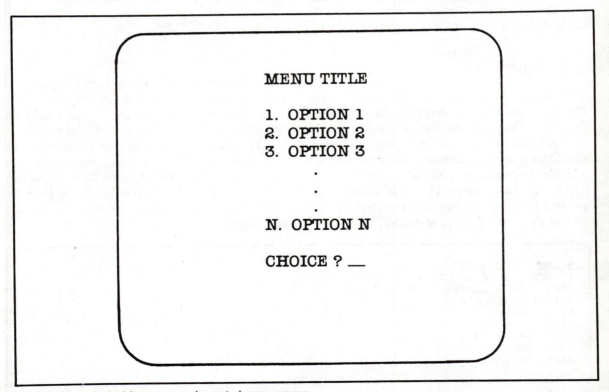

Fig. 4-29. Hypothetical format on main control menu screen.

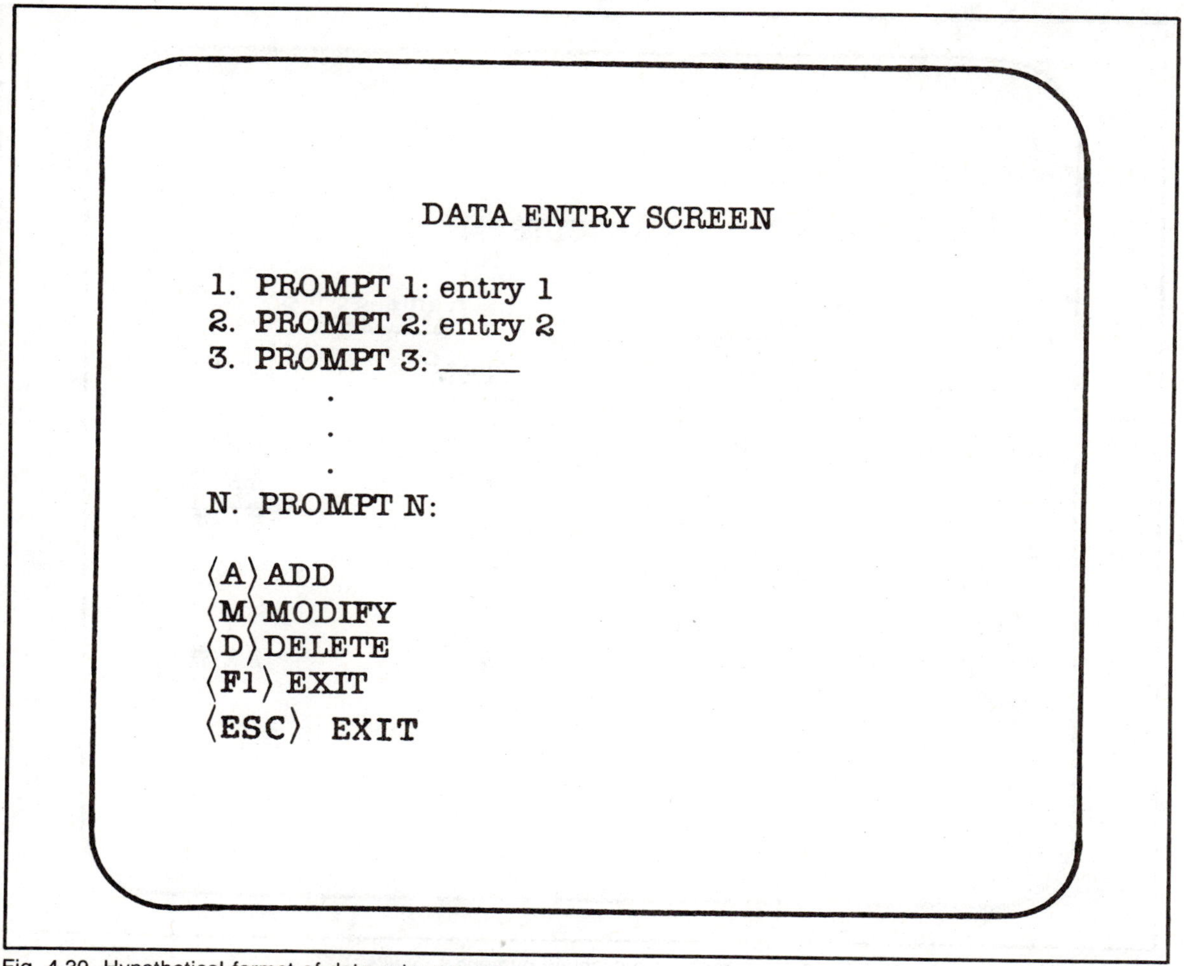

```
                 DATA ENTRY SCREEN

      1.  PROMPT 1: entry 1
      2.  PROMPT 2: entry 2
      3.  PROMPT 3: _____
                  .
                  .
                  .

      N.  PROMPT N:

      〈A〉 ADD
      〈M〉 MODIFY
      〈D〉 DELETE
      〈F1〉 EXIT
      〈ESC〉  EXIT
```

Fig. 4-30. Hypothetical format of data-entry screen.

consistent, analyze what types of screens you need in your program. Determine what classes of information you must present. Then lay out one or more general screen plans for use as models in building your screens. Find the smallest number of screen plans—ideally one—that you can use throughout your program.

To illustrate, Figs. 4-29 through 4-31 show screen plans for a hypothetical program. Screen 1 (Fig. 4-29) is the main control menu screen. This program uses several control menus. All are formatted according to this model. The title appears at the top, menu options at the center, prompt line at the bottom.

Screen 2 (Fig. 4-30) is the data entry screen. The title appears at the top. Numbered data entry fields are at the center. The bottom contains a menu for adding, modifying, or deleting entries, or for exiting the program.

Screen 3 (Fig. 4-31) is the display screen for presenting numeric results. the title appears at the top. Subtitle, column headings, and numeric information fill the center.

The models you develop depend upon your program. Follow the models as you code the program to assure consistency among your screens. Of course, once you sit down and start coding your program, there may be exceptions to each model. Do

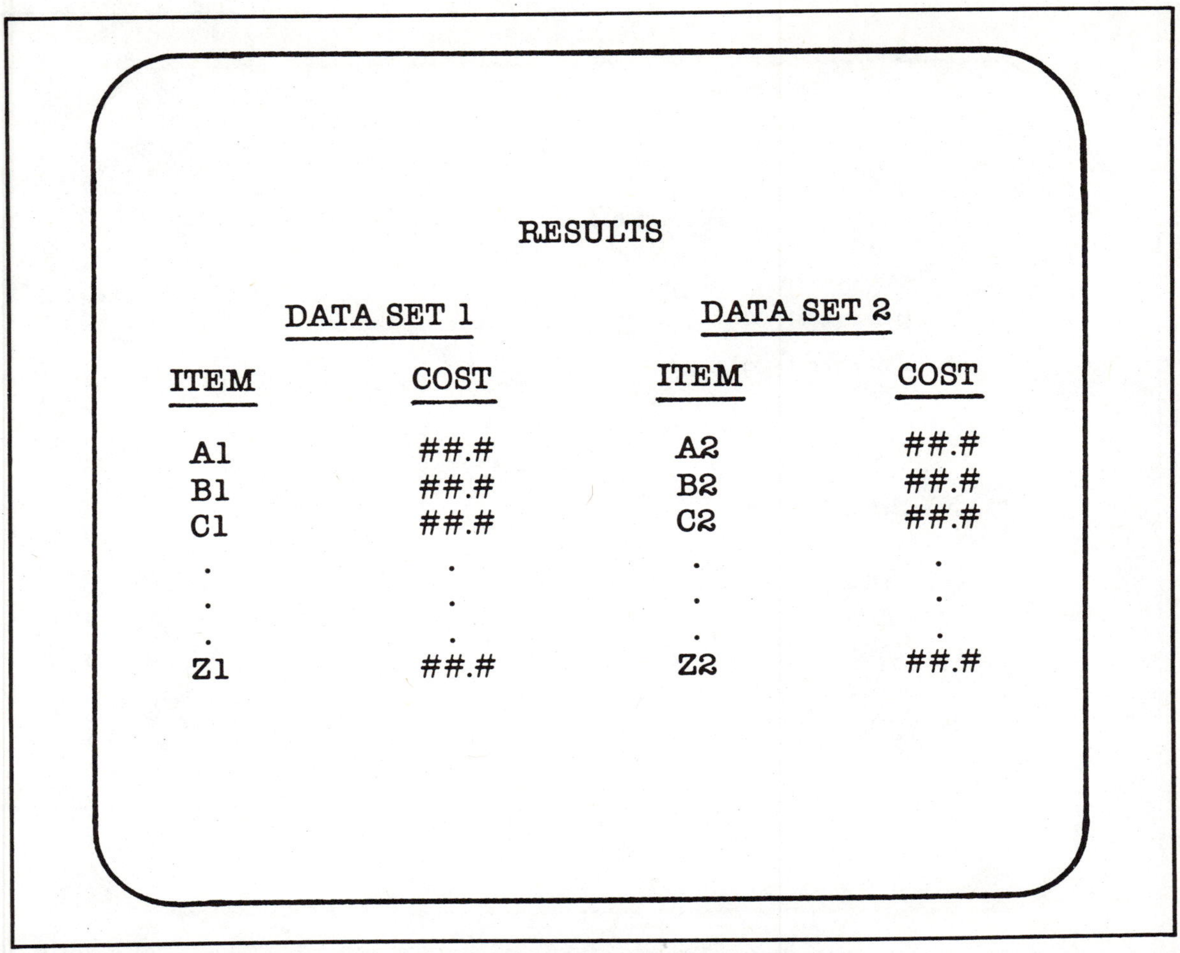

RESULTS

DATA SET 1		DATA SET 2	
ITEM	COST	ITEM	COST
A1	##.#	A2	##.#
B1	##.#	B2	##.#
C1	##.#	C2	##.#
.	.	.	.
.	.	.	.
	.	.	
Z1	##.#	Z2	##.#

Fig. 4-31. Hypothetical format of display screen for presenting numerical results.

not force fit things. Consistency is a good idea to keep in mind, but the primary goal of any display is to do a job—convey information, permit control of the program, take data entries, or whatever.

When a screen contains more than one type of information, label the different types and separate them from one another. If you do not do this properly, the user may have difficulty making sense of the screen. The best way to illustrate this point is by example. Figure 4-32 is an example of a poorly-designed display screen. Here is what is wrong with it:

- The display has no title

- There are three different data areas, but they overlap.
- The column heading are meaningless abbreviations.
- The prompt at the bottom of the screen is ambiguous.
- Headings and prompts are difficult to separate from data.

Figure 4-33 shows a better way to design this screen. A few changes improve the screen a great deal. Here are the differences:

- The display is titled.

- The center of the screen is divided into three distinct data areas, separated by lines. Each area is separately titled.
- Column headings are complete words, not abbreviations.
- The prompt gives explicit directions.
- Headings and prompts are in reverse video to make them stand out.

Using inverse video for titles, headings, and prompt lines is optional, but these three items must stand out. Instead of using inverse video, the items could be printed in high intensity, underlined, or enclosed in boxes.

Avoid abbreviations if you can. Many programmers have the mistaken ideas that abbreviations are expected on computer displays, and they are easy to understand. On the first point, they may be correct, but on the second wrong. Abbreviations are harder to understand. For this reason, avoid them.

The data area may be divided in a number of different ways. In Fig. 4-33, lines were printed between areas to separate them. The areas could also be separated by leaving at least two extra spaces.

A third way is to use color to divide the screen up into blocks and print each block with a different background and character color. While this is more difficult to program, you do not need as much space

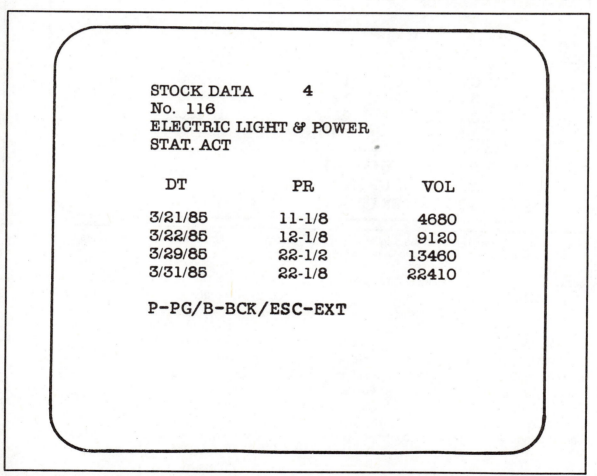

```
STOCK DATA       4
No. 116
ELECTRIC LIGHT & POWER
STAT. ACT


    DT              PR              VOL

3/21/85          11-1/8            4680
3/22/85          12-1/8            9120
3/29/85          22-1/2           13460
3/31/85          22-1/8           22410


P-PG/B-BCK/ESC-EXT
```

Fig. 4-32. Example of poorly designed display screen. There are no titles, data areas overlap, headings and data appear similar, and abbreviations and prompt are ambiguous.

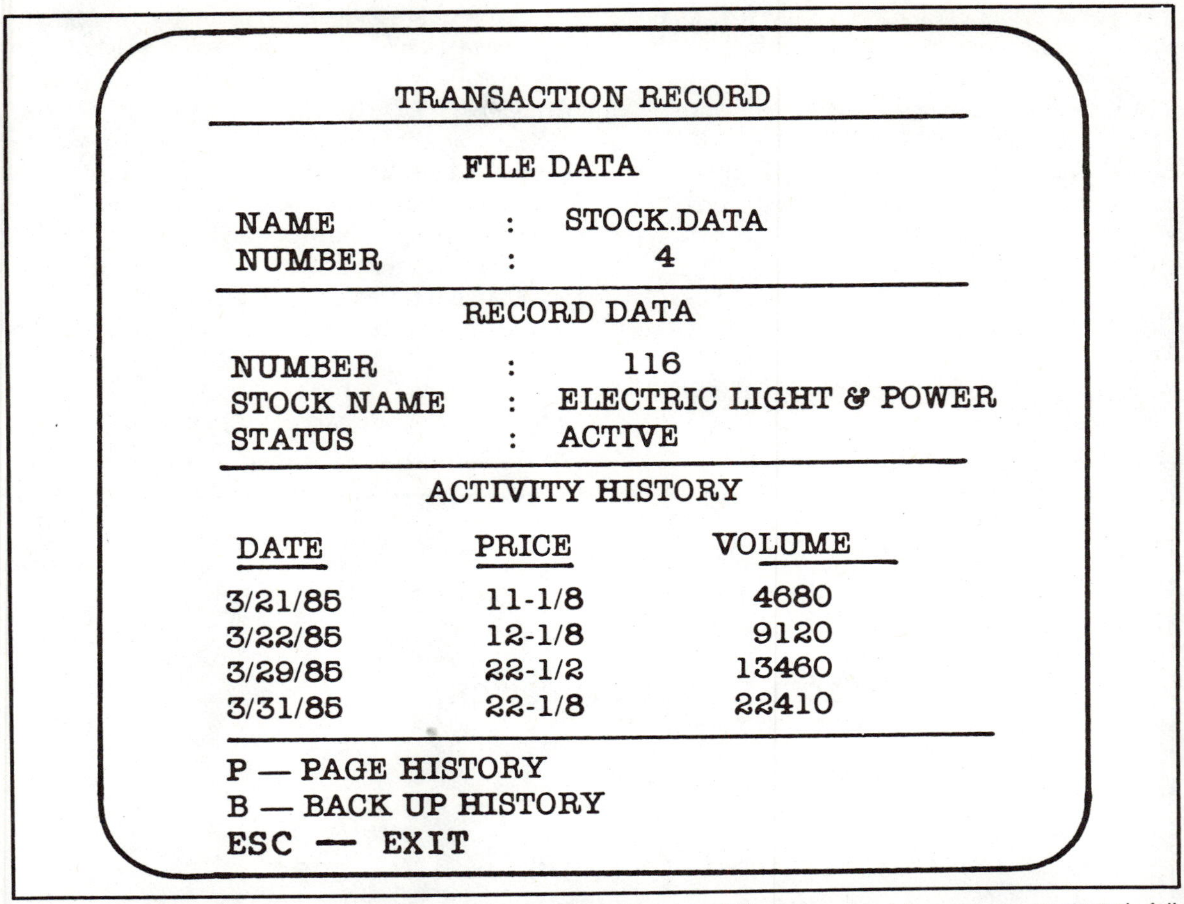

```
           TRANSACTION RECORD
   ──────────────────────────────────────

              FILE DATA
   NAME           :   STOCK.DATA
   NUMBER         :   4
   ──────────────────────────────────────

             RECORD DATA
   NUMBER         :   116
   STOCK NAME     :   ELECTRIC LIGHT & POWER
   STATUS         :   ACTIVE
   ──────────────────────────────────────

           ACTIVITY HISTORY

   DATE         PRICE         VOLUME
   3/21/85      11-1/8        4680
   3/22/85      12-1/8        9120
   3/29/85      22-1/2        13460
   3/31/85      22-1/8        22410
   ──────────────────────────────────────

   P — PAGE HISTORY
   B — BACK UP HISTORY
   ESC — EXIT
```

Fig. 4-33. An improved version of the display screen shown in Fig. 4-32. Titles are used, data areas are separated, full words are used instead of abbreviations, prompt is explicit.

between screen areas because they are clearly separated by their colors. When you use color this way, make sure that the different color blocks have approximately the same brightness levels so that the eye does not have to adapt to different light levels within a single display. The worst possible error is to divide up the screen into some areas which display black characters on a white background, and other areas which display white characters on a black background. Keep the backgrounds within a narrow contrast range.

HOW TO DISPLAY TEXT

Text consists of words combined in sentences to communicate information. It may be used in many different ways in a program, such as:

- Written directions
- Error messages
- Warnings
- Explanations
- Descriptions
- Definitions

Here are the rules for presenting text:

- Left-justify text.
- Use upper- and lowercase rather than all uppercase letters.

- Do not break a word between lines. Avoid splitting words with hyphens, if possible.
- Avoid abbreviations and jargon.
- Use a simple, direct style, with commonplace words.
- To make extended text more readable, break it into short paragraphs.
- In giving directions, or describing a procedure, list each step separately, and in the order it occurs or should be performed. Avoid treating it as a long block of text, or describing steps in some other order than they are performed.
- Present text in a color and against a background field that will be easy on the eyes.

Let the user control the rate at which text is presented. For example, if you have several pages of text to present, let the user page through them by pressing the space bar, Return key, or taking some other action. Do not pace the pages with a timing loop—that is, force the user to adapt his or her reading speed to the rate at which the program presents the information.

In general, text displayed in mixed upper- and lowercase letters is more legible and easier to read than text in all capital letters. Many programmers get into the habit of working with all upper case, and regard it as quite natural to create screens that contain nothing but capital letters. This is similar to the old convention of filling displays with abbreviations and computer jargon. Neither of these is very communicative to the user. It is much better to employ full, natural language, avoiding abbreviations and jargon, and to use both alphabet cases available.

HOW TO DISPLAY NUMBERS

As noted above, the convention for presenting text is to left-justify it by aligning the text against a common left margin. A different convention is fol-

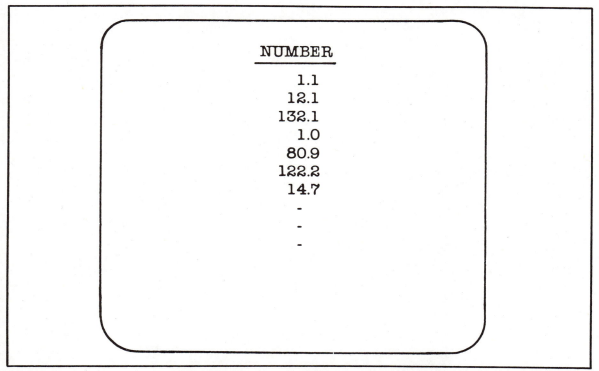

Fig. 4-34. A column of numbers aligned on the decimal point. This is the proper way to present numerical information.

lowed for presenting numbers: Numbers are aligned on their decimal point (Fig. 4-34). In addition, they are usually displayed with the same number of significant digits (numbers to the right of the decimal point). Aligning numbers on the decimal point is called "$ Formatting," since the technique is widely used for printing columns of monetary values. For example, bills are formatted this way, and so are checkbook reconciliation statements sent out by banks. The convention is followed for displaying columns of most numerical quantities.

Displaying numbers this way makes them easier to read. Compare, for example, Fig. 4-34 ($ formatted) and 4-35 (unformatted) and ask yourself these questions:

- Which looks neatest?
- Which helps you find the largest and smallest number most quickly?

In addition to alignment on the decimal point, a set of related numbers is usually displayed in a column beneath a heading that tells what the numbers represent. Never display a set of numbers like text, in rows that the reader must scan (Fig. 4-36).

If you are displaying a single number, or a series of unrelated numbers, place a header to the left of each number and separate it from the number with a colon, like this:

PRICE: $105.16

In short, there are two conventions for displaying numbers:

- List of numbers—In a column, aligned on the decimal point, with a header at the top.
- Single number—Heading at left, colon in middle, number at right.

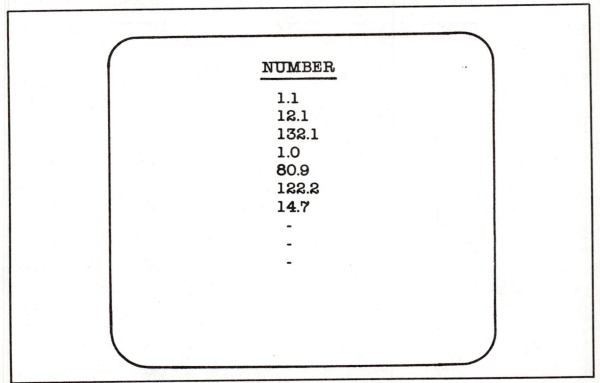

Fig. 4-35. Numbers left-justified. This is a poor way to present numerical information.

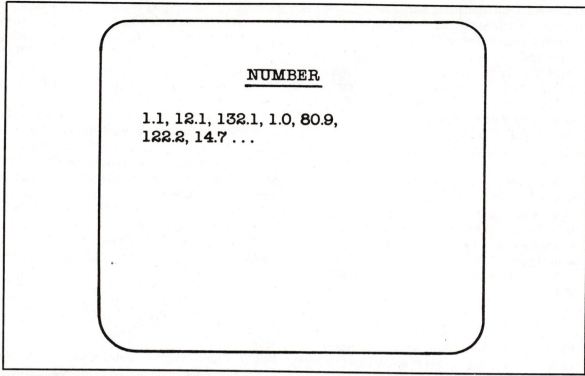

NUMBER

1.1, 12.1, 132.1, 1.0, 80.9,
122.2, 14.7 . . .

Fig. 4-36. Numbers printed like text, in rows. This is a bad way to present numerical information.

If your computer has a PRINT USING statement, numbers can be formatted easily. (If your BASIC lacks PRINT USING, construct a subroutine to do $Formatting, as described below.)

Number Formatting with PRINT USING

PRINT USING permits you to define a formatting string to use by the PRINT statement to set the format of the output. With the IBM PC, for example, to print the variable X with two significant digits, a formatting string such as "###.##" is used, where the # signs represent the character positions to the left and right of the decimal point. A statement such as the following is used to print and format X:

PRINT USING "###.##";X

If the same format is used repeatedly, it is a good idea to define the format string as a constant

to make the PRINT USING code more compact. For example, define string constants such as the following:

```
10   C1$ = "###.#"
20   C2$ = "###.##"
30   C3$ = "###.###"
```

Then use the predefined strings in the PRINT USING statements to display variables showing one, two, or three significant digits. For example, to display two significant digits, use C2$. That is

PRINT USING C2$;X

This discussion only gives an idea of the many things that you can do with the PRINT USING statement. Refer to your BASIC manual for details.

Displaying Numbers without PRINT USING

If your computer lacks the PRINT USING

statement, then formatting numbers for display is more difficult, but still quite straightforward. There are two aspects to the problem: setting the number of decimal places, and $ Formatting. PRINT USING does both of these and, without it, you must do them both yourself, as described below.

Many hand-held calculators have a feature that permits you to set the number of decimal places to be displayed. You know, you set a switch to 2 if you want two significant digits, to 4 if you want four, or to 0 if you are interested in rounding things to whole numbers. Most microcomputers lack this feature. If you start performing mathematical calculations that involve decimals, the number of decimal places displayed sometimes increases to preposterous lengths. Often you wind up with nine decimal places when all you want is one or two.

For example, sit down at your keyboard and type in the following:

PRINT 1/6

When you press the Return key of most computers, you'll see .166666667. It is easy enough to round this off in your head, but it would be nice to have the computer do it for you. You would probably be happy to know this value to two or three decimal places and, if it was produced by a calculation, might not trust a displayed value with any more places than that anyway.

The simplest way to round numbers is with a user-defined function. The following is the general form of a function that can be used for this purpose:

FN ROUND (X) = INT(X * 10 * Number of Places + .5)/10 * Number of Places

You can tailor this general function to suit a specific purpose by substituting a number for the parameter Number of Places. To illustrate, Fig. 4-37 shows three definitions of specific functions for rounding X. Line 410 contains the definition of FN C1(X), which rounds X to one place. Line 420 defines FN C2(X), which rounds to two places. Line 430 defines FN (C3(X), which rounds to three places.

In the improbable event that you have not used a user-defined function in a program before, here is a quick lesson. First, define the function early in the program. When you want to use it during the program, simply use it like any other BASIC statement. For example, to have the function round the value of your variable Y1 to three places, insert a statement setting Y1 = FN C3(Y1).

Try these functions out for yourself. Type in the listing in Fig. 4-37 and add the following lines.

```
10000    INPUT "X" ";X
10010    PRINT FN C1(X)
10020    PRINT FN C2(X)
10030    PRINT FN C3(X)
```

Run this little program, enter a value of X, and watch the rounded values be displayed.

$ Formatter

Figure 4-38 contains the listing of a $ formatting subroutine for the Apple. The arguments of this subroutine are N, N0, and T. N is the number to format. N0 is the number of decimal places to round the number to. T is the tab value at which the decimal point should appear.

To illustrate the subroutine's use, suppose that you calculated the value of variable X1 during a program and wanted to round and display this variable with three significant digits and with the decimal point appearing at tab position 32. You could round

```
0   REM  FIG 4-37
400    REM --DEFINE FUNCTIONS--
410    DEF  FN C1(X) =  INT (X * 10 + .5) / 10: REM     ROUND TO 1 PLACE
420    DEF  FN C2(X) =  INT (X * 100 + .5) / 100: REM     ROUND TO 2 PLACES
430    DEF  FN C3(X) =  INT (X * 1000 + .5) / 1000: REM     ROUND TO 3 PLACES
```

Fig. 4-37. User-defined functions to round numbers to 1, 2, or 3 decimal places.

```
0    REM   FIG 4-38
1    REM   $FORMATTER
2000  REM --$FORMATTER--
2010 N =   INT (N * 10 ^ N0 + .5) / 10 ^ N0: REM   SET DECIMAL PLACES
2020 N$ =   STR$ (N)
2030 L =   LEN (N$)
2040 T0 = L + 1: REM   INITIALIZE TAB OFFSET
2050   FOR A = 1 TO L
2060   IF   MID$ (N$,A,1) = "." THEN T0 = A: REM   LOCATE DECIMAL POINT
2070   NEXT
2080   POKE 36,T - T0
2090   PRINT N$;
2100   RETURN
```

Fig. 4-38. Apple $ Formatting subroutine.

and display the number by inserting the following statements in your program:

```
10010   N = X1
10020   N0 = 3
10030   T = 32
10040   GOSUB 2000
```

The arguments are assigned in lines 10010 – 10030, and the subroutine is called in line 10040. Simple enough.

Here is how the subroutine works. Line 2010 rounds the value of N to the number of places specified by its argument N0. You may recognize the formula on this line as identical to the general formula described above in the discussion of user-defined functions for rounding numbers. Line 2020 converts N to the string N$. Line 2030 computes L, the length of the string.

The next few lines locate the position of the decimal point, if present, within the number. To ensure that the decimal point is later printed at the correct tab position, the first character in the number must be printed starting as far left of the decimal point as there are spaces between the first character and the decimal point. For example, if you want to print the number 123.45 with the decimal point at tab position 23, then the first character must be printed starting at tab position 20. If the number does not contain a decimal point, then it must be printed its entire length to the left of the designated tab position. This distance to the left of the position of the decimal point is referred to as the *tab offset*.

Line 2040 initializes the tab offset to L + 1, the length of the number plus 1. The 1 is added in case the number does not contain a decimal point; this has the effect of defining the location of the decimal point to the right of the number.

Lines 2050 – 2070 search through N$, from left to right, looking for a decimal point. If one is found, its location is defined by setting T0 = A. For example, if the decimal point is the fourth character in N$, then T0 = 4. If no decimal point is located, then the number is an integer and it retains the initial T0 value set in line 2040. Line 2080 prints N$ at tab position T – T0.

Try this subroutine out for yourself. Type it in. Add the following lines so that you can enter values and see what results you get on your screen:

```
100   INPUT "N:";N
110   INPUT "N0:";N0
120   INPUT "T:";T
130   GOSUB 2000
140   PRINT
150   GOTO 100
```

Note that line 2090 ends with a semicolon so that no line feed is issued when this line is executed, thereby permitting you to format several numbers on the same print line. If the last thing you print on a line is a formatted number, however, you must issue a separate PRINT statement to cause a line feed.

```
2000 REM--$ FORMATTER--
2010 N=INT(N*10↑N0+.5)/10↑N0:REM SET DECIMAL PLACES
2020 N$=STR$(N)
2030 L=LEN(N$)
2040 T0=L+1:REM INITIALIZE TAB OFFSET
2050 FOR A=1 TO L
2060 IF MID$(N$,A,1)="."THEN T0=A:REM LOCATE DECIMAL POINT
2070 NEXT
2080 PRINT TAB(T-T0)N$;
2090 RETURN
```

Fig. 4-39. C-64 $ Formatting subroutine.

Figure 4-39 is an equivalent $ formatting subroutine for the C-64.

DESIGNING PRINTED REPORTS

A printed report is the hard copy output produced by your computer. The report may contain words, numbers, graphics, or a combination of all three. A printed report has two main advantages over a screen display. First, it is permanent. It goes on existing after you turn your computer off—a day, week, month, or a year later you can still hold it in your hand. Second, it can be as long as you want to make it. You are not limited to the narrow window of your video display.

One disadvantage of a printed report is that it exists outside the context of a computer program. That is, when you use a program and work your way to a particular display screen, you view that screen in relation to the screens that came before and the particular path you followed. On the other hand, when you pick up a printed report, that is all there is. It is like pulling a page out of a book without being able to see what came earlier. This is one reason why it is important to identify your reports clearly. Put a title or label on each report, and identification information on the different parts of the report. It often is important to include information

that you would not put on a screen report—for example, a date. When you use a computer program, you know the date. However, when you pull your printed budget report out of the file, you may not know when the report was generated.

The general lesson here is to take into account the effects of time on the interpretation of the report. What will the report user need to know? It may be the report generation date, who generated the report, certain report generation factors, or whatever. You must decide.

Most of the guidelines for screen design discussed earlier in this chapter apply also to the design of printed reports. The key rules are:

- Title the report and its various sections.
- Divide the report up into logical areas.
- When presenting text, use upper- and lower-case; avoid abbreviations and jargon; use a simple, direct style, with commonplace words; break extended text up into short paragraphs; present procedures in list form.
- In displaying columns of numeric information, separate columns by at least two blank spaces; align columns on the decimal point.

Plan your report carefully with a design matrix (Fig. 4-14) before you start coding.

Chapter 5

Data Entry, Error-Testing, and Validation

One of the first things a novice BASIC programmer learns is the INPUT statement. It is easy to use, and most new programmers master it within their first few hours of programming. Only later do they learn that there is much more to collecting data from program users than this simple statement. Not only are there other ways to intercept keystrokes—the INKEY$ or GET statements, for example—but many complications arise whenever a program must handle data entries.

To begin with, users do not always know what to enter. The prompts the programmer has written may be unclear, or the user may not have read the user's guide. In their confusion or ignorance, program users then type in information that the programmer had never in the wildest flights of imagination expected. The user will press the Return key with no typed entry, enter numbers where letters were expected and vice-versa, invent creative syntaxes for typing in dates, times, and telephone numbers, and perform other tricks to confound the programmer's neat and orderly view of the world. Well, when these things happen, it does not take the programmer long to wise up. He or she then concludes that something more than the INPUT statement is required.

But what?

Good prompting, for one thing with it, the user is less likely to make incorrect entries. But this, by itself, is not enough. Since errors will still occur some of the time, the programmer realizes that all user entries must be tested before they are accepted by the program. No programmer can read the minds of all program users, or anticipate every possible entry error, any more than he or she can write code to test for every error. Error-testing, it suddenly becomes clear, is more complex and difficult by far than using BASIC statements to convert those keystrokes into variables in memory.

Once the programmer finds a practical way to handle error-testing, the next problem comes to light. After making entries, the user reconsiders or recognizes an error, and wants to change the entry. Is it too late? Should it be too late? Should it be possible to start the entry process all over again? In short, what next?

This chapter attempts to provide reasonable answers to these and related data entry questions. The word "reasonable" is used because the truth is that it is impossible to write prompts that everyone understands, test for and protect against every possible entry error, or satisfy the user's every whim. It is possible, however, to do these things reasonably well, which is about all that should be expected from any reasonably sane, reasonably compulsive programmer.

The chapter begins with a discussion of data entry statements: INPUT, LINE INPUT, INKEY$, and GET. Next, the various steps in the data-entry process—prompting, collecting keystrokes, error-testing, verification—are discussed, and programming techniques, examples, and relevant subroutines are described. Tips and hints are then provided for integrating data entry routines with on-screen displays.

DATA-ENTRY STATEMENTS

Different versions of BASIC offer different sets of data-entry statements. Virtually all have the INPUT statement, which collects several characters, is somewhat selective in the characters it accepts, and requires the operator to press the Return key. Some computers have a LINE INPUT statement, which is similar to INPUT except that it is usually less selective of the characters it accepts and gives better screen control. Most computers have a statement that enables the collection of a single keystroke, without pressing the Return key; common forms are INKEY$ and GET. And in many cases the particular BASIC allows the programmer to modify file-handling statements—such as INPUT#—for keyboard input; if the other data-entry statements in the BASIC repertoire are limited, this often makes good sense. (C-64 owners should refer to Appendix B.)

The following discussion covers the two main categories of data-entry statements:

- INPUT and LINE INPUT
- INKEY$ and GET

Since BASIC dialects vary, the descriptions of the

statements and their properties differ somewhat from computer to computer, although the main points should be accurate for most.

INPUT and LINE INPUT

The main characteristics of the INPUT statement are as follows:

- It presents a flashing cursor on the screen, which attracts attention.
- It can be used for collecting long entries.
- The user can modify the entry before it is assigned to the statement's variable. The entry is verified by pressing the Return key.
- The user can disrupt the appearance of the display by making inappropriate entries. For example, if a real variable follows the INPUT statement (such as INPUT A) and the user types in a letter and presses the Return key, an error message usually appears on the screen and the screen scrolls. The same thing happens if the user types in a comma as part of the entry. If the user types in too-long an entry, the screen scrolls.
- The INPUT statement usually accepts an embedded prompt string, which it prints on the display when the INPUT statement is executed. For example, in IBM PC BASIC, an INPUT statement in the form

    INPUT "Name: ";NA$

will print **Name:** on the screen followed by a question mark and flashing cursor, like this:

    Name: ? _

The question mark can usually be suppressed by varying the syntax. For example, in IBM PC BASIC, an INPUT statement in the form

    INPUT "Name: ",NA$

will print a prompt that looks like this:

Name: __

The LINE INPUT statement works like the INPUT statement with the exception that it accepts any characters that the user types in, including commas and quotation marks. This makes it better for many uses than the INPUT statement, which regards a comma as indicating the end of the entry. To illustrate, enter and run this little program:

```
10  INPUT A$
20  PRINT A$
```

In response to the prompt, type something with a comma in it, such as "Traven, B," and see what happens. If the LINE INPUT statement is substituted for INPUT, the entry will be assigned, as typed in, to the prompt string, commas and all. Since the LINE INPUT statement is more tolerant of what it accepts, it is generally better than the INPUT statement.

INKEY$ and GET

INKEY$ is a fairly standardized data-entry statement. GET is not. In many forms of BASIC (usually those with a separate INKEY$ statement) it is used to read data from files. In a BASIC without INKEY$, such as the Apple and C-64 versions, it is often used for keyboard input, and behaves similarly to INKEY$. The Applesoft form of GET does more than INKEY$, and is much like the Improved INKEY$ described below. The following discussion of INKEY$ applies both to INKEY$ and to forms of GET which do not produce a flashing cursor and pause the program waiting for a keyboard entry.

The main characteristics of INKEY$ are as follows:

- It does not produce a visual cue on the screen—no flashing cursor or question mark. (A flashing cursor must be produced with separate code.)
- It collects one character.
- It does not echo the entry to the screen. The

typed entry is taken by the computer but not displayed.
- It does not permit the user to verify the entry. Once typed, the entry is assigned to its variable.
- Since INKEY$ collects only one character, there is little chance of disrupting the appearance of the display through improper data entry.

INKEY$ is a different kind of data entry statement than INPUT or LINE INPUT. It takes one keystroke at a time, and does not require the user to press the Return key to verify the entry. It would seem that the naked INKEY$ is useless in most programs, since it does not have a flashing cursor or echo entries to the screen. Don't jump to this conclusion, however.

Actually, there are three possible ways to think about INKEY$—sort of like buying a car with different options. Let us consider the three models:

"Naked" or "Economy" INKEY$. This is INKEY$ in its simplest form. Here is an example:

```
10  PRINT "Do you accept? (y/n):";
20  A$ = INKEY$: IF A$ = " " GOTO 20
30  IF A$< >"y" AND A$< >"n" GOTO 20
```

This little program is used to verify a result that was previously displayed to the program user. If the user accepts the result, he or she types *y*. If not, an *n* is typed. In this program, line 10 displays the prompt, 20 contains the INKEY$ loop, and 30 runs an error test to make sure that the routine cannot be exited until either a *y* or *n* is typed. In a simple situation like this, no flashing cursor is placed on the screen and the typed entry is not displayed. The routine would be better if they were, but in such a simple application, these additional features are not critical.

Improved INKEY$. The improved INKEY$ has two features not included in the Economy Model: a flashing cursor and display of the entry. With the IBM PC, we can obtain these features by adding two lines to the above code. Here is the modified listing:

```
10  PRINT "Do you accept? (y/n)";
```

```
15    COLOR 23,0:PRINT"___";:REM flash cursor
16    COLOR 7,0:REM normal video
20    A$ = INKEY$:IF A$ = " " GOTO 20
30    IF A$< >"y" AND A$< >"n" GOTO 20
40    LOCATE,  POS(0) – 1:PRINT  A$;:REM
      display keystroke
```

The modifications are the addition of three lines—15, 16, and 40. Line 15 converts to flashing video mode and prints an underline character which looks like the cursor. Line 16 converts back to normal video. Line 40 determines the location of the cursor—which is one space to the right of the flashing underline—and subtracts one from it and prints the keyboard entry there. Note that the entry is printed only if it is a lowercase *y* or *n*; other characters are filtered out by line 30.

An equivalent form of this routine for the C-64 is shown below.

```
10    PRINT "DO YOU ACCEPT THE RESULT?
      (Y/N):";
15    POKE 204,0:REM FLASH CURSOR
20    GET A$: IF A$ = " " GOTO 20
30    IF A$< >"Y" AND A$< >"N" GOTO 20
40    PRINT A$:REM DISPLAY KEYSTROKE
```

The Apple version of the routine, shown below, is simpler yet, since Applesoft's GET produces its own flashing cursor.

```
10    PRINT "DO YOU ACCEPT? (Y/N):";
20    GET A$
30    IF A$< >"Y" and A$< >"N" GOTO 20
40    PRINT A$;:REM DISPLAY KEYSTROKE
```

Note that, as written, all of these routines look either for uppercase or lowercase characters, and will accept only those tested for and accepted. To accept both upper and lower characters, the tests would have to be modified.

"Deluxe" INKEY$. The Deluxe INKEY$ does everything that the Improved INKEY$ does, and also allows multiple-keystroke entries. It allows entry of commas, permits you to filter what the user types in by ignoring certain characters, and limits the entry to a minimum and maximum length. This INKEY$ is more powerful than the INPUT or LINE INPUT statements, and would be used in place of them in certain types of programs.

In the form described below, it can be used to create complete data entry screens, such as Fig. 5-1. Such a screen contains several data-entry fields, and the user types in the entries for one field at a time. After completing field one, the cursor moves to field two, three, and so on. In such screens, it is important to have complete control of what the user types in and to prevent any keystrokes from disrupting the screen. Without this control, a few unfortunate keystrokes can turn the screen into an unreadable mess.

The code for the Deluxe INKEY$ is a bit involved, and the best way to describe how it works is with a flow chart that shows its logic and the functions that must be performed. After going through the chart, we will look at the actual code.

In using INKEY$ to collect an entry that is more than one character long, the code must still collect one character at a time. It then concatenates the characters together into a longer string. However, not all characters can be treated equally. Pressing the Return key (CHR$(13)) signals the end of data entry. Pressing the Delete or Cursor Left key (for the IBM PC) means that one character must be removed from the current entry. Characters can also be selectively ignored.

Figure 5-2 is a flow chart showing the logic of the Deluxe INKEY$. Each of the steps in the flow chart has a number on the left. The number on the right of each step is the line number in the corresponding BASIC listing shown in Fig. 5-3. In both the flow chart and the listing, the entire entry is represented as A$ and the single character being collected via INKEY$ is B$.

Step 1 positions the cursor to a particular part of the screen, and Step 2 prints the prompt. (Note that no upward arrows return to either of these steps. This means that it is possible to fill a complete screen with prompts, and then go through Steps 3 through 11 of each data entry sequence separately.)

Step 3 positions the cursor again—this time at the end of the prompt, at the beginning of the data-entry field. Step 4 prints whatever has been typed

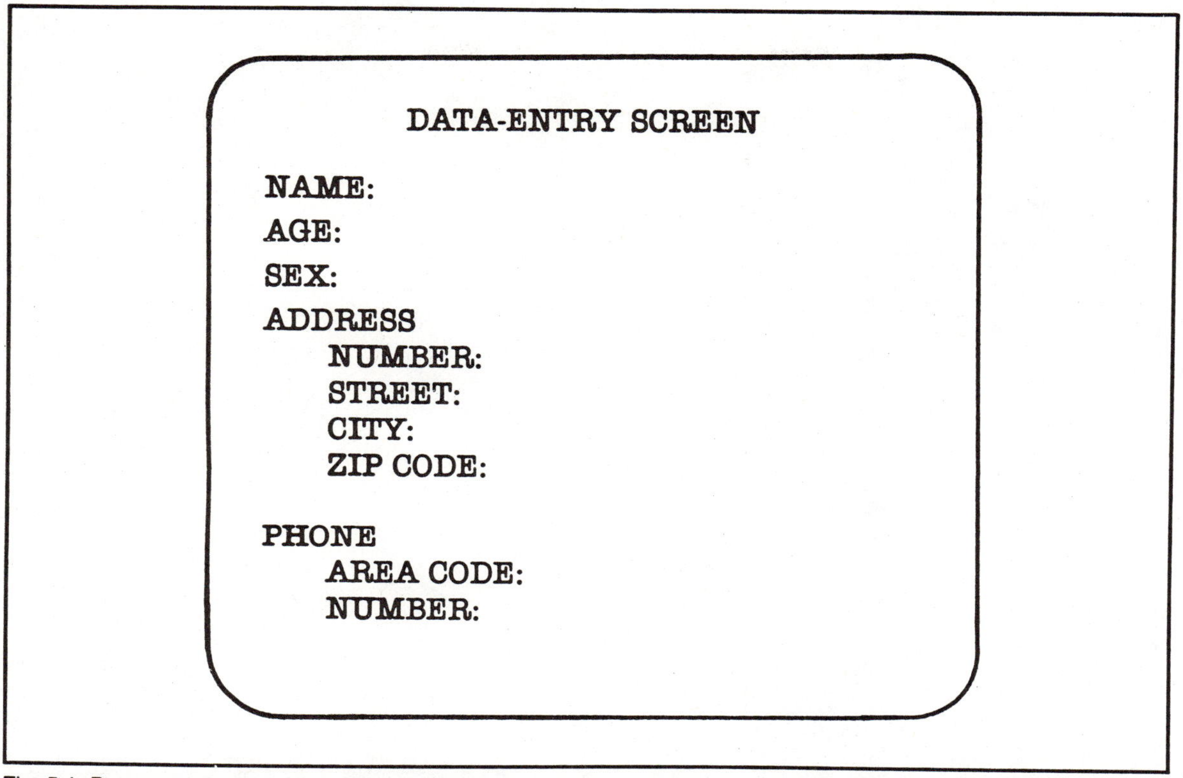

```
┌─────────────────────────────────────────────────────┐
│    ╭─────────────────────────────────────────────╮   │
│    │                                             │   │
│    │          DATA-ENTRY SCREEN                  │   │
│    │                                             │   │
│    │   NAME:                                     │   │
│    │   AGE:                                      │   │
│    │   SEX:                                      │   │
│    │   ADDRESS                                   │   │
│    │       NUMBER:                               │   │
│    │       STREET:                               │   │
│    │       CITY:                                 │   │
│    │       ZIP CODE:                             │   │
│    │                                             │   │
│    │   PHONE                                     │   │
│    │       AREA CODE:                            │   │
│    │       NUMBER:                               │   │
│    │                                             │   │
│    ╰─────────────────────────────────────────────╯   │
└─────────────────────────────────────────────────────┘
```

Fig. 5-1. Data-entry screen. All prompts are printed on the screen, and the cursor moves from field to field as the user types in data.

in so far. These three steps reprint the entire current entry each time a key is pressed. The main reason for doing this is to handle deletions or backspaces, as will be apparent below.

Step 5 prints a flashing cursor on the screen. Step 6 gets one keystroke via INKEY\$. Step 7A tests whether the keystroke is a Return key press. If so, Step 7B tests whether the length of the current entry (A\$) is less than the minimum allowable length (L_{min}). L_{min} can be set to any value less than or equal to L_{max}(maximum length), including zero. However, it is usually desirable to limit minimum length to at least one character. If the minimum length test is failed, then control jumps back to Step 6 so that another character can be retrieved via INKEY\$. If it is passed, then control exits the routine.

Step 8A tests for a Delete or Cursor Left key press. If one occurred, Step 8B tests whether the length of A\$ is greater than zero and, if this test is passed, Step 8C removes the rightmost character from A\$. In Step 8D, the data-entry field is erased so that, when the current entry is rewritten in Step 4, it will not contain the deleted character.

Step 9 tests whether the length of A\$ is equal to L_{max}. If so, control returns to Step 7. If A\$ has reached the length of L_{max}, control will continue to recycle to Step 7 until the Return key is pressed or a character is deleted from A\$.

Step 10 is the keyboard filter. It checks whether the ASCII values of the keystrokes meet acceptable criteria—comma, number, letter, or space bar. If the test is failed, control returns to Step 6. This has the effect of ignoring keystrokes that fail the test.

Step 11 concatenates the single character B\$ with A\$, the string comprising the entry so far.

Now let us consider the code that performs

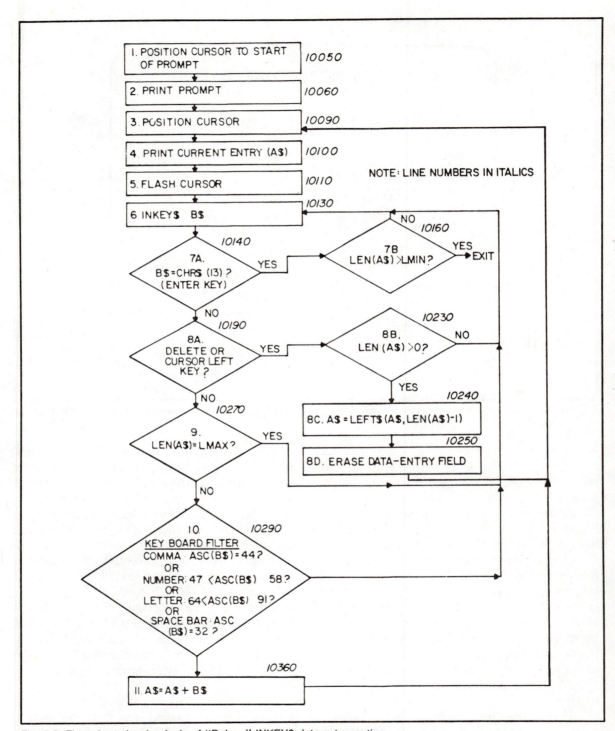

Fig. 5-2. Flow chart showing logic of "Deluxe" INKEY$ data-entry routine.

```
0 REM "Deluxe" INKEY$ Data-Entry Routine
1 REM SAVE"FIG5-3",A
980 WIDE%=80
990 GOTO 10000
1300 REM--Clear One Line--
1310 LOCATE V,H:REM position cursor
1320 PRINT SPACE$(WIDE%+1-H);:REM clear to end of line
1330 LOCATE V,H:REM reposition cursor
1340 RETURN
10000 REM--"Deluxe" INKEY$ Data-Entry Routine--
10010 L1=1:REM set minimum length
10020 L2=12:REM set maximum length
10030 A$="":REM initialize data entry
10040 CLS:REM clear screen
10050 V=10:H=1:GOSUB 1300:REM clear line & position prompt
10060 COLOR 0,7:REM inverse
10070 PRINT"Name (up to 12 char):";
10080 COLOR 7,0:REM normal video
10090 LOCATE 10,23
10100 PRINT A$;:REM print current entry
10110 COLOR 23,0:PRINT "_";:REM flash cursor
10120 COLOR 7,0:REM normal video
10130 B$=INKEY$:IF B$="" GOTO 10130
10140 REM--Enter key pressed?--
10150 IF B$()CHR$(13) GOTO 10190
10160 IF LEN(A$)<L1 THEN BEEP:GOTO 10130:REM minimum length test
10170 PRINT
10180 END:REM end of data-entry sequence
10190 REM--Delete or Cursor Left key pressed?
10200 IF LEN(B$)=1 GOTO 10270
10210 B1$=RIGHT$(B$,1)
10220 IF B1$()"K" AND B1$()"S" GOTO 10270
10230 IF LEN(A$)=0 GOTO 10130:REM minimum length test
10240 A$=LEFT$(A$,LEN(A$)-1):REM subtract right-most character from A$
10250 V=10:H=23:GOSUB 1300:REM erase entry
10260 GOTO 10090
10270 REM--Maximum Length Test--
10280 IF LEN(A$)=L2 THEN BEEP:GOTO 10130
10290 REM--Filter--
10300 IF ASC(B$)=44 GOTO 10360:REM comma entered
10310 IF ASC(B$)>47 AND ASC(B$)<58 GOTO 10360:REM number
10320 IF ASC(B$)>64 AND ASC(B$)<123 GOTO 10360:REM letter (capital)
10330 IF ASC(B$)=32 GOTO 10360:REM space bar
10340 BEEP
10350 GOTO 10130
10360 A$=A$+B$
10370 GOTO 10090
```

Fig. 5-3. IBM PC Deluxe INKEY$ data-entry routine corresponding to logic shown in Fig. 5-2.

these wonders. Figure 5-3 contains the listing of the IBM PC version of the Deluxe INKEY$ routine whose logic was just described. Note that the program requires the line-clearing subroutine presented in Chapter 4 (Fig. 4-8). This subroutine is needed in the present program to position the cursor and to clear the prompt line.

The data entry code is contained in lines 10000 through 10370. A rather long listing to do what an INPUT statement could do, you might be thinking, but recognize that this code does considerably more.

Lines 10010 and 10020 set L1 (minimum length of A$) and L2 (maximum length). Line 10030 initializes the string A$. Line 10040 clears the screen. Line 10050 uses the line-clearing subroutine to position the cursor to row 10, column 1. Line 10060 sets inverse video mode, and line 10070 prints the data entry prompt. This prompt indicates that the maximum length of the name is 12 characters (the value of L2). Line 10080 then sets the display back to normal video. Line 10090 locates the cursor at row 10, column 23, and line 10100 then prints A$, the entry so far. Line 10110 displays the flashing cursor, and line 10120 sets normal video. Line 10130 is an INKEY$ loop that collects one keystroke.

Line 10150 tests whether the Return key was pressed. If not, control jumps to line 10190. Lines 10160 and 10170 are executed only if the Return key was pressed. Line 10160 tests whether A$ satisfies the minimum length requirement. If not, a beep is emitted and control is sent back to line 10130 to INKEY$ another character. In this listing, line 10170 contains a PRINT statement (to provide a carriage return following the printing of A$;) and then END. In an actual program, END would be replaced by a GOTO directing control to the next step in the data entry sequence.

Lines 10190 – 10260 test whether the Delete or Cursor Left keys were pressed and take appropriate action. What happens during these lines is not obvious and deserves a short explanation. With the IBM PC, the Delete or Cursor Left keys do not have normal ASCII codes and cannot be detected in the usual manner. Instead, they have what are referred to as *extended ASCII codes*, meaning that, when they are pressed, the INKEY$ variable returns two characters instead of one. The first character is a blank and the second character is the character whose ASCII code corresponds to the key's scan code (discussed in Chapter 3). The scan code of the Cursor Left key is 75 and of the Delete key is 83. The characters corresponding to these two numbers as ASCII values are the letters K and S.

Here is how the test works. Line 10200 tests the length of B$, the character that was just returned by INKEY$. If the length is 1, then B$ could not be either the Cursor Left or Delete key, and control is sent to line 10270. If the length is not 1, then control flows to line 10210. Line 10210

extracts the rightmost character from B$ and line 10220 tests whether this character is a letter K or S and, if the test is failed (meaning that neither the Cursor Left nor Delete key was pressed), control is sent to line 10270. However, if one of these keys was pressed, control flows to line 10230.

Line 10230 tests whether the length of A$ is zero characters. If so, control is directed to line 10130 to INKEY$ another character. If not, then line 10240 removes the rightmost character from A$, line 10250 clears the data-entry field, and control is sent to line 10090, where the revised A$ is rewritten. Line 10280 performs the maximum length test. As long as the length of A$ equals L2, control will continue to recycle to line 10130.

Lines 10290 – 10350 comprise the filter. These lines test whether the key press B$ is an acceptable character. If so, control is sent to line 10360, where B$ is concatenated with A$. If none of the tests succeeds, line 10350 sends control back to line 10130 to INKEY$ another character. After concatenation, control is sent to line 10090 to rewrite the new version of A$.

Equivalent data-entry routines for the Apple and C-64 are shown in Figs. 5-4 and 5-5, respectively.

Comparing Data Entry Methods

Which data-entry method—INPUT, LINE INPUT, or INKEY$ (or GET)—is best? It depends upon the program.

INPUT is fine for use in programs that have limited data-entry requirements, but not good for serious programs. The main reason is that pressing the Return key can sometimes disrupt the display. In addition, its inability to digest certain characters (such as the comma) is another limitation. LINE INPUT overcomes these limitations and is much better for data entry.

INKEY$ (or GET) may be used to collect a single keystroke or several keystrokes. In single-keystroke form, it is good for presenting verification statements to the user. For example, present a prompt such as the following to the user after several data entries have been made:

```
0    REM   FIG 5-4
1    REM   "DELUXE" GET DATA-ENTRY ROUTINE
980  COLS = 40
990   GOTO 10000
1300   REM --CLEAR ONE LINE--
1310   VTAB V: HTAB H: REM  POSITION CURSOR
1320   CALL  - 868
1330   VTAB V: HTAB H: REM  REPOSITION CURSOR
1340   RETURN
10000  REM --"DELUXE" GET DATA-ENTRY ROUTINE--
10010 L1 = 1: REM  SET MINIMUM LENGTH
10020 L2 = 12: REM  SET MAXIMUM LENGTH
10030 A$ = "": REM  INITIALIZE DATA ENTRY
10040  HOME : REM  CLEAR SCREEN
10050 V = 10:H = 1: GOSUB 1300: REM  CLEAR LINE AND POSITION CURSOR
10060   INVERSE
10070   PRINT "NAME (UP TO 12 CHAR):"
10080   NORMAL
10090   VTAB 10: HTAB 23
10100   PRINT A$;: REM  PRINT CURRENT ENTRY
10110   GET B$
10120   REM  --RETURN KEY PRESSED?--
10130   IF B$ < >  CHR$ (13) GOTO 10170
10140   IF  LEN (A$) < L1 THEN  CALL  - 198: GOTO 10110: REM  MINIMUM
       LENGTH TEST
10150   PRINT
10160   END : REM  END OF DATA-ENTRY SEQUENCE
10170   REM --DELETE OR CURSOR LEFT KEY PRESSED?--
10180   IF  ASC (B$) < > 127 AND  ASC (B$) < > 8 GOTO 10240
10190   IF  LEN (A$) = 0 THEN  CALL  - 198: GOTO 10110: REM  MINIMUM
       LENGTH TEST
10200   IF  LEN (A$) = 1 THEN A$ = "": GOTO 10220
10210 A$ =  LEFT$ (A$, LEN (A$) - 1): REM  SUBTRACT RIGHT-MOST CHARACTER
      FROM A$
10220 V = 10:H = 23: GOSUB 1300: REM  ERASE ENTRY
10230   GOTO 10090
10240   REM --MAXIMUM LENGTH TEST--
10250   IF  LEN (A$) = L2 THEN  CALL  - 198: GOTO 10110
10260   REM --FILTER--
10270   IF  ASC (B$) = 44 GOTO 10330: REM  COMMA ENTERED
10280   IF  ASC (B$) > 47 AND  ASC (B$) < 58 GOTO 10330: REM  NUMBER
10290   IF  ASC (B$) > 64 AND  ASC (B$) < 91 GOTO 10330: REM  LETTER
    (CAPITAL)
10300   IF  ASC (B$) = 32 GOTO 10330: REM  SPACE BAR
10310   CALL  - 198
10320   GOTO 10110
10330 A$ = A$ + B$
10340   GOTO 10090
```

Fig. 5-4. Apple Deluxe GET data-entry routine.

Do you want to change anything? (y/n)

The user types a *y* or *n* to indicate the choice. Pressing the Return key following the entry should not be required. Single-keystroke entry such as this is not good for normal data entry; the user needs to

see the data entry displayed, and be able to verify the entry with the Return key before it becomes final.

When INKEY$ is used in the multiple-keystroke Deluxe INKEY$ form described above, it becomes an alternative to the INPUT or LINE

```
10000 REM--GET ROUTINE FOR EXTENDED INPUT--
10010 L1=1:REM SET MINIMUM LENGTH
10020 L2=12:REM SET MAXIMUM LENGTH
10030 A$="":REM INITIALIZE DATA ENTRY
10040 PRINT CHR$(147);:REM CLEAR SCREEN
10050 SYS C0,0,12,1:REM POSITION PROMPT
10060 PRINT"NAME (UP TO 12 CHAR): ";
10070 SYS C0,1,12,23:REM CLEAR LINE TO RIGHT OF CURSOR
10080 SYS C0,0,12,23:REM POSITION CURSOR
10090 PRINT A$;:REM PRINT CURRENT ENTRY
10100 POKE 204,0:REM FLASH CURSOR
10110 GET B$:IF B$="" GOTO 10110
10120 REM-RETURN KEY PRESSED?-
10130 IF B$<>CHR$(13) GOTO 10170
10140 IF LEN(A$)<L1 GOTO 10110:REM MINIMUM LENGTH TEST
10150 PRINT
10160 END:REM END OF DATA-ENTRY SEQUENCE
10170 REM-DELETE OR BACKSPACE KEY PRESSED?-
10180 IF B$<>CHR$(20) AND B$<>CHR$(157) GOTO 10220
10190 IF LEN(A$)=0 GOTO 10110:REM MINIMUM LENGTH TEST
10200 A$=LEFT$(A$,LEN(A$)-1):REM SUBTRACT RIGHT-MOST CHARACTER FROM A$
10210 GOTO 10070
10220 REM-MAXIMUM LENGTH TEST-
10230 IF LEN(A$)=L2 GOTO 10110
10240 REM-FILTER-
10250 IF ASC(B$)=44 GOTO 10300:REM COMMA ENTERED
10260 IF ASC(B$)>47 AND ASC(B$)<58 GOTO 10300:REM NUMBER
10270 IF ASC(B$)>64 AND ASC(B$)<91 GOTO 10300:REM LETTER
10280 IF ASC(B$)=32 GOTO 10300:REM SPACEBAR
10290 GOTO 10110
10300 A$=A$+B$
10310 GOTO 10070
```

Fig. 5-5. C-64 Deluxe GET data-entry routine. (Requires assembly-language subroutine loader; see Appendix B.)

INPUT statements. It can monitor the keystrokes one by one, filter some out, and prevent the entry from getting too long. In short, it provides complete control of the data-entry process, and provides insurance against disruption of the display. Where these factors are critical, use INKEY$ instead of INPUT or LINE INPUT.

Using Strings as Assignment Variables

Always use string variables in your INPUT, LINE INPUT, INKEY$, and GET statements. String variables can be anything, and your computer will not choke if the user just presses the Return key, or types a letter, number, or symbol. If you ask your computer to INPUT a real variable or an integer, it is more picky. For example, if you

execute this statement in your program:

10   INPUT A

and the user types in "Rose is no rose" and presses the Return key when the prompt appears, the computer will probably display an error message and then redisplay the ?.

Attempting to INPUT an integer variable is like playing roulette: Some numbers win, some numbers lose. Valid integer variables are between −32768 and 32767 (give or take 1, depending on the computer). Type in something outside this range and computer goes "Aargh!" You lose.

Assign all keyboard entries to strings. If what you are looking for is a number, convert the string to its equivalent numeric value with the VAL statement. That is, insert code like the following:

```
10   INPUT A$
20   A = VAL(A$)
```

THE INPUT PROCESS

A well-designed data-entry routine must do more than collect the user's keystrokes and convert them to variables in memory. This is all that some data-entry routines do, and it is not enough. A good routine:

- Prompts the user, telling what entry is required.
- Collects the entries from the keyboard with a BASIC statement.
- Tests the entries.
- Permits the user to verify (observe and modify) the entries.

A poor data-entry routine omits some steps, or performs them poorly. Only when all of these pieces are in place do you have an adequate data-entry routine.

Each of these four functions—prompting, collecting keystrokes, error-testing, verification—poses certain design requirements. There are right ways and wrong ways to do each one. The discussion that follows covers each function in a separate section.

The examples use the LINE INPUT statement, mainly to keep the code simple. As discussed above, it is sometimes better to use the Deluxe INKEY$ method.

Prompting

The prompt tells the user what entry to make. A prompt should do the following:

- Tell what type of entry is required. It should be both descriptive and brief. Being descriptive is more important than being brief. This prompt is both:

Type your monthly salary: $

This prompt is brief, but not descriptive enough:

Enter amount:

Amount of what? It is not clear what is being asked for. It could be pounds, gallons, dollars, or anything measurable.

- Give the entry format, if a special one is required. For example, if a time, telephone number, or date must be entered in a special format, the prompt should show it. For example:

Type your birthdate
(month/day/year, example: 4/15/54):__

This tells the user to type the month, day, and year, separated by slashes. Without this prompting, the date might be entered in any one of a number of different ways, such as 4,15,54; 4-15-54; or 04151954.

- Attract attention. A prompt is a question and requires an answer. However, it cannot be answered if the user does not see it or realize that some action is required. It must be conspicuous. Use a flashing cursor if you can. A flashing cursor attracts attention and draws the eyes to the prompt. It is also helpful to print the prompt in inverse video, or in a bright color that differs from the rest of what is on the screen. An additional way to make the prompt stand out is to print it in all capital letters.

Remember the principle of consistency. Prompt similar entries consistently. Do no ask for the same type of information in two different ways in the same program.

Collecting Keystrokes

Normally, a program collects the user's keystrokes while presenting the user with a data-entry screen. A data-entry screen is the display screen that the user views while typing keyboard entries. Some screens are dedicated solely to this purpose (Fig. 5-6). Others may also display information that relates, directly or indirectly, to the required entries (Fig. 5-7).

Full-Screen Data Entry. You have probably used a program that has a data entry screen similar to Fig. 5-6. The screen looks like a data-entry form (Fig. 5-8). In fact, the screen may be based on a paper form, and the more the screen looks like the form, the better. Typically, the user sits before the computer and types entries from the form. On the screen, the cursor starts at the first data-entry field. After the user types the entry and presses the Return key, the cursor jumps to the next field. The user then types the next entry, the next, and so on, until the entire screen is filled in.

This data-entry method is called *full-screen data entry*.

It is good to use full-screen data entry if users will type in data from standard forms or formatted paper copy such as checks. Having the screen look like the copy makes it easier for the user to see the connection between the two. It is also good to use full-screen data entry if users make a series of related entries—such as a set of stock prices—and may want to refer to previous entries while making the current one. By keeping previous entries on the screen, the user can remain oriented and reduce chances of skipping an entry or making an entry twice.

Let us go through the exercise of designing a simple data-entry screen and then creating the code necessary to generate the screen and permit full-screen data entry. The example that follows can be

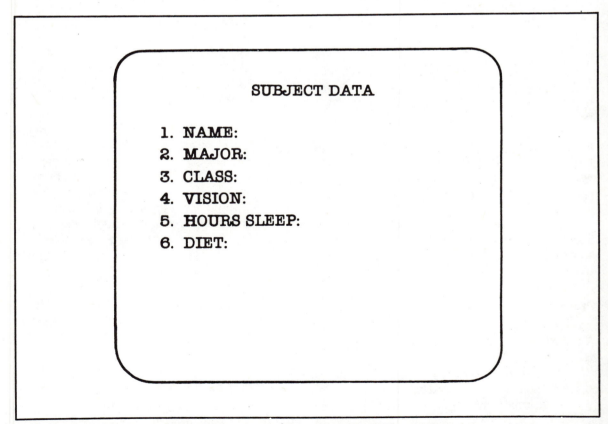

Fig. 5-6. A data-entry screen fully committed to data entry, and without displayed information.

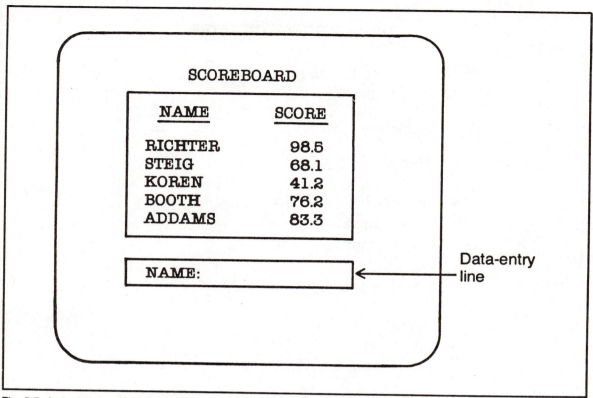

SCOREBOARD

NAME	SCORE
RICHTER	98.5
STEIG	68.1
KOREN	41.2
BOOTH	76.2
ADDAMS	83.3

NAME:

Data-entry line

Fig. 5-7. A display screen with information at the top and a data-entry line at the bottom.

extended to much more complex screens than the one described. This screen will collect three entries: Name, Age, and Sex, which will be assigned to the program variables NAMES\$, AGE, and SEX\$, respectively.

To keep things simple, assume that any value of any variable is legal. This is obviously not true, but let us ignore the error tests for now; they are covered later in the chapter.

We will start by laying out the screen on a design matrix. The result is shown in Fig. 5-9. Three prompts appear, in rows 4, 8, and 12 of column 1 of the screen.

Take it on faith for now that it is useful to create a data-entry subroutine that we can use to collect the keystrokes. Figure 5-10 is the listing of an IBM PC subroutine that will do the job. (Equivalent subroutines for other computers can be created based on this model. If the LINE INPUT

statement is not available, use the Deluxe INKEY\$ method.) This makes use of the line-clearing subroutine described in Chapter 4 (Fig. 4-8), although the cursor could also be positioned and the line cleared without it. The arguments of the data-entry subroutine are V, H, and P\$. V is the number of the row and H the number of the column at which the prompt is to be printed. P\$ is the prompt. When these arguments are defined and the subroutine is called, the prompt is printed in inverse video at the designated location and the LINE INPUT statement collects the data entry, returning it as the variable A\$.

Here is how the subroutine works. Line 3020 clears the prompt line and positions the cursor. Line 3030 turns on inverse video and line 3040 prints the prompt, attaching a colon to it. Line 3050 turns inverse video off. Line 3060 collects the keystrokes, using the LINE INPUT statement, and assigns

SUBJECT QUESTIONNAIRE

Please write in the answers to the
following questions.

1. Name (last, first) _____

2. Major _____

3. Class (check one)
    Freshman ____
    Sophomore ____
    Junior ____
    Senior____

4. Vision (check one)
    Normal ____
    Corrected ____

5. Hours sleep per night _____

6. Diet (check one)
    None ____
    High carbohydrate ____
    High protein ____

Fig. 5-8. A questionnaire corresponding to the data-entry screen shown in Fig. 5-6.

them to the variable A$.

Now let's create the code to generate the data entry screen. Since all of the prompts must appear on the screen when the data-entry routine begins, we must print each prompt twice. We will start by clearing the screen, and then print all of the prompts for the entire screen. Then we will set up and call the subroutine to display the first prompt and collect its keystrokes, do the same for the second prompt, and repeat for the third. (By redesign-ing the data-entry subroutine not to display the prompt, we could save having to print prompts twice, but it is handy to have it print the prompt in other types of data-entry situations.)

Figure 5-11 shows the code required to generate the data-entry screen and collect the data entries. The data-entry subroutine runs from lines 3000 – 3070. Line 10020 clears the screen. Line 10030 sets inverse video mode. Line 10040 positions the cursor, and line 10050 prints the first

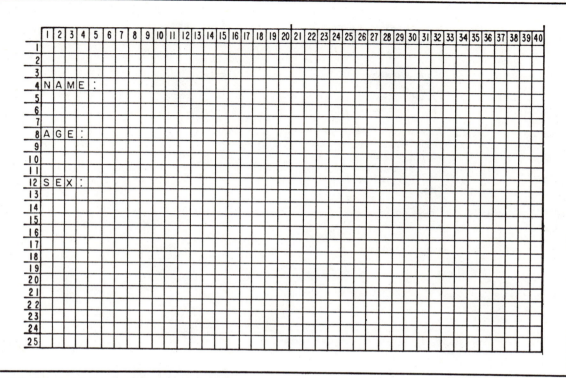

Fig. 5-9. Use of a design matrix to lay out a data-entry screen.

prompt in inverse video. Lines 10060 and 10070 do the same for the second prompt, and 10080 and 10090 for the third. Line 10100 sets normal video. After these lines have been executed, the data-entry screen has been created.

Lines 10130, 10140, and 10150, respectively, define the row (V) and column (H) at which the prompt is to appear, and what the prompt is to say (P$). Line 10160 calls the data-entry subroutine. After it has been executed, the value it returns is

```
Ø REM LINE INPUT Data-Entry Subroutine
1 REM SAVE"FIG5-10.BAS",A
1300 REM--Clear One Line--
1310 LOCATE V,H:REM position cursor
1320 PRINT SPACE$(WIDE%+1-H);:REM clear to end of line
1330 LOCATE V,H:REM reposition cursor
1340 RETURN
3010 REM--LINE INPUT Data Entry--
3020 GOSUB 1300:REM clear line & position prompt
3030 COLOR 0,7:REM inverse
3040 PRINT P$+":";:REM print prompt
3050 COLOR 7,0:REM normal video
3060 LINE INPUT A$
3070 RETURN
```

Fig. 5-10. IBM PC subroutine to collect keystrokes with LINE INPUT statement.

```
0 REM Full-Screen Data-Entry Program
1 REM SAVE"FIG5-11.BAS",A
980 WIDE%=80
990 GOTO 10000
1300 REM--Clear One Line--
1310 LOCATE V,H:REM position cursor
1320 PRINT SPACE$(WIDE%+1-H);:REM clear to end of line
1330 LOCATE V,H:REM reposition cursor
1340 RETURN
3010 REM--LINE INPUT Data Entry--
3020 GOSUB 1300:REM clear line & position prompt
3030 COLOR 0,7:REM inverse
3040 PRINT P$+":";:REM print prompt
3050 COLOR 7,0:REM normal video
3060 LINE INPUT A$
3070 RETURN
10000 REM--Full-Screen Data-Entry Program--
10010 REM-Initialize Screen-
10020 CLS
10030 COLOR 0,7:REM inverse
10040 LOCATE 4,1
10050 PRINT"Name:"
10060 LOCATE 8
10070 PRINT"Age:"
10080 LOCATE 12
10090 PRINT"Sex:"
10100 COLOR 7,0:REM normal video
10110 REM-Prompt & Collect Keystrokes-
10120 REM-Name-
10130 V=4
10140 H=1
10150 P$="Name"
10160 GOSUB 3010
10170 NAMES$=A$
10180 REM-Age-
10190 V=8
10200 P$="Age"
10210 GOSUB 3010
10220 AGE=VAL(A$)
10230 REM-Sex-
10240 V=12
10250 P$="Sex"
10260 GOSUB 3010
10270 SEX$=A$
10280 END
```

Fig. 5-11. IBM PC full-screen data-entry program based on screen design shown in Fig. 5-9.

assigned in line 10170 to the program variable NAMES$. Lines 10180–10220 do likewise for AGE and lines 10230–10270 for SEX$.

Single-Line Data Entry. A much simpler data entry method is to take all entries on a single line of the screen. Not only is this easier to code, but it makes sense if the user might need to refer to information on another part of the screen. For example, the screen might contain a directory of names, a list of parts, or something else that could influence the entries (see Fig. 5-7).

Writing a program to do single-line data entry is fairly easy, especially if we use a data-entry subroutine such as the one in Fig. 5-10 (it is no longer necessary to accept the value of this subroutine on faith). Figure 5-12 is the listing of a program that collects the same three variables— NAMES\$, AGE, SEX\$—as the full-screen data entry program described earlier. However, the current program will display the prompts, and collect the entries, one at a time, from row 22 of the screen.

The main program consists of lines 10000 – 10160. Line 10010 clears the screen. Lines 10030 – 10050 define the arguments V, H, and P\$ for the first variable. Line 10060 calls the data-entry subroutine. And line 10070 assigns the value of A\$ returned by the subroutine to the program variable NAMES\$. Lines 10080 – 10110 do the same thing for the AGE variable, and lines 10120 – 10150 for the SEX\$ variable.

The Scrolling Screen Method. Now we come to what is probably the most common method of taking data entries. Try to remember back to the first program you ever wrote for taking a series of data entries. It may very well have consisted of a series of INPUT statements such as these:

```
10   INPUT "Name";N$
20   INPUT "Age";AGE
30   INPUT "Sex";SEX$
```

And so on.

What happens when the program executed depends mainly on where the first prompt appears. If it starts at the top of the screen (Fig. 5-13), then subsequent prompts work their way down the screen toward the bottom, one below the other. If it starts at the bottom (Fig. 5-14), then old prompts scroll up each time a new prompt appears. While this data entry method is simple, it produces either

```
0 REM Single-Line Data-Entry Program
1 REM SAVE"FIG5-12.BAS",A
980 WIDE%=80
990 GOTO 10000
1300 REM--Clear One Line--
1310 LOCATE V,H:REM position cursor
1320 PRINT SPACE$(WIDE%+1-H);:REM clear to end of line
1330 LOCATE V,H:REM reposition cursor
1340 RETURN
3010 REM--LINE INPUT Data Entry--
3020 GOSUB 1300:REM clear line & position prompt
3030 COLOR 0,7:REM inverse
3040 PRINT P$+":";:REM print prompt
3050 COLOR 7,0:REM normal video
3060 LINE INPUT A$
3070 RETURN
10000 REM--Single-Line Data-Entry Program--
10010 CLS
10020 REM-Name-
10030 V=22
10040 H=1
10050 P$="Name"
10060 GOSUB 3010
10070 NAMES$=A$
10080 REM-Age-
10090 P$="Age"
10100 GOSUB 3010
10110 AGE=VAL(A$)
10120 REM-Sex-
10130 P$="Sex"
10140 GOSUB 3010
10150 SEX$=A$
10160 END
```

Fig. 5-12. IBM PC single-line data-entry program.

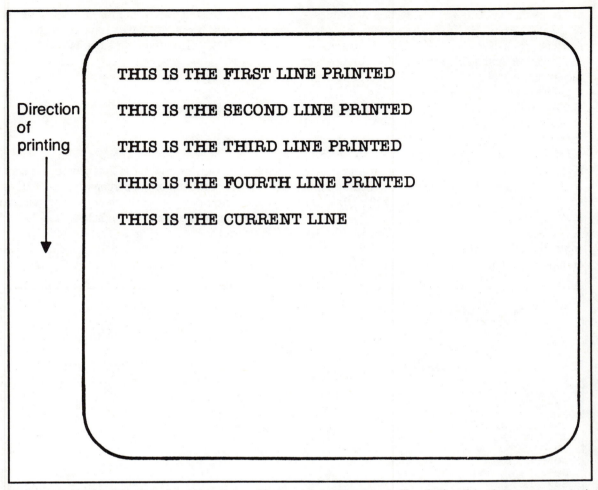

Direction of printing

THIS IS THE FIRST LINE PRINTED

THIS IS THE SECOND LINE PRINTED

THIS IS THE THIRD LINE PRINTED

THIS IS THE FOURTH LINE PRINTED

THIS IS THE CURRENT LINE

Fig. 5-13. If the screen is cleared and then data entries are taken without controlling the location of the prompts, each successive prompt will appear one row further down the screen.

a shifting center of focus, as the prompt line moves down the screen, or undesirable scrolling of the screen. More bluntly, it makes for sloppy data-entry programs. Avoid it if you can.

Error-Testing

Most data-entry routines require error tests. An error test is code that examines the user's data entry according to certain rules to determine whether that entry makes sense. The simple data-entry programs we have been working with have

three items to be entered: Name, Age, and Sex. Though we did not build error tests into the programs described earlier, we would certainly do so in any program that we wanted to use to collect valid data. The types of error tests depend upon the nature of the data. For example:

- We would conduct a length test on Name to assure that the number of characters in the name fell within certain limits, such as between 2 and 24 characters.

- We would conduct a range test on Age to assure that the value fell between, say, 2 and 99 years.
- Sex would have to be either *m* or *f*.

If we did not conduct such tests, data entry errors made by users would find their way into our database, and cause problems later on. The best time to catch such errors is early, as the user types in the data, so we must write code that detects the errors. However, that alone is not enough. When an error occurs, we must tell the user about it, and provide enough additional information so that the error can be corrected. This is what error messages are for. In this section, then, we are concerned with two issues: error detection, and error messages. These two factors together comprise error-testing.

Error Detection. The simplest type of error test is the *identity* test. For example, in this prompt:

Please type your sex ('m' or 'f'):

the only acceptable entries are *m* or *f*. The code

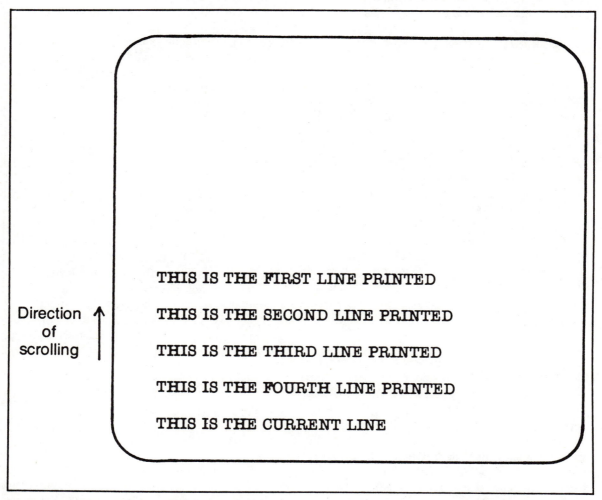

Direction of scrolling ↑

THIS IS THE FIRST LINE PRINTED

THIS IS THE SECOND LINE PRINTED

THIS IS THE THIRD LINE PRINTED

THIS IS THE FOURTH LINE PRINTED

THIS IS THE CURRENT LINE

Fig. 5-14. If the first prompt is printed at the bottom of the screen, and the location of subsequent prompts is not controlled, old prompts scroll up the screen as each new prompt is printed on the bottom row.

to generate the prompt and conduct the test is as follows:

```
10  INPUT"Please type in your sex ('m' or 'f'):"
    ;SEX
20  IF SEX$< > "m" AND SEX$< > "f"
    GOTO 10
```

The identity test is useful in some data-entry programs. More often than not, however, we want to know whether a value falls within a particular range. Suppose that you write a simple data-entry program that looks like this:

```
10  INPUT"Age:";A$
20  AGE = VAL(A$)
```

This particular prompt is looking for someone's age. An excited user might press the Return key without making a numeric entry. The value of AGE returned by the VAL function would then be zero. The value zero would also be returned if the user typed in a letter or symbol key. Alternatively, if the user struck the key too many times, a very large number might result. The user's age of 22 might, for example, be typed in as 222. It is fairly easy to check the numeric range of entries and reject those outside of it. We must, of course, set a lower and upper limit on what will be acceptable. Assume that this is from 2 to 99 years. By adding the following line to our program, we can have it make a *range test*:

```
30  IF AGE < 2 OR AGE > 99 GOTO 10
```

Line 30 tests whether AGE is less than 2 or greater than 99. If so, then it is outside the legal range and control is sent back to line 10, which forces the user to re-enter the value. If the value is within the acceptable range, then the routine is finished.

The lines of code that perform error tests invariably make use of relational and logical operators: =, <, >, AND, OR, NOT. Simple tests (such as the range test just illustrated) involve simple expressions. However, sometimes the expressions used in a test become quite complicated. For example, if the acceptable range of entries is

disjoint—ages from 1–23 or from 43–63, or the age 99 are acceptable—then the logical expression for making the tests gets a little hairy:

```
30  IF NOT ((AGE > = 1 AND AGE < = 23)
    OR (AGE > = 43 AND AGE < = 63)
    OR AGE = 99)
    GOTO 10
```

The lesson is that, if you are not up on your operators, and you do need to perform complex error tests, do a little homework. In what follows, it is assumed that you have a good understanding of the logic involved, and the logical expressions stand alone, without explanation.

Let us explore some additional error tests. We just examined the simplest type of range test, one that tests whether the data entry falls between a lower and upper numeric bound. Range tests are not limited to numbers. Every character that can be displayed on your computer has an ASCII (American Standard Code for Information Interchange) code. This is a number that amounts to the character's pecking order in the character set. The ASCII values for your computer's character should be given in your computer's BASIC manual. Use your manual to find the ASCII values of the characters %, &, 4, and E. The values should be 37, 38, 52, and 69. The character with the highest ASCII value is E and that with the lowest is %.

Your computer knows the ASCII value of each character. You can use the ASC statement to obtain the ASCII value of any character. For example, to find the ASCII value of the character %, type the following statement:

```
PRINT ASC("%")
```

Now type this:

```
PRINT "E" > "%"
```

The result you get from this is −1 (or +1, in some versions of BASIC), which means that character E is greater than character %. Your computer arrived at this answer by comparing the ASCII values of the two characters. Since the

ASCII value of E is greater than the ASCII value of %, the statement is true, and its logical result is −1 (or +1).

What all this is leading up to is that you can perform a range test not just on numbers, but also on characters and symbols. To illustrate, suppose, for the sake of argument, that you want to design a data entry routine that accepts any letter between A (ASCII value 65) and E (ASCII value 69). The code to perform this test is as follows:

```
10  INPUT "Letter:";A$
20  IF A$<"A" OR A$>"E" GOTO 10
```

To make it more interesting, suppose that acceptable entries are characters A through E, or numbers 1 through 4. The code to perform this test is:

```
10  INPUT "Character:";A$
20  IF NOT ((A$> = "A" AND A$< = "E") OR
    A$> = "1" AND A$ < = "4") GOTO 10
```

(This test illustrates what is meant about the importance of feeling comfortable with operators.)

Note that tests such as these can be posed in either of two ways: to detect an unacceptable condition, or to detect acceptable conditions. For example, in this program:

```
10  INPUT "Letter:";A$
20  IF A$<"A" OR A$>"E" GOTO 10
```

the test looks for an unacceptable condition—a character outside the range. We could change the test to look for an acceptable condition by rewriting line 20 to read:

```
20  IF A$ >"@" AND A$ <"F" THEN continue
    program
```

If you want to bounce control back to a particular place when an error occurs, then it is best to look for the unacceptable condition. If you detect an acceptable condition, as in the most recent line 20, then you need a separate line to handle the error condition. The following listing illustrates an alternate version of the earlier program. The error test in this one looks for the acceptable condition:

```
10  INPUT "Letter: ";A$
20  IF A$> = "A" AND A$< = "E" GOTO 40
30  GOTO 10
40  END
```

And, as you are aware, you can change a positive test to a negative test by adding NOT at the beginning. For example,

```
IF NOT (A$ > "@" AND A$ < "F")
```

is the same as

```
IF A$ <"A" OR A$ > "E"
```

You can use character range tests on entries that are longer than a single character. Most versions of BASIC evaluate the entire character string. To illustrate, suppose that we want to design a data-entry routine for collecting the names of people, but only if their names fall between the letters A and E in the alphabet. The little program we have been working with can be used for this purpose. Type the last program, run it, and then enter some names that start with letters between A and E, and some that do not.

Another common test is the *length test*. This is used to assure that the number of characters in a typed entry does not fall below or exceed a certain limit (such as between 2 and 24 characters). The simplest way to perform a length test is by using the LEN statement in code such as the following:

```
10  INPUT "Name (2–24 char): ";A$
20  IF LEN(A$) < 2 OR LEN(A$)  >24 GOTO
    10
```

The program permits the user to type in any string. Line 20 uses the LEN function to calculate the length of the string. If the length is shorter than two characters or greater than 20 characters, then control returns to line 10. As you can see, the length test works much like the range test.

These examples illustrate the basic concepts underlying error tests. Of course, the examples were simplified and do not tell the whole story. The code used the INPUT statement (you know what its shortcomings are), and if an error condition occurred, control bounced back to re-present the prompt, causing scrolling. You can make everything much neater by using the LINE INPUT subroutine described earlier in this chapter (or an equivalent Deluxe INKEY$ subroutine), since it positions the prompt before it prints it, thereby preventing scrolling.

Another simplification was to use either all uppercase or all lowercase letters. Since many entries may contain either upper- or lowercase letters, or both, the tests should usually handle both. If your computer has true upper/lowercase characters, it can distinguish between the two. Thus, if you want your code to accept either, then tests must include both. On the other hand, if you want the tests to accept only uppercase or only lowercase characters, then make sure that program users understand the rules. There is nothing more frustrating to a user than to observe a prompt such as this,

Do you want to continue? (y/n)

type *Y*, and then have nothing happen.

Figure 5-15 is a version of the full-screen data-entry program presented earlier in Fig. 5-11. A few lines have been added to the program to provide error-testing.

Line 10172 conducts a length test on NAMES$. Line 10222 conducts a range test on AGE. And line 10272 conducts an identity test on SEX$. These tests are straightforward enough. However, if a test is failed, control now jumps back to a line that regenerates the prompt at a specific location on the screen. When you handle error-testing this way, there is no need for the screen to scroll.

Error Messages. Detecting errors in fine, but not quite enough to stay on good terms with program users. They appreciate it when you keep them from filling their databases with garbage, but they do not appreciate it when they respond to a prompt by typing an invalid entry, and the prompt keeps reappearing. Almost everyone who has used a computer has been in a situation where they faced a prompt line, typed something, and the computer did not accept it and kept repeating the prompt. In these situations, the computer sometimes displays a cryptic message such as ILLEGAL INPUT or SYSERR 401 that makes some users want to perform an act of violence upon the computer.

What is lacking in these situations is a good error message. Each time the user types in something that is invalid, display an error message before repeating the prompt. The message should do these things:

- Attract attention—Have your computer beep and make the message flash.
- Define the error—Tell the user what is wrong with the entry.
- Give the recovery action, if it is something other than retyping the entry.

Display the error message close to the prompt so that the user can relate it to the data entry.

Let us concentrate for a moment on the mechanical aspects of displaying error messages by devising a subroutine to beep and display a flashing error message at a definable location on the screen. After doing this, we will discuss in more detail what an error message should contain.

Figure 5-16 contains the listing of an IBM PC subroutine for displaying an error message. The subroutine consists of lines 3200–3280, and this subroutine also requires that the line-clearing and time delay subroutines be present. The arguments of the subroutine are V, H, and ERRORS$, which are the row number, column number, and error message, respectively. The subroutine clears whatever line it is on from the column number to the right edge of the display, and so the error message can be as long as the space available.

Here is how the subroutine works. Line 3210 clears the display row, 3220 sets flashing video mode, 3230 prints the error message, 3240 beeps the speaker, 3250 sets normal video, and 3260 introduces a 5-second time delay. Line 3270 then clears the prompt line, thereby erasing the message.

```
0 REM Full-Screen Data Entry Program with Simple Error Tests
1 REM SAVE"FIG5-15.BAS",A
980 WIDE%=80
990 GOTO 10000
1300 REM--Clear One Line--
1310 LOCATE V,H:REM position cursor
1320 PRINT SPACE$(WIDE%+1-H);:REM clear to end of line
1330 LOCATE V,H:REM reposition cursor
1340 RETURN
3010 REM--LINE INPUT Data Entry--
3020 GOSUB 1300:REM clear line & position prompt
3030 COLOR 0,7:REM inverse
3040 PRINT P$+":";:REM print prompt
3050 COLOR 7,0:REM normal video
3060 LINE INPUT A$
3070 RETURN
10000 REM--Full-Screen Data-Entry Program--
10010 REM-Initialize Screen-
10020 CLS
10030 COLOR 0,7:REM inverse
10040 LOCATE 4,1
10050 PRINT"Name:"
10060 LOCATE 8
10070 PRINT"Age:"
10080 LOCATE 12
10090 PRINT"Sex:"
10100 COLOR 7,0:REM normal video
10110 REM-Prompt & Collect Keystrokes-
10120 REM-Name-
10130 V=4
10140 H=1
10150 P$="Name"
10160 GOSUB 3010
10170 NAMES$=A$
10171 REM-Error Test-
10172 IF LEN(NAMES$))=2 AND LEN(NAMES$)<=24 GOTO 10180
10173 GOTO 10160
10180 REM-Age-
10190 V=8
10200 P$="Age"
10210 GOSUB 3010
10220 AGE=VAL(A$)
10221 REM-Error Test-
10222 IF AGE)=2 AND AGE <=99 GOTO 10230
10223 GOTO 10210
10230 REM-Sex-
10240 V=12
10250 P$="Sex"
10260 GOSUB 3010
10270 SEX$=A$
10271 REM-Error Test-
10272 IF SEX$="m" OR SEX$="f" GOTO 10280
10273 GOTO 10260
10280 END
```

Fig. 5-15. IBM PC full-screen data entry program based on Fig. 5-9, with the addition of error testing.

```
0 REM Error Message Subroutine
1 REM SAVE"FIG5-16.BAS",A
1300 REM--Clear One Line--
1310 LOCATE V,H:REM position cursor
1320 PRINT SPACE$(WIDE%+1-H);:REM clear to end of line
1330 LOCATE V,H:REM reposition cursor
1340 RETURN
3200 REM--Error Message--
3210 GOSUB 1300:REM clear line
3220 COLOR 23,0:REM flash
3230 PRINT ERRORS$:REM print error message
3240 BEEP
3250 COLOR 7,0:REM normal video
3260 TX=5:GOSUB 4100:REM 5-second time delay
3270 GOSUB 1300:REM erase message
3280 RETURN
4100 REM--TX-Second Delay--
4110 FOR A=1 TO TX*987
4120 NEXT
4130 RETURN
```

Fig. 5-16. IBM PC subroutine (lines 3200-3280) for generating a flashing error message at a designated row and column.

This subroutine can be used to print a flashing message anywhere on the screen, and is not restricted to error messages. It is also useful for attracting attention to other matters of concern. Note, however, that while this subroutine is being ex-ecuted, everything else going on in the program stops.

Equivalent subroutines for the Apple and C-64 are shown in Fig. 5-17 and 5-18, respectively.

To illustrate the subroutine's use, insert these

```
0   REM   FIG 5-17
1   REM   ERROR MESSAGE SUBROUTINE
1300   REM --CLEAR ONE LINE--
1310   VTAB V: HTAB H: REM   POSITION CURSOR
1320   CALL  - 868
1330   VTAB V: HTAB H: REM   REPOSITION CURSOR
1340   RETURN
3350   REM --ERROR MESSAGE--
3360   GOSUB 1300: REM   CLEAR LINE
3370   FLASH : REM   DELETE THIS LINE IF USING 80-COLUMN CARD
3380   PRINT ERR$
3390   CALL  - 198
3400   NORMAL
3410 TX = 5: GOSUB 4100: REM   5-SECOND TIME DELAY
3420   GOSUB 1300: REM   ERASE MESSAGE
3430   RETURN
4100   REM --TX-SECOND DELAY--
4110   FOR A = 1 TO TX * 960
4120   NEXT
4130   RETURN
```

Fig. 5-17. Apple subroutine (lines 3350-3430) for generating a flashing error message at a designated row and column.

```
3200 REM--ERROR MESSAGE--
3210 SYS C0,1,V,H:REM CLEAR LINE
3220 FOR B=1 TO 10
3230 TX=.2:GOSUB 4100:REM .2 SEC DELAY
3240 SYS C0,0,V,H:REM POSITION CURSOR
3250 PRINT CHR$(18)ER$:REM PRINT ERROR MESSAGE IN REVERSE VIDEO
3260 TX=.2:GOSUB 4100:REM .2 SEC DELAY
3270 SYS C0,0,V,H
3280 PRINT CHR$(146)ER$:REM PRINT ERROR MESSAGE IN NORMAL VIDEO
3290 NEXT
3300 SYS C0,1,V,H
3310 RETURN
4100 REM--TX SECOND DELAY--
4110 FOR A=1 TO TX*870
4120 NEXT
4130 RETURN
```

Fig. 5-18. C-64 subroutine (lines 3200-3310) for generating a flashing error message at a designated row and column. (Requires assembly-language subroutine loader; see Appendix B.)

lines into the listing shown in Fig. 5-16 and try it out. (If you are using the Apple or C-64 version of Fig. 5-16, change ERRORS$ on line 10020 to ER$.)

```
990   GOTO 10000
10000   INPUT "V: ";V
10010   INPUT "H: ";H
10020   INPUT "Errors$: ";ERRORS$
10030   GOSUB 3200
10040 GOTO 10000
```

Now that you see how the subroutine works, let us add it to the data-entry program in Fig. 5-15 so that we can generate error messages in response to invalid data entries. Figure 5-19 is the data-entry program we examined earlier, but with a few changes:

- Two subroutines have been added: Error Message (lines 3200–3280), and Time Delay (lines 4100–4130)
- Error messages and subroutine calls have been added at lines 10173, 10174; 10223, 10224; and 10273, 10274.

This program permits full-screen data entry. If an invalid entry is typed in, an error message is printed in place of the prompt for about five

```
0 REM Full-Screen Data Entry Program with Error-Message Subroutine
1 REM SAVE"FIG5-19.BAS",A
980 WIDE%=80
990 GOTO 10000
1300 REM--Clear One Line--
1310 LOCATE V,H:REM position cursor
1320 PRINT SPACE$(WIDE%+1-H);:REM clear to end of line
1330 LOCATE V,H:REM reposition cursor
1340 RETURN
3010 REM--LINE INPUT Data Entry--
3020 GOSUB 1300:REM clear line & position prompt
3030 COLOR 0,7:REM inverse
3040 PRINT P$+":";:REM print prompt
3050 COLOR 7,0:REM normal video
```

Fig. 5-19. IBM PC full-screen data-entry program based on Fig. 5-15, with the addition of error messages.

```
3060 LINE INPUT A$
3070 RETURN
3200 REM--Error Message--
3210 GOSUB 1300:REM clear line
3220 COLOR 23,0:REM flash
3230 PRINT ERRORS$:REM print error message
3240 BEEP
3250 COLOR 7,0:REM normal video
3260 TX=5:GOSUB 4100:REM 5-second time delay
3270 GOSUB 1300:REM erase message
3280 RETURN
4100 REM--TX-Second Delay--
4110 FOR A=1 TO TX*987
4120 NEXT
4130 RETURN
10000 REM--Full-Screen Data-Entry Program--
10010 REM-Initialize Screen-
10020 CLS
10030 COLOR 0,7:REM inverse
10040 LOCATE 4,1
10050 PRINT"Name:"
10060 LOCATE 8
10070 PRINT"Age:"
10080 LOCATE 12
10090 PRINT"Sex:"
10100 COLOR 7,0:REM normal video
10110 REM-Prompt & Collect Keystrokes-
10120 REM-Name-
10130 V=4
10140 H=1
10150 P$="Name"
10160 GOSUB 3010
10170 NAMES$=A$
10171 REM-Error Test-
10172 IF LEN(NAMES$))=2 AND LEN(NAMES$)(=24 GOTO 10180
10173 ERRORS$="Name must be 2-24 characters long"
10174 GOSUB 3200
10175 GOTO 10160
10180 REM-Age-
10190 V=8
10200 P$="Age"
10210 GOSUB 3010
10220 AGE=VAL(A$)
10221 REM-Error Test-
10222 IF AGE)=2 AND AGE (=99 GOTO 10230
10223 ERRORS$="Age must be between 2 and 99 years"
10224 GOSUB 3200
10225 GOTO 10210
10230 REM-Sex-
10240 V=12
10250 P$="Sex"
10260 GOSUB 3010
10270 SEX$=A$
10271 REM-Error Test-
10272 IF SEX$="m" OR SEX$="f" GOTO 10280
10273 ERRORS$="Please enter 'm' or 'f'"
10274 GOSUB 3200
10275 GOTO 10260
10280 END
```

seconds, and then the prompt reappears, permitting re-entry of the data.

Let us see how the code works by examining the data-entry steps for the first variable, NAMES$. Most of this code was described earlier, so we'll focus on how the error message is generated. Line 10172 performs the error test. If this test is passed, then control is sent to line 10180, permitting entry of the next variable. If the test is failed, then control drops first to line 10173, which defines the error message ERRORS$, and then to line 10174, which calls the error message subroutine. This subroutine displays the message at row V and column H (these two arguments were defined in lines 10130 and 10140 and are the same for both the LINE INPUT and error message subroutines). After the return from the subroutine, control drops to line 10175, which sends it back to line 10160, where the LINE INPUT subroutine again presents the data-entry prompt.

There are a lot of steps in this process, but nothing earthshakingly complex. It is fairly easy to build such error-messaging into your programs by using these procedures. However, even if you can present such messages, you must know what to say and avoid that INVALID ENTRY and other such insensitive and antisocial stuff.

How do you write a good error message? A simple question, right? Well, the answer may be simple, but it is not obvious. $E = mc^2$ is simple, too, but it took Albert a lot of work to get there. Admittedly, writing error messages is not in the same league as relativity, but you get the idea.

Make your error messages short, but be sure they tell the story. Do not leave the user guessing. Avoid sarcastic messages. These will turn program users against both you and the program. It is not generally a good idea to use humor in your error messages, either. The message you find in your first fortune cookie is fun, but if you keep finding it again and again, it kind of gets on your nerves.

The error message must alert the user that something is wrong, identify the problem, and, if it is not obvious, tell what to do about it. Flashing and a beep usually take care of the alerting part, but if you are not sure they will do the job, have your computer make some other kind of pained noise when something goes wrong.

You must take care of identifying the error and telling what to do about it with the written message. The first part of this—identifying the error—is required. All of the messages used in our example identify the error condition. Here they are:

- Name test: **Name must be 2-24 characters long**
- Age test: **Age must be between 2 and 99 years**
- Sex test: **Please enter either 'm' or 'f'**

The first two messages identify the condition but do not tell what to do, since it can be considered obvious. The third message tells what to do and implicitly defines the error. Telling what to do may be considered optional in most data-entry programs since the ongoing activity is data entry and a data-entry error calls for reentry.

In some programs, telling the corrective action is more important. This is often the case when the user is engaged in keying in entries that control the program, and may have gotten the program into a state that requires some non-obvious action for recovery.

Error messages are a form of written communication, and the types of messages you provide tell a lot about your personality. We all have recollections of messages (or non-messages) we have encountered in our work with computer programs. The way error-messaging is handled provides insight into the programmer's mentality, and is somewhat like handwriting analysis. If your program provides informative error messages, it is rather like the flowing and elliptical handwriting of John Hancock. If the error messages are cryptic, uninformative, or insulting, they are like the handwriting of someone with a personality disorder who writes in little, broken, disconnected letters.

Verification

To verify something is to confirm its truth. In

a data-entry program, verification occurs when the user views an entry that has been typed in and gives it the OK. Until that point, the entry is not finalized. When the user verifies it, it stops being a potential entry and becomes an actual entry. Verification is important because program users often make mistakes or simply change their minds. They need to be able to change their entries.

The three most common verification techniques used in microcomputer programs are:

- Return key verification
- Line verification
- Page verification

Return Key Verification. The simplest verification technique is Return key verification. You use this all the time and probably do not think of it as a verification technique. It is built into the INPUT and LINE INPUT statements. Whenever your program executes one of these statements, it requires the user to type in an entry and follow it by pressing the Return key. The entry is not final until the Return key is pressed. The Return key, in other words, verifies what has been typed in.

Return key verification allows the user to recognize and modify entries before the Return key has been pressed, but not afterward. Still, it is desirable and you should use it for entries that the user may want to change, like data entries or selecting the options on a program control menu.

Return key verification does not require use of the INPUT or LINE INPUT statements. It can also be built into data-entry routines that use the INKEY$ or GET statement, such as the Deluxe INKEY$ method described earlier in this chapter. The INKEY$ statement by itself does not have Return key verification—whatever key is pressed is assigned immediately to the relevant variable, without giving the user a chance to verify it. For this reason, the naked INKEY$ statement is not good as a way of taking data entries.

Line Verification. Line verification consists of permitting the user to back up and change the previous entry. A prompt such as this appears:

Do you want to change your entry? (y/n)

If the user types y, then control is sent back to the data-entry prompt and permits the user to reenter the item. If the user types n, then the entry is verified and the program proceeds.

To illustrate, the following program collects a single data entry and then permits the user to verify it:

```
10   INPUT"Name: ";NAMES$
20   PRINT"Okay? (y/n) ";
30   A$ = INKEY$:IF A$ = " " GOTO 30
40   PRINT
50   IF A$ = "n" GOTO 10
60   IF A$ = "y" THEN END
70   GOTO 30
```

Line 10 collects the data entry. Line 20 prints the prompt "Okay? (y/n)." Line 30 then uses INKEY$ to get a single character. Line 50 tests whether the entered character is an n and, if so, sends control back to line 10, which permits the user to reenter the data. If a y is typed, the program ends (line 60). If neither y nor n is typed, line 70 sends control back to line 30 to collect another keystroke.

The nice thing about line verification is that it allows the user to make a change after the item has been entered, after the Return key has been pressed. Line verification works well if there are only a few entries to verify. However, imagine what it would be like to make 20 entries and verify each one. It all becomes very tedious very quickly, and the program moves along very slowly. If a program requires many data entries that must be verified, it is better to use page verification, as described below.

Page Verification. Page verification is similar to line verification except that the user makes a series of entries before verifying them. It is often used with full-screen data entry. After the last data-entry field is completed, a prompt such as the following appears on the display:

Do you have changes? (y/n)

If the entries are okay, the user types n and the program proceeds. If not, the user types y and a prompt such as the following appears:

Select item # to change: ___

The user then types in the number of the item and the cursor moves to the appropriate data-entry field, allowing reentry. After making the change, the "Do you have changes?" prompt reappears, permitting additional changes, as necessary, until the user is completely satisfied.

One requirement of this type of verification is that each prompt be numbered so that the user can identify it to make changes. Page verification does not actually require full-screen data entry, although it helps. If full-screen entry is not used, then all of the entries must somehow be displayed simultaneously after they are entered.

How do you write code that permits page verification? It seems straightforward enough. You must number the prompts. This is easy. After data entry, you must generate a prompt that says "Do you have changes? (y/n)," and, if the user enters y, another that allows the user to select the item number to change. This is also easy.

Suppose that the user enters a y and selects an item to change. What then? This is where it gets harder. If the user wants to change something, then the program must re-present the data-entry prompt and collect the keystrokes, doing all of the error testing and other things that went with data entry the first time. If your data-entry program consists of a series of routines, you cannot simply send control back to the one for the variable the user wants to change or it may require re-entry of data that the user does not want to change. For example, if the program collects three items of data and the user wants to change the first one, when you send control back to the first data-entry routine the user will be forced to reenter all three items before being able to continue the program.

The only solution to this dilemma is to make each of the date entry routines into a subroutine that operates independently of the others. In this way, if the user wants to change item #1, the program can access the appropriate data-entry subroutine without affecting other data entries.

In short, if you want to do page verification, you must reorganize your program. The reorganization is not complex, but it may require some reorientation to get used to. We will see how to reorganize the program presently, but first let's develop a subroutine to handle verification prompting.

Verification prompting can be done with or without a subroutine, although if you do very much of it a subroutine is a definite help. Even if you prefer not to use a subroutine, the techniques employed in the verification subroutine described below will be useful.

Figure 5-20 contains a revised version of the full-screen data-entry program shown earlier in Fig. 5-19. This version has all of the features of the earlier version and, in addition, permits page verification.

Let us begin by examining the verification subroutine, which consists of lines 3350–3500. Note that the subroutine shown in Fig. 5-20 calls subroutines 1300, 3010, and 3200, and that subroutine 3200 calls subroutine 4100. Thus, all four subroutines—1300, 3010, 3200, 4100—must be present in the program. (Equivalent subroutines for the Apple and C-64 are shown in Figs. 5-21 and 5-22, respectively.)

The arguments of the verification subroutine are V, H, and N. V is the row number and H the column number at which the verification prompt is to be printed. N is the number of verification options available (the number of prompts displayed on the screen). When this subroutine is called, it first presents this prompt:

Do you have changes? (y/n)

If the user types n, then the variable A is set equal to zero and control returns to the program. If the user types y, then A is set equal to the number of the item to change. Thus A carries back with it the message of change or no change to the displayed item.

Now let us see how this subroutine works. Line 3360 clears the line and positions the cursor. Line 3370 sets inverse video mode. Line 3380 prints the first verification prompt in inverse video. Line 3400

```
0 REM Full-Screen Data Entry Program with Error Tests, Messages, and Entry
Verification
1 REM SAVE"FIG5-20.BAS",A
980 WIDE%=80
990 GOTO 10000
1300 REM--Clear One Line--
1310 LOCATE V,H:REM position cursor
1320 PRINT SPACE$(WIDE%+1-H);:REM clear to end of line
1330 LOCATE V,H:REM reposition cursor
1340 RETURN
3010 REM--LINE INPUT Data Entry--
3020 GOSUB 1300:REM clear line & position prompt
3030 COLOR 0,7:REM inverse
3040 PRINT P$+":";:REM print prompt
3050 COLOR 7,0:REM normal video
3060 LINE INPUT A$
3070 RETURN
3200 REM--Error Message--
3210 GOSUB 1300:REM clear line
3220 COLOR 23,0:REM flash
3230 PRINT ERRORS$:REM print error message
3240 BEEP
3250 COLOR 7,0:REM normal video
3260 TX=5:GOSUB 4100:REM 5-second time delay
3270 GOSUB 1300:REM erase message
3280 RETURN
3350 REM--Verification Prompt--
3360 GOSUB 1300:REM clear line
3370 COLOR 0,7:REM inverse
3380 PRINT"Do you have changes? (y/n):";
3390 COLOR 7,0:REM normal video
3400 A$=INKEY$:IF A$="" GOTO 3400
3410 IF A$<>"y" AND A$<>"n" GOTO 3400
3420 IF A$="n" THEN A=0:GOTO 3500:REM no changes
3430 P$="Select item # to change"
3440 GOSUB 3010:REM call data-entry subroutine
3450 A=VAL(A$)
3460 IF A)=1 AND A<=N GOTO 3500
3470 ERRORS$="Number must be between 1 and"+STR$(N):REM define error message
3480 GOSUB 3200:REM call error message subroutine
3490 GOTO 3430:REM have user select another item#
3500 RETURN
4100 REM--TX-Second Delay--
4110 FOR A=1 TO TX*987
4120 NEXT
4130 RETURN
10000 REM--Full-Screen Data-Entry Program--
10010 REM-Initialize Screen-
10020 CLS
10030 COLOR 0,7:REM inverse
10040 LOCATE 4,1
10050 PRINT"1. Name:"
10060 LOCATE 8
10070 PRINT"2. Age:"
10080 LOCATE 12
10090 PRINT"3. Sex:"
10100 COLOR 7,0:REM normal video
10110 REM-Collect Data Entries-
```

Fig. 5-20.   IBM PC full-screen data-entry program based on Fig. 5-15, with the addition of error messages and data-entry verification.

```
10120 GOSUB 10240:REM Name
10130 GOSUB 10360:REM Age
10140 GOSUB 10470:REM Sex
10150 REM-Verification-
10160 V=22:REM verification row
10170 H=1:REM verification column
10180 N=3:REM number of prompts
10190 GOSUB 3350:REM call verification subroutine
10200 IF A=0 GOTO 10230:REM all entries okay
10210 ON A GOSUB 10240,10360,10470:REM verify Name, Age, or Sex
10220 GOTO 10160
10230 END:REM all entries verified
10240 REM-Name-
10250 V=4
10260 H=1
10270 P$="1. Name"
10280 GOSUB 3010
10290 NAMES$=A$
10300 REM-Error Test-
10310 IF LEN(NAMES$))=2 AND LEN(NAMES$) <=24 GOTO 10350
10320 ERRORS$="Name must be 2-24 characters long"
10330 GOSUB 3200
10340 GOTO 10280
10350 RETURN
10360 REM-Age-
10370 V=8
10380 P$="2. Age"
10390 GOSUB 3010
10400 AGE=VAL(A$)
10410 REM-Error Test-
10420 IF AGE)=2 AND AGE <=99 GOTO 10460
10430 ERRORS$="Age must be between 2 and 99 years"
10440 GOSUB 3200
10450 GOTO 10390
10460 RETURN
10470 REM-Sex-
10480 V=12
10490 P$="3. Sex"
10500 GOSUB 3010
10510 SEX$=A$
10520 REM-Error Test-
10530 IF SEX$="m" OR SEX$="f" GOTO 10570
10540 ERRORS$="Please enter 'm' or 'f'"
10550 GOSUB 3200
10560 GOTO 10500
10570 RETURN
```

grabs a single character, and line 3410 tests it to make sure that it is either *y* or *n*, recycling control to line 3400 if it is not.

Line 3420 tests whether the entry is *n*. If so, A is set equal to 0 and control is sent to line 3500, which returns to the program, thereby ending the subroutine.

If the user types *y*, then lines 3430–3490 are executed. Line 3430 defines a prompt, P$, which is displayed when line 3440 calls the data-entry subroutine at line 3010. Line 3450 evaluates the variable returned from the data-entry subroutine, and line 3460 conducts a range test, sending control to line 3500 if the test is passed. If the test is failed, then the user has entered an invalid Item # to change and line 3470 defines an error message, which is displayed when the error message subroutine is called at line 3480. Line 3490 then

```
0    REM    FIG 5-21
1    REM      FULL-SCREEN DATA ENTRY PROGRAM WITH ERROR MESSAGES, AND ENTRY VER
       IFICATION
990   GOTO 10000
1300  REM --CLEAR ONE LINE--
1310  VTAB V: HTAB H: REM   POSITION CURSOR
1320  CALL  - 868
1330  VTAB V: HTAB H: REM   REPOSITION CURSOR
1340  RETURN
3010  REM --"DELUXE" GET DATA-ENTRY SUBROUTINE--
3020 A$ = ""
3030  GOSUB 1300
3040  INVERSE
3050  PRINT P$ + ":"
3060  NORMAL
3070  VTAB V: HTAB H +  LEN (P$) + 1
3080  PRINT A$;: REM   PRINT CURRENT ENTRY
3090  GET B$
3100  REM  --RETURN KEY PRESSED?--
3110  IF B$ < >  CHR$ (13) GOTO 3150
3120  IF  LEN (A$) < 1 THEN   CALL  - 198: GOTO 3090: REM    MINIMUM LENGTH
       TEST
3130  PRINT
3140  RETURN
3150  REM --DELETE OR CURSOR LEFT KEY PRESSED?--
3160  IF  ASC (B$) < > 127 AND  ASC (B$) < > 8 GOTO 3210
3170  IF  LEN (A$) = 0 THEN   CALL  - 198: GOTO 3090: REM    MINIMUM LENGTH
       TEST
3180  IF  LEN (A$) = 1 THEN A$ = "": GOTO 3200
3190 A$ =  LEFT$ (A$, LEN (A$) - 1): REM    SUBTRACT RIGHT-MOST CHARACTER
       FROM A$
3200  GOTO 3030
3210  REM --MAXIMUM LENGTH TEST--
3220  IF  LEN (A$) = L2 THEN   CALL  - 198: GOTO 3090
3230  REM --FILTER--
3240  IF  ASC (B$) = 44 GOTO 3300: REM   COMMA ENTERED
3250  IF  ASC (B$) > 47 AND  ASC (B$) < 58 GOTO 3300: REM   NUMBER
3260  IF  ASC (B$) > 64 AND  ASC (B$) < 91 GOTO 3300: REM     LETTER
       (CAPITAL)
3270  IF  ASC (B$) = 32 GOTO 3300: REM   SPACE BAR
3280  CALL  - 198
3290  GOTO 3090
3300 A$ = A$ + B$
3310  GOTO 3070
3350  REM --ERROR MESSAGE--
3360  GOSUB 1300: REM   CLEAR LINE
3370  FLASH : REM   DELETE THIS LINE IF USING 80-COLUMN CARD
3380  PRINT ERR$
3390  CALL  - 198
3400  NORMAL
3410 TX = 5: GOSUB 4100: REM   5-SECOND TIME DELAY
3420  GOSUB 1300: REM   ERASE MESSAGE
3430  RETURN
3450  REM --VERIFICATION PROMPT--
3460  GOSUB 1300: REM   CLEAR LINE
3470  INVERSE
3480  PRINT "DO YOU HAVE CHANGES? (Y/N):";
```

Fig. 5-21. Apple verification subroutine (lines 3450-3600) and related subroutines required for full-screen data entry with error messages and verification (like that in Fig. 5-20).

```
3490   NORMAL
3500   GET A$
3510   IF A$ < > "Y" AND A$ < > "N" GOTO 3500
3520   IF A$ = "N" THEN A = 0: GOTO 3600: REM   NO CHANGES
3530   P$ = "SELECT ITEM # TO CHANGE"
3540   GOSUB 3010: REM   CALL DATA-ENTRY SUBROUTINE
3550   A =  VAL (A$)
3560   IF A >  = 1 AND A < = N GOTO 3600
3570   ERR$ = "NUMBER MUST BE BETWEEN 1 AND " +  STR$ (N): REM   DEFINE ERROR
       MESSAGE
3580   GOSUB 3350: REM   CALL ERROR MESSAGE SUBROUTINE
3590   GOTO 3530: REM   HAVE USER SELECT ANOTHER ITEM #
3600   RETURN
4100   REM --TX-SECOND DELAY--
4110   FOR A = 1 TO TX * 960
4120   NEXT
4130   RETURN
```

sends control back to line 3430 so that the user can type in a different Item#.

Now let us consider how the actual program works, starting with the data-entry subroutines. The data-entry program consists of lines 10000 – 10570. There are three data-entry subroutines, starting at lines 10240, 10360, and 10470. Each of these has the same structure, so let us focus on the one starting at line 10240, which collects the NAMES$ variable. This subroutine consists of lines 10240 – 10350. It should look very familiar to you, since it is almost identical to lines 10120 – 10175 of Fig. 5-19, which was discussed earlier in this chapter. Other than line numbers, only two changes have been made: the prompt is now preceded by the number "1", and a RETURN statement has been added at the end. Analogous changes have been made to the routines for collecting the AGE and SEX$ variables.

Now let us examine the control code, which consists of lines 10000 – 10230. Lines 10000 – 10100 create the data-entry screen. These lines are identical to the corresponding lines in Fig. 5-19. Line 10120 calls the first data entry subroutine at line 10240. Lines 10130 and 10140 call the other two data-entry subroutines.

The verification part of the program begins at line 10150 and continues to the end of the control code. Lines 10160 – 10180 set the arguments for the verification subroutine. These arguments will cause the verification prompt to appear at row 22 and column 1 of the display, and to accept any "Item number to change" between 1 and 3. The verification subroutine is called at line 10190. If the value of A returned by the subroutine is 0, then there are no changes to make, and line 10200 sends control to line 10230, terminating the program.

If the value of A returned by the verification subroutine is 1, 2, or 3, then one of the lines 10210 – 10220 will execute, calling the appropriate data-entry subroutine, and then sending control back to line 10160, where the user can reverify and select further changes to make, if necessary.

This program may seem a bit convoluted to you if you are not used to constructing programs out of building blocks such as subroutines. If you have more experience, you may still find it difficult to follow what is going on. On the other hand, it may all be perfectly clear to you.

Whatever your state of mind, spend a little time going over the code and the explanation given above. This is an example of how your control code shrinks when you construct a program of powerful subroutines. Note that, though there are many lines of code in this program, the controlling part consists of only lines 10110 through 10230—a total of 14 lines, two of which are REMs and one of which is END. In other words, the intelligence of this program is contained in only 11 lines, which do their job mainly by calling on their friends, the subroutines. When you look at the program from this perspective, you see that it is much simpler

```
3010 REM--INPUT# DATA ENTRY--
3020 SYS C0,1,V,H :REM CLEAR LINE
3030 SYS C0,0,V,H:REM POSITION PROMPT
3040 PRINT CHR$(18);:REM REVERSE ON
3050 PRINT P$+":";:REM PRINT PROMPT
3060 PRINT CHR$(146);:REM REVERSE OFF
3070 OPEN 1,0
3080 INPUT#1,A$
3090 PRINT
3100 CLOSE 1
3110 RETURN
3200 REM--ERROR MESSAGE--
3210 SYS C0,1,V,H:REM CLEAR LINE
3220 FOR B=1 TO 10
3230 TX=.2:GOSUB 4100:REM .2 SEC DELAY
3240 SYS C0,0,V,H:REM POSITION CURSOR
3250 PRINT CHR$(18)ER$:REM PRINT ERROR MESSAGE IN REVERSE VIDEO
3260 TX=.2:GOSUB 4100:REM .2 SEC DELAY
3270 SYS C0,0,V,H
3280 PRINT CHR$(146)ER$:REM PRINT ERROR MESSAGE IN NORMAL VIDEO
3290 NEXT
3300 SYS C0,1,V,H
3310 RETURN
3350 REM--VERIFICATION PROMPT--
3360 SYS C0,1,V,H:REM CLEAR LINE
3370 SYS C0,0,V,H:REM POSITION PROMPT
3380 PRINT CHR$(18)"DO YOU HAVE CHANGES? (Y/N): ";
3390 POKE 204,0:REM FLASH CURSOR
3400 GET A$:IF A$="" GOTO 3400
3410 IF A$<>"Y" AND A$<>"N" GOTO 3400
3420 IF A$="N" THEN A=0:GOTO 3500:REM NO CHANGES
3430 P$="SELECT ITEM # TO CHANGE"
3440 GOSUB 3010:REM CALL DATA ENTRY SUBROUTINE
3450 A=VAL(A$)
3460 IF A>=1 AND A<=N GOTO 3500
3470 ER$="NUMBER MUST BE BETWEEN 1 AND"+STR$(N):REM DEFINE ERROR MESSAGE
3480 GOSUB 3200:REM CALL ERROR MESSAGE SUBROUTINE
3490 GOTO 3430:REM HAVE USER SELECT ANOTHER ITEM#
3500 RETURN
4100 REM--TX SECOND DELAY--
4110 FOR A=1 TO TX*870
4120 NEXT
4130 RETURN
```

Fig. 5-22. C-64 verification subroutine (lines 3350-3500) and related subroutines required for full-screen data entry with error messages and verification (like that in Fig. 5-20).   (Requires assembly-language subroutine loader; see Appendix B.)

than it could be without subroutines. If you are not convinced of this, consider how you might write a program that does what this one does without them.

Figure 5-20 illustrates the basic structure and logic for doing page verification of prior data entries. This technique is also useful in programs that make use of a database which users need to query and modify. The programming requirements for a database editing program are much the same as those for page verification. The main difference between the two types of programs is how long after the entries are made that they are reviewed and edited. In a verification routine, this is a few seconds or minutes. In a database editing program, on the other hand, it may be days, weeks, or months afterward.

Chapter 6

Program Control

To make a computer program do something, the user must exercise control over it. In a game, for example, this may be done with a joystick which tells a gunnery platform where to move and when to fire at descending invaders. In a more serious program, control is usually exercised through the keyboard. A popular method of control in microcomputer programs is the *menu*. This is simply a list of the functions that the program can perform. The user looks at the menu to find the function desired, and then uses the keyboard to type in the selection with a number, letter, or function key. The computer then, like an obedient servant, carries out its master's command. Though the menu is popular, other control methods may be used in addition to menus or in place of them. This chapter describes the control methods most popular with microcomputers—menus, simple choices, and typed-in commands.

To use any control method, the user must enter information into the computer. Since entries are made, users may make errors, and all of the error-testing methods described in Chapter 5 apply. If

you are not familiar with these methods or have not read Chapter 5, do so before starting this chapter.

Data entry and program control are similar in more ways than they differ. Both involve user entry of data which are assigned to variables. Error tests and user verification of entries are required in both cases. However, there is at least one big difference. The entries made during a data-entry program become part of the program's database and affect the content of the displays the user views. The entries made for program control govern what the program does. They decide, for example, whether the user views an analysis display, updates files, or exits the program. If you think of a program as a sort of network of roads, with each road leading to a different program function, then the control entries decide what routes are taken. To extend the metaphor, conventional data entry decides what data are processed—who gets in and out of the vehicles, and when and where they do it.

The method of control has a big effect on how easy it is to learn and use a program. Several trade-offs must be made in selecting the control method, and making them is not always easy. The three primary trade-off factors are *ease of learning, ease of use,* and *speed.*

Ease of learning is always a desirable goal, despite what some misguided teachers and writers may think. No virtue accrues to he or she who learns things the hard way, and in fact it is more the other way around. What makes one control method easier or more difficult to learn than another? Several things matter, but one of the main ones is how much the user must commit to memory. Since menus display what is available, the user does not have to memorize their content, and this makes them relatively easy to learn. If the program's functions are not displayed on a menu, then the user must memorize what is available and create an internal list of program options. This is harder to learn, obviously, but not necessarily a bad thing. Another thing that influences ease of learning is the logic (or lack thereof) that holds the program's control structure together. Is that structure a nice, geometric spider's web, or a rat's nest of confusion?

Some control methods are easier to use than others. Also, given a particular method, the way you implement it affects how difficult it is to use. A complicating factor is that making something easy to learn often makes it more difficult to use, and vice-versa. For example, providing extensive on-screen prompting makes a program easy to learn. However, after a user masters a program, such prompting often gets in the way, making the program more difficult to use.

Speed is important, and in some programs it is more important than ease of learning or use. Some control methods are faster than others. However, the fastest control method is not always the best.

Often, you must make a trade-off among making your program easy to learn, easy to use, or fast. In general, programs with menus are the easiest to learn and use, but they are also among the slowest. It seems—on the surface at least—that you cannot have everything. As this chapter eventually shows, it is not really as bad as it might seem, because there are ways to combine the control

methods to get the best of both worlds. But before you can do this intelligently, you must understand each control method and its strengths and weaknesses in terms of the three trade-off factors.

The chapter begins by presenting design guidelines for program control, and then covers three common control methods: menus, simple choices, and typed-in commands. The main emphasis is on menus. Menus are not necessarily the answer to every programmer's design problem, but they are becoming increasingly popular and widely used in microcomputer programs for very good reasons. The final section shows how to combine menus and typed-in commands to get the best of at least two worlds. As in the earlier chapters, this one presents many examples of code and more than a few useful subroutines.

PROGRAM CONTROL DESIGN GUIDELINES

Guess which two design principles are (again) important for designing program control? As always, they are simplicity and consistency.

Let's start with simplicity. Consider the analogy between program control and a road network. In this analogy, the various roads are the links between the functions the program can perform (its subprograms), and the crossroads are where control actions occur. This network is often referred to as a *control structure.* Well, the more complex this network becomes, the more difficult it is for someone to master the program. Have you ever been to a city where the roads were poorly laid out or the maps were bad? You know, lots of dead ends, roads that ran off at odd angles, roundabouts, and other nonstandard interconnections that broke up the regularity of the pattern. If you live in a city that has such roads, eventually you get used to them. However, if you are a stranger who is used to a more regular pattern—one that is simple and that follows conventional rules for how streets should interconnect—then finding your way around can be very difficult. When you move to a city with such roads, you must go through a learning phase. At first it all seems very confusing. But with a map and time, you master the roads. Eventually, you may discover that there was method to the madness of the road patterns after all. That is, some of the crazy interconnections, odd angles or roads, and so forth make it possible to get between points more quickly. After learning the road system, you may grow to like it. It may not be good for strangers, you realize, but it is fine for old hands who live there, such as yourself.

It may not be obvious, but there is a very close analogy between this and the control structure you build into your program. A simple control structure is easy to learn and use at first, but may be more difficult to use later. A more complex control structure may be faster, once you have mastered it, but be harder to learn.

In microcomputer programs, it is best to keep things simple, and to lean in the direction of making your program easy to learn. This chapter will show some concrete examples of how to do this in the discussion of menu networks.

Another way simplicity applies is in what you name things; that is, your use of language. Find the simplest, most descriptive labels that you can. This applies universally to anything in a computer program that needs a label—the name of a program, a display's title, a procedure that must be performed. Avoid the complex, technical, computer-sounding, and abstract. Instead, use simple, concrete, descriptive terms. To illustrate, if you just loaded up a new program for the first time, which menu do you think would be the easiest to understand, that in Fig. 6-1 or that in Fig. 6-2?

Keep it simple.

Now take consistency. Following the consistency rule makes it easier for someone to learn something because it reduces the number of different things that must be learned. This rule requires you to do similar things in similar ways. How does it apply to program control?

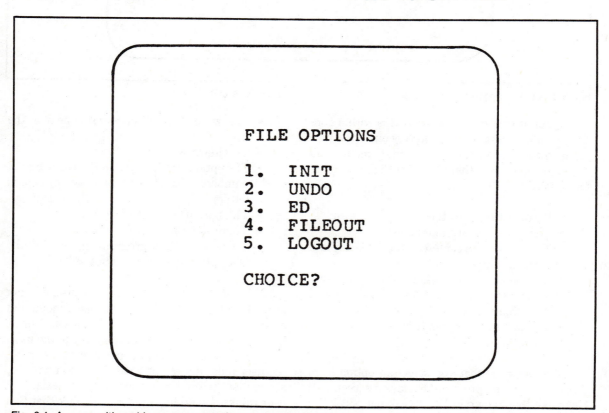

```
FILE OPTIONS

1.   INIT
2.   UNDO
3.   ED
4.   FILEOUT
5.   LOGOUT

CHOICE?
```

Fig. 6-1. A menu with ambiguous menu options—what do they mean?

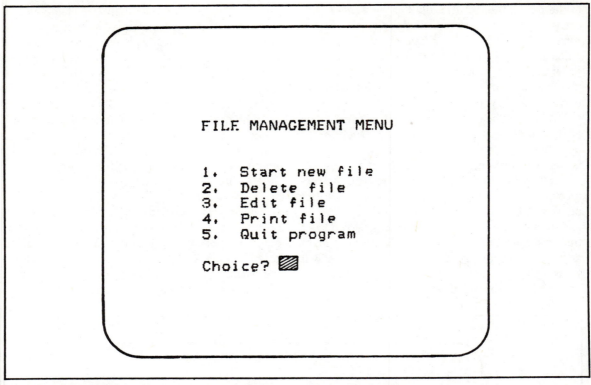

FILE MANAGEMENT MENU

1. Start new file
2. Delete file
3. Edit file
4. Print file
5. Quit program

Choice? ▨

Fig. 6-2. A menu whose options are simple verb-noun pairs, and easy to understand.

Again, it is helpful to answer this with a concrete example. Suppose that you try out a new program that uses menus. The first menu you encounter looks like that shown in Fig. 6-2. Some features of this menu are:

- It has a title with the word *menu* in it.
- Menu options are numbered.
- The options are centered both vertically and horizontally.
- The menu options consist of verb-noun pairs.
- A prompt directs the user to type Choice.
- A flashing cursor follows the prompt.
- The last menu option is labeled "Quit program."

Now, suppose that you select an option from this menu and the program displays a screen that looks like that shown in Fig. 6-3. What is this? In some ways it looks like a menu, but:

- The word "menu" does not appear in the title.
- The items are left-justified.
- The options (if that is what they are) are not numbered, but they are preceded by capital letters.
- The options consist of verbs.
- There is no prompt or cursor.
- There is no "Quit program" option, but the last option is labeled "Escape."

What do you make of this? It is probably not difficult to figure out that this is also a menu, but it is not like the first one. Since its format differs, it poses a certain amount of ambiguity to the user. Making sense of it is a problem-solving task. First, the user must figure out what the screen is. Like a scientist, he or she develops a hypothesis. The user thinks something such as, "I think that that is a menu. Let's see, now. Menus have properties

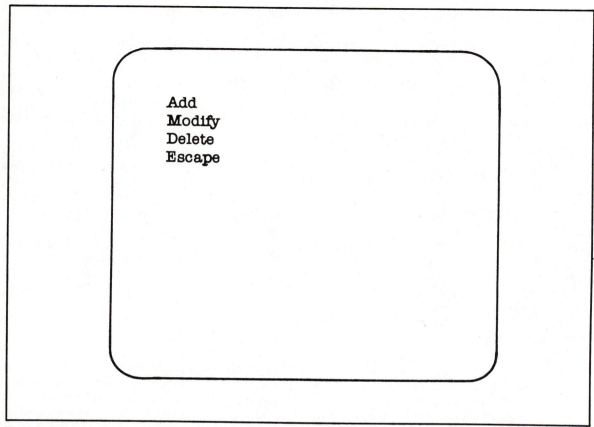

Add
Modify
Delete
Escape

Fig. 6-3. A menu is not always obviously a menu. This one lacks a title and prompt line, and it is not clear how options are to be selected.

A, B, and C. Let me test my hypothesis by examining the content of this screen. No, it does not have property A. I think it has property B. I am not sure about property C."

You get the idea. Why make it necessary for the user to act the role of a scientist? Make it easy on the user. Be consistent.

MENUS

A menu was defined in general terms, but for the record (and the sake of consistency) let us define it a little more formally. A *menu* consists of a list of program options and a data-entry routine that allow the user to select one of the options. This is the minimum, of course. A menu can and usually should include more than just these two things.

Advantages of Menus

Software publishers, in advertising their programs, often mention that they are "user-friendly" and have menus. Many of the programs whose listings appear in books and magazines use menus. There must be something good about them, or else they would not be so widely used. Well, what is it?

Perhaps the best way of answering this question is to consider the alternative: a blank screen. This, in fact, is all that many programs—especially advanced ones—provide. To use a program such as this, the user must pull the program options out of his or her memory. A program menu is, well, a menu. It is aptly named. Walk into most restaurants and they hand you a menu or have a menu posted. Walk into a fast-food place and the menu is simple and easy to figure out. Walk into a Chinese restaurant and it may take you hours. Walk into a fancy restaurant, or one that has such pretensions, and the menu is not written down, but related verbally by a fancily dressed maître d' with a real or phony foreign accent. However the menu is delivered to you, it fulfills a need you have to know what is available. Without it you could not order without either already knowing what was available, or asking someone. In a computer program, you do not usually have the second option.

Menu Drawbacks

Some people do not like menus. Many sophisticated users regard them with about the same amount of enthusiasm that an Olympic miler would regard training with a high school track team. The problem for these experts is that they do know the bill of fare and do not need a menu to tell them what they can order. When the waiter hands it to them, they hand it right back, and order on the spot. They do not like delays. They want to get on with things. Some programs have many menus, and to get to the program you want, you may have to work your way there, menu by menu. This can be time consuming and tedious for the expert. But, although menus are not the answer for every program, they are the answer for many.

Menus can be designed in a number of different ways. This section describes two types: the full-screen menu, and the partial-screen menu. A full-screen menu is a menu of the type illustrated in Fig. 6-1 through 6-3. Full-screen menus are typically used as main control menus. When they are on the display, nothing else appears. A partial-screen menu is typically displayed on one part of the display while something else is on the rest of the display. Such a menu is often used to control the information on the display. For example, it might be used to modify the scale or other graphic features of the display. Both types of menus are useful, but usually for different purposes. Let us start with the full-screen menu.

Full-Screen Menus

Figure 6-2 is a typical full-screen menu. The main features of this menu are as follows:

- Menu title—This is centered at the top of the display. It is in all capital letters, inverse video, and contains the word *menu*.
- Menu options—This menu contains five options, numbered 1 through 5.
- Prompt line—This is the line on which the user types in the menu choice.

As mentioned earlier, a menu may contain more than just these three features. In a moment, we will discuss what these might be. But let us start with the main features and see why these three simple features are not as simple as they seem.

Title. The title, of course, is straightforward. Center this at the top of the display, or perhaps a few lines down from the top, if you can compose a better-looking screen that way. It is best to use all capital letters. The use of inverse video is optional, somewhat a matter of style. In this book, the style followed is to use all capital letters and inverse video for titles, headings, and most prompts. While following this particular convention is not critical, it is important to follow some convention that permits the user to discriminate among titles, headings, prompts, and the other information on the display.

Options. Now let us consider the menu options. There are a number of dos and don'ts here. First, the way the options are identified is somewhat arbitrary. In Fig. 6-2, each option has a number beside it. Options may also be identified with letters (Fig. 6-4). A third way is to list them with function key assignments (Fig. 6-5).

When numbers are used, the lowest-numbered option should be the number 1. You often see a menu with an option numbered zero on it. Avoid this. These numbers stand for real things—programs or program options. A zero implies the absence of something, and is an abstract notion at best. It took the human race a long time to discover the concept of zero, and many of us still have difficulty with it. Please help us out by not using zeros in your menus.

Using letters as option identifiers is good if your

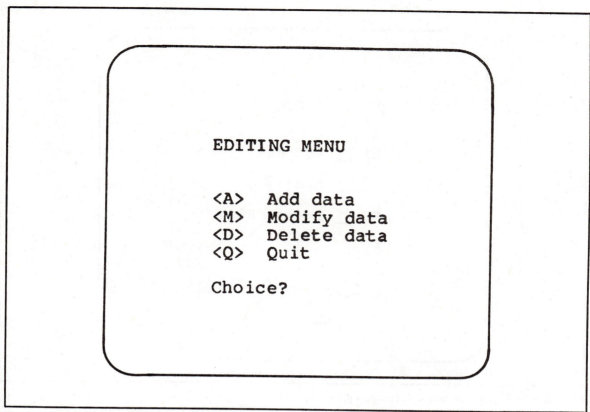

```
EDITING MENU


<A>    Add data
<M>    Modify data
<D>    Delete data
<Q>    Quit

Choice?
```

Fig. 6-4. A menu where options are selected with a letter.

program has a few menus and you can assign letters that relate mnemonically to the options. For example, let the user type in "A" to add something, "M" to modify something, and so forth. Users tend to expect the identifiers to relate semantically to the options. If they lack a semantic component (that is, an intrinsic meaning), then you are better off using numbers.

Now we come to function keys. Some computers have them and they are nice. You can use function keys for menu selection, although doing this has some complications. In using menus to control a program, one ought to start with the premise that menu options are active only while a menu is displayed on the screen. That is, the user should not be able to leave the menu and still activate the options by pressing certain keys. It is true that some program control techniques (such as command

languages) do permit control this way, but that is now how a menu is supposed to work.

True function keys are activated with statements such as KEY(n) ON and ON KEY(n) GOSUB and remain active anywhere in the program. If you want to make them active only when a menu is displayed, then they must be activated when that menu is first displayed and deactivated when the menu is no longer displayed. The code required to do this is extra overhead to the program.

An additional problem is that true function keys are supposed to be active all or most of the time, and turning them on and off in this manner runs counter to the convention. As noted, there are a few complications in using the function keys. In the end, you must weigh these factors and decide whether or not to use them. In some cases they may be perfect, but if you are in doubt, leave them alone.

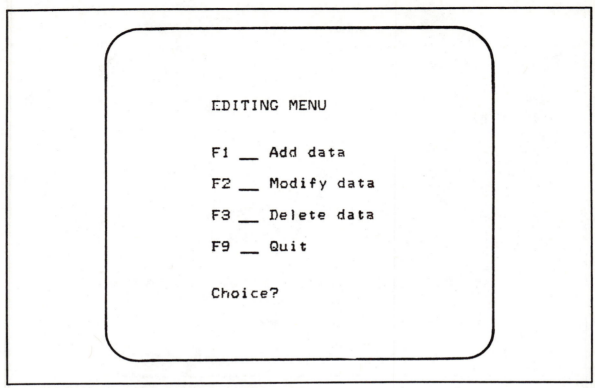

```
EDITING MENU

F1 __ Add data

F2 __ Modify data

F3 __ Delete data

F9 __ Quit


Choice?
```

Fig. 6-5. A menu where options are selected with a function key.

No menu should have more than about nine options. The ideal number is somewhere in the five-to-seven range. This is not a number that was dreamed up, but one that has been established through research. When a menu is longer than about nine items, it becomes more like a directory. It takes a fairly long time to read such a menu. Have you ever used a program with a menu that had 20 or 30 options on it? Creating a menu this long shows a lack of awareness that it takes time for people to search for and read things.

If you create a menu with more than five options, it is a good idea to separate the list of options into two parts, separated by a space (Fig. 6-6). This makes it easier for the user to read.

In general, it is desirable for menu options to be concise and descriptive. If the user rarely uses the program, then it makes sense for the options to be longer and more descriptive. Short options can be read more quickly, and save time for the ex-

perienced user. However, it is hard to make short options as descriptive as longer ones, which argues for longer options on menus that are rarely used.

Menu options can take on several different forms, such as:

- Short action object. Examples are *Update files, Exit program,* and *Start new file.* These define an action and something to be acted upon by the user.
- Short descriptive label. Examples are *File update, Exit,* and *New file.* These may be the names of the programs, or define an implicit action and object. This form of label is less explicit than the action-object form.
- Long descriptive label. Sometimes these are framed as questions, such as *Do you want to update your files?* Alternatively, they may just describe an action: *Start a new file.*

Options can be constructed in other ways than

these, although these are the common ones. It is difficult to say which is best, since this depends upon the program and the user. It is clear that an option form that gives an action and something to be acted upon is more meaningful than a descriptive label, especially for the inexperienced user. Long labels are also better for the inexperienced user. However, longer labels take more time to read, and may be less desirable in programs that are frequently used.

I prefer the short action-object form since it is both short and reasonably descriptive. Whatever form is used, it is important to avoid mixing options in different forms on the same menu or within the same program. Doing so can cause confusion. For example, if most of your menu options take the short descriptive label form, a user may be confused by an option with the label *Update file*. Does this refer to a file named UPDATE or the act of updating any file?

In programs that involve many menus, linked together in a network, it is often desirable to make the final option of all menus the same, and to use this option for exiting the current menu and returning to the previous menu. To illustrate, Fig. 6-7 shows one of a family of menus that are linked together in a hierarchical fashion. The last option of each menu permits the user to exit from that menu

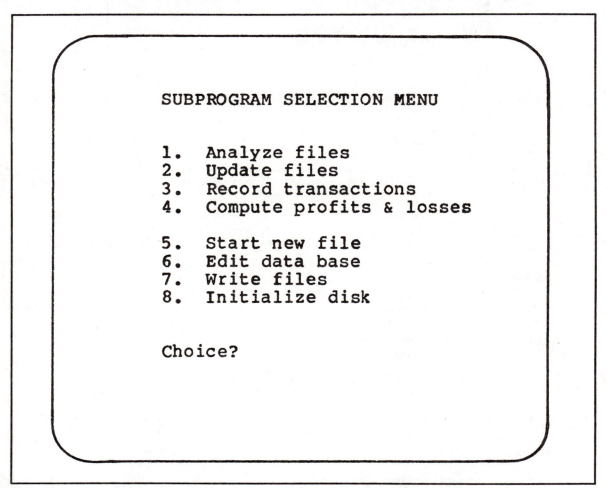

```
SUBPROGRAM SELECTION MENU


1.   Analyze files
2.   Update files
3.   Record transactions
4.   Compute profits & losses

5.   Start new file
6.   Edit data base
7.   Write files
8.   Initialize disk


Choice?
```

Fig. 6-6. A long menu, the option block of which is broken into two parts to make it easier to read.

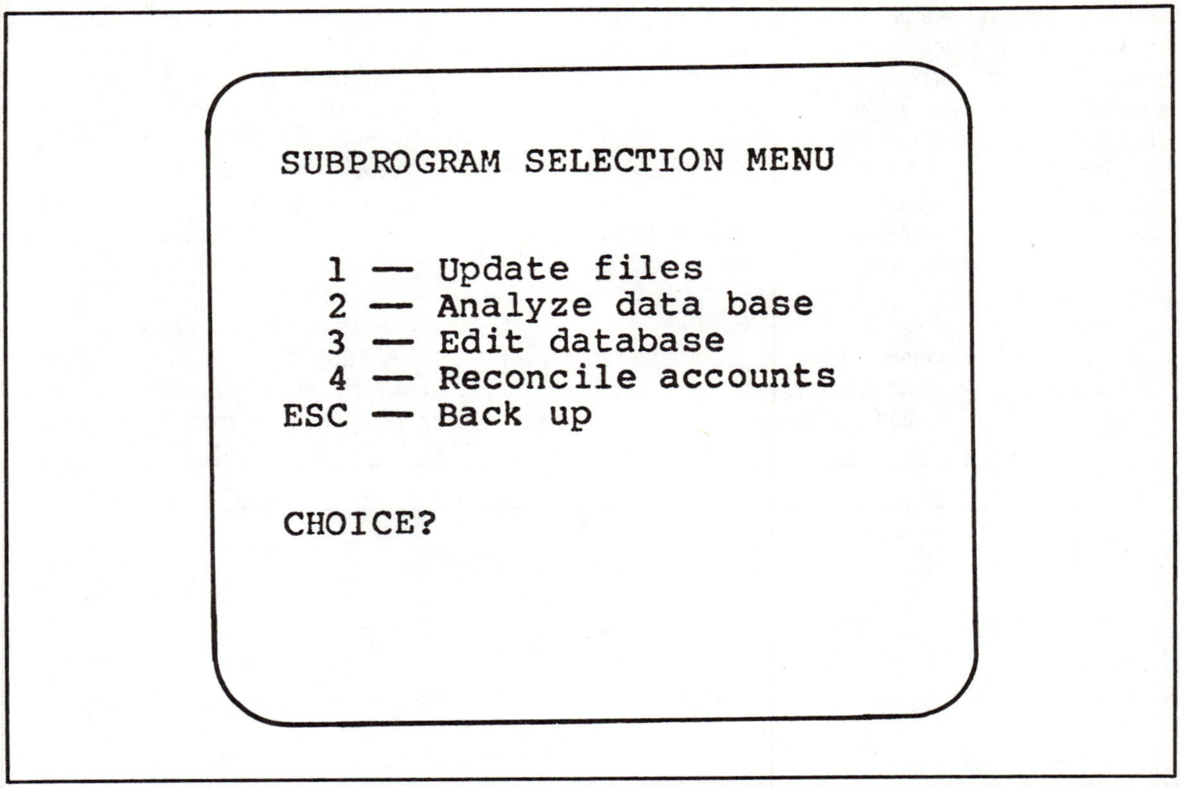

```
┌─────────────────────────────────────────┐
│   ╭─────────────────────────────────╮   │
│   │                                 │   │
│   │  SUBPROGRAM SELECTION MENU      │   │
│   │                                 │   │
│   │                                 │   │
│   │    1 — Update files             │   │
│   │    2 — Analyze data base        │   │
│   │    3 — Edit database            │   │
│   │    4 — Reconcile accounts       │   │
│   │  ESC — Back up                  │   │
│   │                                 │   │
│   │                                 │   │
│   │  CHOICE?                        │   │
│   │                                 │   │
│   │                                 │   │
│   │                                 │   │
│   ╰─────────────────────────────────╯   │
└─────────────────────────────────────────┘
```

Fig. 6-7. A menu where the final option, selected with the ESC key, brings back (backs up to) the previous menu.

and return to the previous one. In this case, the last option on every menu is called by pressing the ESC (Escape) key. A user who is deep in the program does not have to look at the menu to know how to back up to a higher-level menu—pressing the ESC key always does this, and pressing it repeatedly brings back the highest-level menu.

The Prompt. The prompt for a menu is like a data-entry prompt in that it must alert the user that an entry is required (a flashing cursor does this), and describe the nature of the entry. Prompts tend to be written in either succinct or descriptive form, depending upon the proclivities and moods of the programmer, and either form is perfectly acceptable. For a descriptive prompt, you might use something such as:

- *Please type the number (or letter) of your choice.*
- *Please type your choice.*

- *Type the number of your program selection.* Some programmers use the term "enter" instead of "type" or "please type." However, "enter" is a bit ambiguous. "Type" is more specific, descriptive, and accurate in terms of what the user must actually do.

I prefer short prompts—something along these lines:

- *Choice*
- *Option*
- *Selection number*

While it is true that these are not particularly descriptive, the form of the menu is such that there is little doubt that what is being viewed is a menu and that what the user must do is type something on the keyboard. After using menus a few times, users tend to ignore the prompt line, anyway.

When the user types a menu selection, the typed entry should appear (that is, be *echoed*) on the prompt line after the prompt. The program should not execute the choice immediately, but should give the user a chance to view the selection and change it, if desired. In other words, the user should be able to verify the entry.

The simplest way to permit user verification of a typed entry is to use the INPUT statement. Using this statement, whatever the user types is echoed to the screen, and nothing takes effect until the Return key is pressed. As noted in Chapter 5, the INPUT statement has the drawback that it allows a careless or mischievous user to wreak havoc on a screen display. For this reason, it is better to use a Return-verified INKEY$ technique similar to that described in Chapter 5. By using such a technique, you can maintain control of the screen and also filter the keyboard entries. The method will be illustrated later in this chapter.

Additional Information that May Be Displayed on a Full-Screen Menu. Depending upon the nature of the program, it sometimes makes good sense to display certain additional information on the menu screen. This is particularly true if the program tends to use a lot of menus and the user frequently has one on the display. In this case, the menu is a convenient place to present status or file information. The information should only be presented on the menu if it is of genuine importance to the user. Otherwise, it is clutter and a distraction from the central purpose of the menu screen.

Here are examples of types of information that might be presented on a menu screen:

- The amount of available memory remaining.
- Dates; current date, date file last updated.
- The name of the file presently active.
- The amount of available file space remaining.

One way to add such information is to put it on the bottom of the menu, below the prompt line. This way the information is accessible, but out of the way. The user can refer to it, if desired.

Generating a Menu

There are two common ways to generate a menu screen: directly, like a display screen; and with a subroutine, by supplying certain arguments, and having the subroutine create the menu from them.

Generating a Menu Directly. If your program uses only one menu, or only a few, then it may be best to generate directly. Lay out the menu on paper, just as you would any other display screen. Then write the code to create the menu.

To illustrate, Fig. 6-8 is the design matrix for a simple program control menu. Figure 6-9 contains code in IBM PC BASIC for generating this menu, line by line. The menu was laid out in such a manner that the block of options is centered vertically; that is, is equidistant from the top and bottom of the screen. It is also centered horizontally. Since the options vary in length, it is a little tricky to center the option block horizontally. Centering is done by computing the average length of an option, subtracting this from the program variable WIDE%, adding 1, and dividing by 2. After computing the horizontal tab position in this manner, lay out the options on the matrix and see how they look. If you have some very short and very long lines, the option block may tend to look off center to the left, because we tend to pay more attention to long lines than short ones. See how the option block looks to the eye. Then readjust the tab until it looks good. This is a subjective, aesthetic judgment. (Apologies for not having a subroutine to do this for you.)

The title is at the top of the display. You might move it down a few lines if it looks better to you that way. This is a matter of personal preference.

The prompt is at the bottom of the display. Move it up a few lines if you like.

If you decide to add additional information below the prompt line, you may want to move everything up, until the display appears balanced. It will probably not look right the first time you lay it out.

IBM PC BASIC code for generating the menu is shown in Fig. 6-9. Line 10010 clears the display. Line 10020 defines the menu title and line 10030

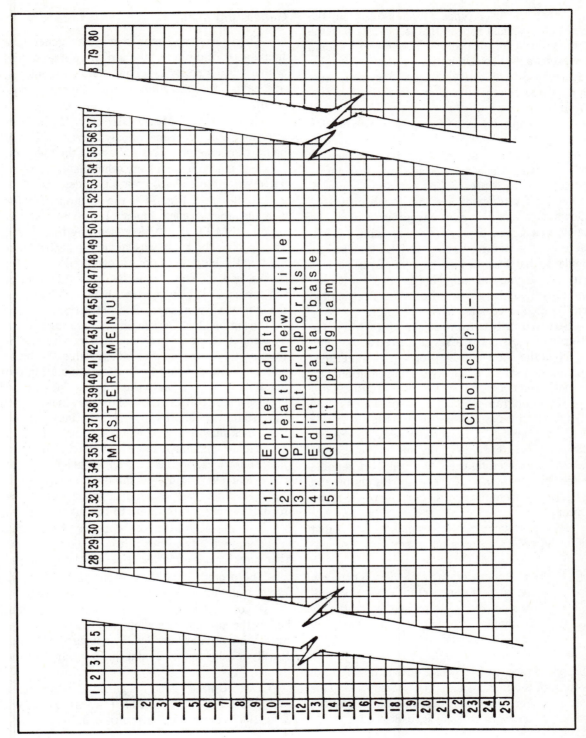

Fig. 6-8. Design matrix for a simple program-control menu.

```
0 REM Menu-Generation Program (direct)
1 REM SAVE"FIG6-9.BAS",A
980 WIDE%=80
990 GOTO 10000
1500 REM--Center & Print Title--
1510 T=(WIDE%+1-LEN(T$))/2
1520 LOCATE ,T:REM position cursor horizontally
1530 COLOR 0,7:REM inverse
1540 PRINT T$
1550 COLOR 7,0:REM normal video
1560 RETURN
10000 REM--Full-Screen Menu Generator--
10010 CLS
10020 T$="MASTER MENU"
10030 GOSUB 1500:REM print title
10040 REM-Display Options-
10050 LOCATE 10:REM position first option to row 10
10060 PRINT TAB(32)"1. Enter data"
10070 PRINT TAB(32)"2. Create new file"
10080 PRINT TAB(32)"3. Print reports"
10090 PRINT TAB(32)"4. Edit data base"
10100 PRINT TAB(32)"5. Quit program"
10110 REM-Print Prompt-
10120 LOCATE 23,37
10130 COLOR 0,7:REM inverse
10140 PRINT"Choice?";
10150 COLOR 23,0:PRINT SPC(1) "_";:REM flash cursor
10160 COLOR 7,0:REM normal video
10170 A$=INKEY$:IF A$="" GOTO 10170
10180 A=VAL(A$)
10190 IF A<1 OR A>5 THEN BEEP:GOTO 10110
10200 LOCATE ,POS(0)-1:PRINT A$:REM display entry
10210 B$=INKEY$:IF B$="" GOTO 10210
10220 IF ASC(B$)<>13 GOTO 10110:REM verification by Enter key?
10230 END
```

Fig. 6-9. IBM PC code for generating the menu shown in Fig. 6-8 directly.

calls the Center & Print subroutine at line 1500. Line 10050 moves the cursor down to row 10, and lines 10060–10100 print the five menu options at tab 32. Lines 10120–10210 print the prompt and collect user entries. Line 10120 positions the cursor, 10130 sets inverse video mode, and 10140 prints the prompt *Choice?*. Line 10150 prints a flashing cursor. Line 10170 uses INKEY$ to get a single keystroke and assign it to A$.

Line 10180 evaluates the keystroke and line 10190 conducts a range test. If the number is between 1 and 5, it is valid. If not, control is sent back to line 10110. Note that, unless the entry falls within the valid range (1 – 5) the user is required to continue reentering it. Invalid entries are filtered out.

Once a valid entry occurs, line 10200 prints it. Line 10210 then INKEY$'s B$, the verification keystroke. This must be a Return keystroke or control is sent back to line 10110, starting data entry over.

Equivalent routines for the Apple and C-64 are shown in Figs. 6-10 and 6-11, respectively.

Generating a Menu with a Subroutine. Laying out a menu and then writing the code for it become a bit tedious if you have more than one or two of them to do. You can save yourself a lot of time by using a subroutine to do the work for you. The trickiest part is to lay out and then display the block of options. This must be centered both vertically and horizontally. However, what is in-

```
0   REM    FIG 6-10
1   REM   MENU-GENERATION PROGRAM (DIRECT)
980 COLS = 40
990   GOTO 10000
1500  REM --CENTER & PRINT TITLE--
1510 T = (COLS + 1 -  LEN (T$)) / 2
1520  HTAB T
1530  INVERSE
1540  PRINT T$
1550  NORMAL
1560  RETURN
10000  REM --FULL-SCREEN MENU GENERATOR--
10010  HOME
10020 T$ = "MASTER MENU"
10030  GOSUB 1500: REM   PRINT TITLE
10040  REM -DISPLAY OPTIONS-
10050  VTAB 9: REM    POSITION FIRST OPTION TO ROW 10
10060  PRINT  TAB( 12)"1. Enter data"
10070  PRINT  TAB( 12)"2. Create new file"
10080  PRINT  TAB( 12)"3. Print reports"
10090  PRINT  TAB( 12)"4. Edit data base"
10100  PRINT  TAB( 12)"5. Quit program"
10110  REM -PRINT PROMPT-
10120  VTAB 22: HTAB 17
10130  INVERSE
10140  PRINT "CHOICE?";
10150  NORMAL
10160  GET A$
10170 A =  VAL (A$)
10180  IF A < 1 OR A > 5 THEN  CALL  - 198: GOTO 10120
10190  PRINT A$;
10200  GET B$
10210  IF  ASC (B$) < > 13 GOTO 10120: REM   VERIFICATION BY RETURN KEY?
10220  END
```

Fig. 6-10. Apple code for generating the menu shown in Fig. 6-8 directly.

```
990 GOTO 10000
1500 REM--CENTER & PRINT T$--
1510 T=(39-LEN(T$))/2
1520 PRINT CHR$(18);
1530 PRINT TAB(T)T$
1540 RETURN
10000 REM--FULL-SCREEN MENU GENERATOR--
10010 PRINT CHR$(147);:REM CLEAR SCREEN
10020 T$="MASTER MENU"
10030 GOSUB 1500:REM PRINT TITLE
10040 REM-DISPLAY OPTIONS-
10050 SYS C0,0,10:REM POSITION FIRST OPTION TO ROW 10
10060 PRINT TAB(12)"1. ENTER DATA"
10070 PRINT TAB(12)"2. CREATE NEW FILE"
10080 PRINT TAB(12)"3. PRINT REPORTS"
10090 PRINT TAB(12)"4. EDIT DATA BASE"
10100 PRINT TAB(12)"5. QUIT PROGRAM"
10110 REM-PRINT PROMPT-
```

Fig. 6-11. C-64 code for generating the menu shown in Fig. 6-8 directly.   (Requires assembly-language subroutine loader; see Appendix B.)

```
10120 SYS C0,1,24,17:REM CLEAR PROMPT LINE
10130 SYS C0,0,24,17:REM POSITION PROMPT
10140 PRINT CHR$(18)"CHOICE?";
10150 POKE 204,0:REM FLASH CURSOR
10160 GET A$:IF A$="" GOTO 10160:REM GET MENU SELECTION
10170 A=VAL(A$)
10180 IF A<1 OR A>5 GOTO 10120
10190 PRINT CHR$(146)" ";A$;:REM DISPLAY KEYSTROKE
10200 GET B$:IF B$="" GOTO 10200:REM ENTRY VERIFICATION
10210 IF ASC(B$)<>13 GOTO 10120:REM VERIFICATION RETURN KEY?
10220 END
```

volved in figuring out the vertical and horizontal positions is reducible to simple mathematics of the sort that your computer does in a flash.

Figure 6-12 is the listing of a subroutine for generating a full-screen menu such as the one shown in Fig. 6-8. Arguments of the subroutine are WIDTH% (number of columns), T$ (title), N (number of valid options, 1 through N), and OPT$ (1) through OPT$(N) (menu options).

To use this subroutine, set the arguments as in any other subroutine and then call the subroutine with a GOSUB statement. Lines 10000 – 10080 in Fig. 6-12 do precisely this. When the subroutine is called, it clears the screen and generates the menu.

The subroutine prints the title on the top row, computes the average length of an option and centers the option block horizontally, centers it vertically based on the number of options, and then prints the prompt on row 23. The aesthetics of a menu with title at top of screen and prompt at bottom are dubious at best, and most menus would look much nicer with the three parts of the menu brought closer together. It is fairly easy to modify the subroutine to change its layout. It is presented in the form shown in Fig. 6-12 mainly to provide a starting point in a menu-generation subroutine that you can later tailor to meet your own particular needs.

```
0 REM Menu-Generation Subroutine (full screen)
1 REM SAVE"FIG6-12.BAS",A
980 WIDE%=80
990 GOTO 10000
1500 REM--Center & Print Title--
1510 T=(WIDE%+1-LEN(T$))/2
1520 LOCATE ,T:REM position cursor horizontally
1530 COLOR 0,7:REM inverse
1540 PRINT T$
1550 COLOR 7,0:REM normal video
1560 RETURN
4200 REM--Full-Screen Menu Generator--
4210 CLS
4220 T$=" "+T$+" MENU "
4230 GOSUB 1500:REM print title
4240 REM-Compute Menu Starting Column-
4250 L=0
4260 FOR A=1 TO N
4270 L=L+LEN(OPT$(A))+3
4280 NEXT
4290 L=L/N
4300 H=(WIDE%+1-L)/2:REM compute tab
4310 REM-Compute Vertical Offset-
4320 V=(26-N)/2
```

Fig. 6-12. IBM PC subroutine (lines 4200-4500) for generating full-screen menu with numbered options.

```
4330 REM-Display Options-
4340 LOCATE V:REM position first option
4350 FOR A=1 TO N
4360 PRINT TAB(H-1)STR$(A);". "OPT$(A)
4370 NEXT
4380 REM-Print Prompt-
4390 LOCATE 23,37
4400 COLOR 0,7:REM inverse
4410 PRINT"Choice?";
4420 COLOR 23,0:PRINT SPC(1) "_";:REM flash cursor
4430 COLOR 7,0:REM normal video
4440 A$=INKEY$:IF A$="" GOTO 4440
4450 A=VAL(A$)
4460 IF A<1 OR A>N THEN BEEP:GOTO 4380
4470 LOCATE ,POS(0)-1:PRINT A$:REM display entry
4480 B$=INKEY$:IF B$="" GOTO 4480
4490 IF ASC(B$)<>13 GOTO 4380:REM verification by Enter key?
4500 RETURN
10000 REM--Generate Menu--
10010 N=5
10020 T$="MASTER"
10030 OPT$(1)="Enter data"
10040 OPT$(2)="Create new file"
10050 OPT$(3)="Print reports"
10060 OPT$(4)="Edit data base"
10070 OPT$(5)="Quit program"
10080 GOSUB 4200
10090 END
```

The subroutine is based on the code shown in Fig. 6-9, which was discussed earlier, and so we will focus here mainly on the differences.

Lines 4220–4230 generate the title. Lines 4250–4290 compute the average length, L, of an option. Line 4250 initializes L to 0. Lines 4260–4280 then add up the total length of all options. Three is added to the length of each option for the number, period, and space that will be added later to precede the option. Line 4290 then divides the total by N (number of options) to compute the average length of an option. Line 4300 computes the horizontal tab position, H, required for printing the options.

Line 4320 computes the first option's vertical offset (row number) based on the number of options. Line 4340 positions the cursor vertically, and lines 4350–4370 print the prompts, adding a selection number, period, and space at the beginning of each. (1 is subtracted from tab position H to correct for the extra space IBM PC BASIC adds to the front of a number when it converts to string form.) Lines 4390–4490 print the prompt and collect user keystrokes. These lines are identical to those in Fig. 6-9 except for line numbers and the use of the variable N in the error test in line 4460.

This subroutine permits you to create a full-screen menu in about as much time as it takes to type in lines with the subroutine's arguments. In this particular example, eight lines of code supply the arguments and subroutine call necessary to generate the five-option menu shown in Fig. 6-8. Using the subroutine is a considerable timesaver, and also eliminates the drudgery of counting the characters of the options and computing the horizontal tab positions and vertical offset.

Equivalent subroutines for the Apple and C-64 are shown in Figs. 6-13 and 6-14, respectively.

Control Switching. Creating a menu directly or with a subroutine is an act of screen generation and does not control anything. In order to execute control, you must convert the user's option selection into a control action. That is, if the user selects option 1 by typing the 1 key and then pressing Return, you must send program control to the part of the program that executes the appropriate function.

```
0   REM    FIG 6-13
1   REM   MENU-GENERATION SUBROUTINE (FULL SCREEN)
980 COLS = 40
990   GOTO 10000
1500   REM --CENTER & PRINT TITLE--
1510 T = (COLS + 1 -  LEN (T$)) / 2
1520   HTAB T
1530   INVERSE
1540   PRINT T$
1550   NORMAL
1560   RETURN
4200   REM --FULL-SCREEN MENU GENERATOR--
4210   HOME
4220 T$ = " " + T$ + " MENU "
4230   GOSUB 1500: REM   PRINT TITLE
4240   REM -COMPUTE MENU STARTING COLUMN-
4250 L = 0
4260   FOR A = 1 TO N
4270 L = L +  LEN (OPT$(A)) + 3
4280   NEXT
4290 L = L / N
4300 H = (COLS + 1 - L) / 2: REM   COMPUTE TAB
4310   REM -COMPUTE VERTICAL OFFSET-
4320 V = (24 - N) / 2
4330   REM -DISPLAY OPTIONS-
4340   VTAB V: REM   POSITION FIRST OPTION
4350   FOR A = 1 TO N
4360   PRINT  TAB( H) STR$ (A);". "OPT$(A)
4370   NEXT
4380   REM -PRINT PROMPT-
4390   VTAB 22: HTAB COLS / 2 - 3
4400   INVERSE
4410   PRINT "CHOICE?";
4420   NORMAL
4430   GET A$
4440 A =  VAL (A$)
4450   IF A < 1 OR A > N THEN   CALL  - 198: GOTO 4390
4460   PRINT A$;
4470   GET B$
4480   IF  ASC (B$) < > 13 GOTO 4390
4490   RETURN
10000   REM  --GENERATE MENU--
10010 N = 5
10020 T$ = "MASTER"
10030 OPT$(1) = "Enter data"
10040 OPT$(2) = "Create new file"
10050 OPT$(3) = "Print reports"
10060 OPT$(4) = "Edit data base"
10070 OPT$(5) = "Quit program"
10080   GOSUB 4200
10090   END
```

Fig. 6-13. Apple subroutine (lines 4200-4490) for generating full-screen menu with numbered options.

This section shows two ways to switch control using BASIC statements: IF-THEN logic, and ON X GOTO. It also shows how and why the two methods are sometimes combined. The code examples that follow use the Menu-Generation subroutine described in the previous section. However, these control-switching methods apply equally when a menu is generated directly.

```
1500 REM--CENTER & PRINT T$--
1510 T=(39-LEN(T$))/2
1520 PRINT CHR$(18);
1530 PRINT TAB(T)T$
1540 RETURN
4200 REM--FULL-SCREEN MENU GENERATOR--
4210 PRINT CHR$(147);
4220 T$=T$+" MENU"
4230 GOSUB 1500:REM PRINT TITLE
4240 REM-COMPUTE MENU STARTING COLUMN-
4250 L=0
4260 FOR A=1 TO N
4270 L=L+LEN(OPT$(A))+3
4280 NEXT
4290 L=L/N
4300 H=(39-L)/2:REM COMPUTE TAB
4310 REM-COMPUTE VERTICAL OFFSET-
4320 V=INT(25-N)/2
4330 REM-DISPLAY OPTIONS-
4340 SYS C0,0,V:REM POSITION FIRST OPTION
4350 FOR A=1 TO N
4360 PRINT TAB(H-1)STR$(A)". "OPT$(A)
4370 NEXT
4380 REM-PRINT PROMPT-
4390 SYS C0,1,24,17:REM CLEAR PROMPT LINE
4400 SYS C0,0,24,17:REM POSITION PROMPT
4410 PRINT CHR$(18)"CHOICE?";
4420 POKE 204,0:REM FLASH CURSOR
4430 GET A$:IF A$="" GOTO 4430:REM GET MENU SELECTION
4435 POKE 204,1
4440 A=VAL(A$)
4450 IF A<1 OR A>N GOTO 4390
4460 PRINT CHR$(146)" ";A$;:REM DISPLAY KEYSTROKE
4470 GET B$:IFB$="" GOTO 4470:REM GET ENTRY VERIFICATION
4480 IF ASC(B$)<>13 GOTO 4390:REM VERIFICATION RETURN KEY?
4490 RETURN
10000 N=5
10010 T$="MASTER"
10020 OPT$(1)="ENTER DATA"
10030 OPT$(2)="CREATE NEW FILE"
10040 OPT$(3)="PRINT REPORTS"
10050 OPT$(4)="EDIT DATA BASE"
10060 OPT$(5)="QUIT PROGRAM"
10070 GOSUB 4200
10080 END
```

Fig. 6-14. C-64 subroutine (lines 4200-4490) for generating full-screen menu with numbered options. (Requires assembly-language subroutine loader; see Appendix B.)

Line 4440 of the Menu-Generation subroutine (Fig. 6-12) uses INKEY$ to get the user's menu selection and assign it to the string variable A$. Line 4450 evaluates A$ and assigns the result to the real variable A. Thus, the subroutine returns its result in two forms, and either can be used for control switching. Also note that since the subroutine does the error-testing—only valid values of A$ or A can be returned—further error-testing of these values is unnecessary.

IF-THEN Logic. Suppose that your program has the five options shown in Fig. 6-7 and that the lines at which these program functions start are as follows:

You can use IF-THEN logic to control switching by inserting the following lines in the listing shown in Fig. 6-12:

```
10090   REM—PROGRAM CONTROL—
10100   IF A=1 GOTO 12000
10110   IF A=2 GOTO 14000
10120   IF A=3 GOTO 20000
10130   IF A=4 GOTO 24000
10140   IF A=5 GOTO 10500
```

The above code uses the real variable A to control switching. You can also use the string form of this variable:

```
10090   REM—PROGRAM CONTROL—
10100   IF A$="1" GOTO 12000
10110   IF A$="2" GOTO 14000
10120   IF A$="3" GOTO 20000
10130   IF A$="4" GOTO 24000
10140   IF A$="5" GOTO 10500
```

Not only can you use either the real or string form of the switching variable, but you could even combine them, if desired:

```
10100   IF A=1 GOTO 12000
10110   IF A=2 GOTO 14000
10120   IF A$="3" GOTO 20000
10130   IF A$="4" GOTO 24000
10140   IF A$="5" GOTO 10500
```

There may not seem to be much point in doing this, but it comes in handy, as will be demonstrated later.

Any one of these three sets of code will do the job, but the most economical is the first, which works with real numbers. Still, this requires five statements, one for each menu option.

ON X GOTO Statement. The ON X GOTO statement is considerably more economical than IF-THEN logic. This statement switches control to the Xth statement following the GOTO. To illustrate, the switching logic given above can be reduced to this statement:

```
10010   ON X GOTO 12000, 14000, 20000,
        24000, 10500
```

This is obviously much shorter, but it requires that X be a number. You cannot use a string in place of X.

Further, if X is zero or a number greater than the number of arguments following GOTO, control falls through to the next line. For example, when this program is executed, control drops to line 30:

```
10   X=0
20   ON X GOTO 40, 50, 60
30   PRINT"LINE 30":END
40   PRINT"LINE 40":END
50   PRINT"LINE 50":END
60   PRINT"LINE 60":END
```

The same result is obtained if X is set equal to a number greater than 3.

Mixing Number and Letter Identifiers. It is sometimes useful to mix number and letter identifiers in menus. Suppose, for example, that you want to use a menu that has these four options:

1 - Enter data
2 - Create new file
3 - Print reports
ESC-Quit program

In order to generate this menu, we must modify the Menu-Generation subroutine so that it allows us to define not only the option label (OPT$(A)), but also the option identifier (the number or letter preceding the label), so that we can precede an option label by anything. In addition, we must modify the subroutine's error test so that it accepts an A$ value of 0. (This is the value of A$ if a non-number key is pressed.) These changes are fairly easy to make.

Lines 4200–4500 of Fig. 6-15 contain a modified version of the Menu-Generation subroutine that provides the additional features needed. Changes were made to the following lines:

- 4270—Length computation based on

```
0 REM Menu-Generation Subroutine (full screen)
1 REM SAVE"FIG6-15.BAS",A
980 WIDE%=80
990 GOTO 10000
1500 REM--Center & Print Title--
1510 T=(WIDE%+1-LEN(T$))/2
1520 LOCATE ,T:REM position cursor horizontally
1530 COLOR 0,7:REM inverse
1540 PRINT T$
1550 COLOR 7,0:REM normal video
1560 RETURN
4200 REM--Full-Screen Menu Generator--
4210 CLS
4220 T$=" "+T$+" MENU "
4230 GOSUB 1500:REM print title
4240 REM-Compute Menu Starting Column-
4250 L=0
4260 FOR A=1 TO N
4270 L=L+LEN(OPT$(A))
4280 NEXT
4290 L=L/N
4300 H=(WIDE%+1-L)/2:REM compute tab
4310 REM-Compute Vertical Offset-
4320 V=(26-N)/2
4330 REM-Display Options-
4340 LOCATE V:REM position first option
4350 FOR A=1 TO N
4360 PRINT TAB(H)OPT$(A)
4370 NEXT
4380 REM-Print Prompt-
4390 LOCATE 23,37
4400 COLOR 0,7:REM inverse
4410 PRINT"Choice?";
4420 COLOR 23,0:PRINT SPC(1) "_";:REM flash cursor
4430 COLOR 7,0:REM normal video
4440 A$=INKEY$:IF A$="" GOTO 4440
4450 A=VAL(A$)
4455 IF A=0 GOTO 4500
4460 IF A<1 OR A>N0 THEN BEEP:GOTO 4380
4470 LOCATE ,POS(0)-1:PRINT A$:REM display entry
4480 B$=INKEY$:IF B$="" GOTO 4480
4490 IF ASC(B$)<>13 GOTO 4380:REM verification by Enter key?
4500 RETURN
10000 REM--Generate Menu--
10010 N=4
10020 N0=3
10030 T$="MASTER"
10040 OPT$(1)="1 - Enter data"
10050 OPT$(2)="2 - Create new file"
10060 OPT$(3)="3 - Print reports"
10070 OPT$(4)="ESC - Quit program"
10080 GOSUB 4200
10090 IF A=1 GOTO 12000:REM key=1
10100 IF A=2 GOTO 14000:REM key=2
10110 IF A=3 GOTO 16000:REM key=3
10120 IF ASC(A$)=27 GOTO 10140:REM ESC key pressed
10130 GOTO 10010
10140 CLS:END:REM end of program
```

Fig. 6-15. IBM PC subroutine (lines 4200-4500) for generating full-screen menu with any option indicators (alternative to Fig. 6-12).

OPT$(A) only, since it will be completely defined as an argument (formerly 3 was added to account for the number, period, and space preceding the option label).

- 4360—TAB (H-1) changed to TAB (H) since no number-to-string conversion occurs.
- 4455—This line was added to permit a return from the subroutine if the value of A is 0. A is 0 if a 0 is typed in or if any non-number key is pressed. Since some such values of A correspond to invalid A$ entries, further error-testing must occur outside of the subroutine. Note that these entries are not verified by the Enter key.
- 4460—The limiting argument N has been changed to N0 to allow for a greater number of options than valid numbers. For example, in the menu shown above, there are four menu options, but only three valid option numbers (1-3).

Equivalent subroutines for the Apple and C-64 are shown in Fig. 6-16 and 6-17, respectively.

Lines 10000–10080 show the code for generating the actual menu. Line 10010 defines the number of menu options (N), and line 10020 defines

```
0    REM    FIG 6-16
1    REM      MENU-GENERATION SUBROUTINE (FULL SCREEN), FULLY-DEFINED OPTIONS
980  COLS = 40
990   GOTO 10000
1500   REM --CENTER & PRINT TITLE--
1510 T = (COLS + 1 -  LEN (T$)) / 2
1520   HTAB T
1530   INVERSE
1540   PRINT T$
1550   NORMAL
1560   RETURN
4200   REM --FULL-SCREEN MENU GENERATOR--
4210   HOME
4220 T$ = " " + T$ + " MENU "
4230   GOSUB 1500: REM   PRINT TITLE
4240   REM -COMPUTE MENU STARTING COLUMN-
4250 L = 0
4260   FOR A = 1 TO N
4270 L = L +  LEN (OPT$(A))
4280   NEXT
4290 L = L / N
4300 H = (COLS + 1 - L) / 2: REM   COMPUTE TAB
4310   REM -COMPUTE VERTICAL OFFSET-
4320 V = (24 - N) / 2
4330   REM -DISPLAY OPTIONS-
4340   VTAB V: REM   POSITION FIRST OPTION
4350   FOR A = 1 TO N
4360   PRINT  TAB( H)OPT$(A)
4370   NEXT
4380   REM -PRINT PROMPT-
4390   VTAB 22: HTAB COLS / 2 - 3
4400   INVERSE
4410   PRINT "CHOICE?";
4420   NORMAL
4430   GET A$
4440 A =  VAL (A$)
4445   IF A = 0 GOTO 4490
4450   IF A < 1 OR A > N0 THEN  CALL  - 198: GOTO 4390
4460   PRINT A$;
```

Fig. 6-16. Apple subroutine (lines 4200-4490) for generating full-screen menu with any option indicators (alternative to Fig. 6-13).

```
4470  GET B$
4480  IF  ASC (B$) < > 13 GOTO 4390
4490  RETURN
10000  REM  --GENERATE MENU--
10010 N = 4
10020 N0 = 3
10030 T$ = "MASTER"
10040 OPT$(1) = "  1 - Enter data"
10050 OPT$(2) = "  2 - Create new file"
10060 OPT$(3) = "  3 - Print reports"
10070 OPT$(4) = "ESC - Quit program"
10080  GOSUB 4200
10090  IF A = 1 GOTO 12000: REM  KEY=1
10100  IF A = 2 GOTO 14000: REM  KEY=2
10110  IF A = 3 GOTO 16000: REM  KEY=3
10120  IF  ASC (A$) = 27 GOTO 10150: REM  ESC KEY PRESSED
10130  CALL  - 198
10140  GOTO 10010
10150  HOME : END : REM  END OF PROGRAM
```

the number of options with number identifiers (N0). Line 10030 defines the menu title. Lines 10040 – 10070 define the four menu options, including identifiers. Line 10080 calls the subroutine.

IF-THEN logic is used to switch control. Lines 10090 – 10120 look for keys 1, 2, 3, and ESC, respectively. If no such key has been pressed, then line 10130 sends control back to line 10080, which regenerates the menu. If the computer lacks an ESC key, then another key (such as a function key) may be used in its place (see Fig. 6-17).

Menu Control Networks. *Network* is the

```
990 GOTO 10000
1500 REM--CENTER & PRINT T$--
1510 T=(39-LEN(T$))/2
1520 PRINT CHR$(18);
1530 PRINT TAB(T)T$
1540 RETURN
4200 REM--FULL-SCREEN MENU GENERATOR--
4210 PRINT CHR$(147);
4220 T$=T$+" MENU"
4230 GOSUB 1500:REM PRINT TITLE
4240 REM-COMPUTE MENU STARTING COLUMN-
4250 L=0
4260 FOR A=1 TO N
4270 L=L+LEN(OPT$(A))
4280 NEXT
4290 L=L/N
4300 H=(39-L)/2:REM COMPUTE TAB
4310 REM-COMPUTE VERTICAL OFFSET-
4320 V=INT(25-N)/2
4330 REM-DISPLAY OPTIONS-
4340 SYS C0,0,V:REM POSITION FIRST OPTION
4350 FOR A=1 TO N
4360 PRINT TAB(H)OPT$(A)
4370 NEXT
4380 REM-PRINT PROMPT-
4390 SYS C0,1,24,17:REM CLEAR PROMPT LINE
4400 SYS C0,0,24,17:REM POSITION PROMPT
```

Fig. 6-17. C-64 subroutine (lines 4200-4490) for generating full-screen menu with any option indicators   (alternative to Fig. 6-14). (Requires assembly-language subroutine loader; see Appendix B.)

138

```
4410 PRINT CHR$(18)"CHOICE?";
4420 POKE 204,0:REM FLASH CURSOR
4430 GET A$:IF A$="" GOTO 4430:REM GET MENU SELECTION
4435 POKE 204,1:REM TURN FLASH OFF
4440 A=VAL(A$)
4445 IF A=0 GOTO 4490:REM NON-NUMBER KEY PRESSED
4450 IF A<1 OR A>N0 GOTO 4390
4460 PRINT CHR$(146)" ";A$;:REM DISPLAY KEYSTROKE
4470 GET B$:IFB$="" GOTO 4470:REM GET ENTRY VERIFICATION
4480 IF ASC(B$)<>13 GOTO 4390:REM VERIFICATION RETURN KEY?
4490 RETURN
10000 REM--DEFINE MENU--
10010 N=4
10020 N0=2
10030 T$="MASTER"
10040 OPT$(1)="1  - ENTER DATA"
10050 OPT$(2)="2  - CREATE NEW FILE"
10060 OPT$(3)="F1 - CHANGE MODE"
10070 OPT$(4)="F2 - BACK UP"
10080 GOSUB 4200
10090 IF A=1 GOTO 12000:REM KEY=1
10100 IF A=2 GOTO 14000:REM KEY=2
10110 IF A$=CHR$(133) GOTO 16000:REM KEY=F1
10120 IF A$=CHR$(137) GOTO 20000:REM KEY=F2
10130 GOTO 10000:REM KEY=INVALID--RE-GENERATE MENU
```

technical term for the structure that results when you create a series of menus and then link them together. Figure 6-18 is an example of a simple three-level, hierarchical network. This particular type of network is referred to as a *tree* because it branches out, downward from the top. Each menu, or node, is linked to only one menu above it, and to those below. The further down the tree, the more menus separate you from the top.

The tree structure is widely used in computer

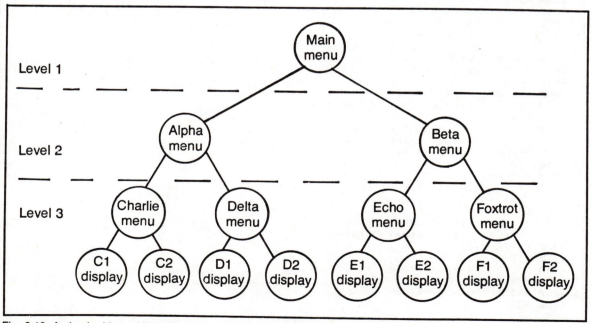

Fig. 6-18. A simple, hierarchical, three-level menu network in the form of a tree.

programs. It provides access to any part of the program, and its simplicity makes it easy to learn. It has one disadvantage, however. In a large network, with many levels, it may take the user a long time to go between programs, particularly if the programs are in different branches of the network. For example, in Fig. 6-18, to go from Delta menu to Foxtrot menu, the user must go through three other menus first: Alpha menu, Main menu, and Beta menu.

By using the Menu-Generation Subroutine (Fig. 6-15) it is fairly easy to write the code that generates a network of menus such as that shown in Fig. 6-18. There are seven menus in this network, but they and their links to other menus can be created in about as much time as it takes to write down their arguments, the subroutine calls, and the control logic—perhaps an hour or two for an average programmer.

To illustrate, Fig. 6-19 contains the code required to generate all of the menus as well as eight dummy displays. You may find it instructive to type this in and try it out for yourself. It shows how quickly you can put together a network of complete and professional-looking menus.

The Main Menu is generated on lines 10000 – 10110. Main Menu links to Alpha Menu (lines 12000 – 12110) and Beta Menu (19000 – 19110).

Alpha Menu links to Charlie Menu (lines

```
0 REM Menu Network Code
1 REM SAVE"FIG6-19.BAS",A
980 WIDE%=80
990 GOTO 10000
1500 REM--Center & Print Title--
1510 T=(WIDE%+1-LEN(T$))/2
1520 LOCATE ,T:REM position cursor horizontally
1530 COLOR 0,7:REM inverse
1540 PRINT T$
1550 COLOR 7,0:REM normal video
1560 RETURN
4010 REM--Temporary Pause Subroutine--
4020 LOCATE 23,WIDE%/2-13
4030 COLOR 16,7:REM inverse flash
4040 PRINT"[Press Space Bar to Continue]";
4050 COLOR 7,0:REM normal video
4060 A$=INKEY$:IF A$<>" " GOTO 4060
4070 PRINT
4080 RETURN
4200 REM--Full-Screen Menu Generator--
4210 CLS
4220 T$=" "+T$+" MENU "
4230 GOSUB 1500:REM print title
4240 REM-Compute Menu Starting Column-
4250 L=0
4260 FOR A=1 TO N
4270 L=L+LEN(OPT$(A))
4280 NEXT
4290 L=L/N
4300 H=(WIDE%+1-L)/2:REM compute tab
4310 REM-Compute Vertical Offset-
4320 V=(26-N)/2
4330 REM-Display Options-
4340 LOCATE V:REM position first option
4350 FOR A=1 TO N
4360 PRINT TAB(H)OPT$(A)
4370 NEXT
```

Fig. 6-19. IBM PC code required to generate menus and dummy displays of control network shown in Fig. 6-18.

```
4380 REM-Print Prompt-
4390 LOCATE 23,37
4400 COLOR 0,7:REM inverse
4410 PRINT"Choice?";
4420 COLOR 23,0:PRINT SPC(1) "_";:REM flash cursor
4430 COLOR 7,0:REM normal video
4440 A$=INKEY$:IF A$="" GOTO 4440
4450 A=VAL(A$)
4455 IF A=0 GOTO 4500
4460 IF A<1 OR A>N0 THEN BEEP:GOTO 4380
4470 LOCATE ,POS(0)-1:PRINT A$:REM display entry
4480 B$=INKEY$:IF B$="" GOTO 4480
4490 IF ASC(B$)<>13 GOTO 4380:REM verification by Enter key?
4500 RETURN
10000 REM--Main Menu--
10010 N=3
10020 N0=2
10030 T$="MAIN"
10040 OPT$(1)="1 - Alpha"
10050 OPT$(2)="2 - Beta"
10060 OPT$(3)="ESC - Quit Program"
10070 GOSUB 4200
10080 IF A=1 GOTO 12000
10090 IF A=2 GOTO 19000
10100 IF ASC(A$)=27 THEN CLS:END:REM end of program
10110 GOTO 10010
12000 REM--Alpha Menu--
12010 N=3
12020 N0=2
12030 T$="ALPHA"
12040 OPT$(1)="1 - Charlie"
12050 OPT$(2)="2 - Delta"
12060 OPT$(3)="ESC - Back up"
12070 GOSUB 4200
12080 IF A=1 GOTO 13000
12090 IF A=2 GOTO 16000
12100 IF ASC(A$)=27 GOTO 10000
12110 GOTO 12010
13000 REM--Charlie Menu--
13010 N=3
13020 N0=2
13030 T$="CHARLIE"
13040 OPT$(1)="1 - C1 display"
13050 OPT$(2)="2 - C2 display"
13060 OPT$(3)="ESC - Back up"
13070 GOSUB 4200
13080 IF A=1 THEN GOSUB 14000
13090 IF A=2 THEN GOSUB 15000
13100 IF ASC(A$)=27 GOTO 12000
13110 GOTO 13010
14000 REM--C1 Display--
14010 CLS
14020 T$="C1 DISPLAY"
14030 GOSUB 1500
14040 GOSUB 4010
14050 RETURN
15000 REM--C2 Display--
15010 CLS
15020 T$="C2 DISPLAY"
15030 GOSUB 1500
15040 GOSUB 4010
```

```
15050 RETURN
16000 REM--Delta Menu--
16010 N=3
16020 N0=2
16030 T$="DELTA"
16040 OPT$(1)="1 - D1 display"
16050 OPT$(2)="2 - D2 display"
16060 OPT$(3)="ESC - Back up"
16070 GOSUB 4200
16080 IF A=1 THEN GOSUB 17000
16090 IF A=2 THEN GOSUB 18000
16100 IF ASC(A$)=27 GOTO 12000
16110 GOTO 16010
17000 REM--D1 Display--
17010 CLS
17020 T$="D1 DISPLAY"
17030 GOSUB 1500
17040 GOSUB 4010
17050 RETURN
18000 REM--D2 Display--
18010 CLS
18020 T$="D2 DISPLAY"
18030 GOSUB 1500
18040 GOSUB 4010
18050 RETURN
19000 REM--Beta Menu--
19010 N=3
19020 N0=2
19030 T$="BETA"
19040 OPT$(1)="1 - Echo"
19050 OPT$(2)="2 - Foxtrot"
19060 OPT$(3)="ESC - Back up"
19070 GOSUB 4200
19080 IF A=1 GOTO 20000
19090 IF A=2 GOTO 23000
19100 IF ASC(A$)=27 GOTO 10000
19110 GOTO 19010
20000 REM--Echo Menu--
20010 N=3
20020 N0=2
20030 T$="ECHO"
20040 OPT$(1)="1 - E1 display"
20050 OPT$(2)="2 - E2 display"
20060 OPT$(3)="ESC - Back up"
20070 GOSUB 4200
20080 IF A=1 THEN GOSUB 21000
20090 IF A=2 THEN GOSUB 22000
20100 IF ASC(A$)=27 GOTO 19000
20110 GOTO 20010
21000 REM--E1 Display--
21010 CLS
21020 T$="E1 DISPLAY"
21030 GOSUB 1500
21040 GOSUB 4010
21050 RETURN
22000 REM--E2 Display--
22010 CLS
22020 T$="E2 DISPLAY"
22030 GOSUB 1500
22040 GOSUB 4010
22050 RETURN
23000 REM--Foxtrot Menu--
```

```
23010 N=3
23020 N0=2
23030 T$="FOXTROT"
23040 OPT$(1)="1 - F1 display"
23050 OPT$(2)="2 - F2 display"
23060 OPT$(3)="ESC - Back up"
23070 GOSUB 4200
23080 IF A=1 THEN GOSUB 24000
23090 IF A=2 THEN GOSUB 25000
23100 IF ASC(A$)=27 GOTO 19000
23110 GOTO 23010
24000 REM--F1 Display--
24010 CLS
24020 T$="F1 DISPLAY"
24030 GOSUB 1500
24040 GOSUB 4010
24050 RETURN
25000 REM--F2 Display--
25010 CLS
25020 T$="F2 DISPLAY"
25030 GOSUB 1500
25040 GOSUB 4010
25050 RETURN
```

13000 – 13110) and Delta Menu (lines 16000 – 16110). Similarly, Beta Menu links to Echo Menu (lines 20000 – 20110) and Foxtrot Menu (lines 23000 – 23110).

Each of the four third-level menus—Charlie, Delta, Echo, Foxtrot—is further linked to two dummy displays.

The control logic used with these menus is of the IF-THEN type, and permits the user to move downward by pressing a number key, or to BACK UP by pressing the ESC key.

Because of the time required to move between branches in a network such as Fig. 6-18, programmers often modify it by providing a quick return to the Main Menu. The resulting network then appears as shown in Fig. 6-20. A Main Menu option is added to all program menus except the Main Menu itself.

You can also, of course, add additional options to specific menus to allow users to move between different parts of the program. A word of caution, however. A menu network is much like the logic of your program. If your program is well designed, and the programs relate to one another in a logical fashion, then it should not be necessary to do very much patching between different parts of the program. Each link between a menu is analogous to

a GOTO statement in a program. When you keep these GOTOs working according to a simple pattern, your program organization is easy to follow. As the links between menus become more arbitrary and disordered, your control network is analogous to program code that is written according to the non-rules of spaghetti logic. Just as you must "beware the GOTO" in writing program code, you must also beware of linking menus in a disordered fashion.

The tree is not the only way to construct a menu network. You can, for example, construct one in the form of a ring (Fig. 6-21A), matrix (Fig. 6-21B) or in other ways. In a ring, there is usually only one menu, and every option is displayed on it. Such a menu can get very long. However, if all of the options are independent—that is, unrelated to each other in some hierarchical way—then a ring network may make sense.

A *matrix*, or net, allows essentially arbitrary connections among menus. This may make sense in some programs, but would be extremely difficult to learn and use.

Actually, there is no ideal control structure that will work with all programs. This is because the control structure should be derived from the interrelationships among the various functions in the

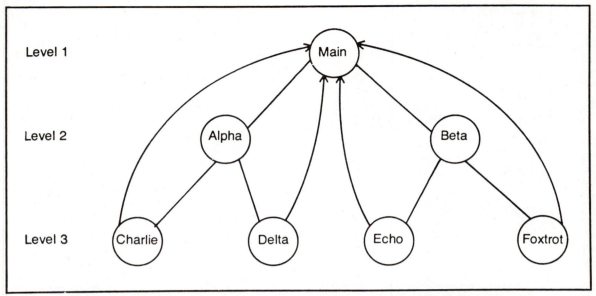

Fig. 6-20. A three-level hierarchical menu network in which all of the menus—even those at the bottom—have a direct route back to the main menu.

program. Often these relationships are hierarchical. If so, it is natural to use a tree as the form of the control structure. The control structure should be derived from the program, not imposed upon it. To derive the structure, start with the subprograms, displays, functions, and other things your program does. Cluster (that is, group) related things together. Look for hierarchical relationships among things. Then plan the network.

Here are a few general guidelines for planning such networks:

- Use a hierarchical network, if possible.
- Try not to allow more than nine options per menu.
- If your network has three or more levels, provide an option on all menus that goes back to the top level (Main Menu or its equivalent).
- In general, it is better to design a network with fewer levels and more options per menu than one with a few options per menu and more levels. For example, if your program has a total of 64 functions, you are better off with two menu levels of eight options each

(Fig. 6-22) than with three levels of four each (Fig. 6-23) or six levels of two each (Fig. 6-24).

Partial-Screen Menus

A partial-screen menu usually takes up only a few lines. Such a menu has a minimum of one line, and may have several. Figures 6-25, 26, and 27 show three typical partial-screen menus. Partial-screen menus, as the name indicates, use only part of the screen—they share it with the information being displayed. The menu may be used to manipulate the display, to control data entry, or to perform other functions relating to the display. In this respect, it differs from a full-screen menu. A full-screen menu usually makes a clean break between display screens. While it is on the screen, other information is not.

Another way in which full-screen and partial-screen menus differ is in their local versus global use. Partial-screen menus are generally used locally, on a particular screen. They allow the user to exercise control of that screen. The full-screen menu is generally used globally, for moving around the program.

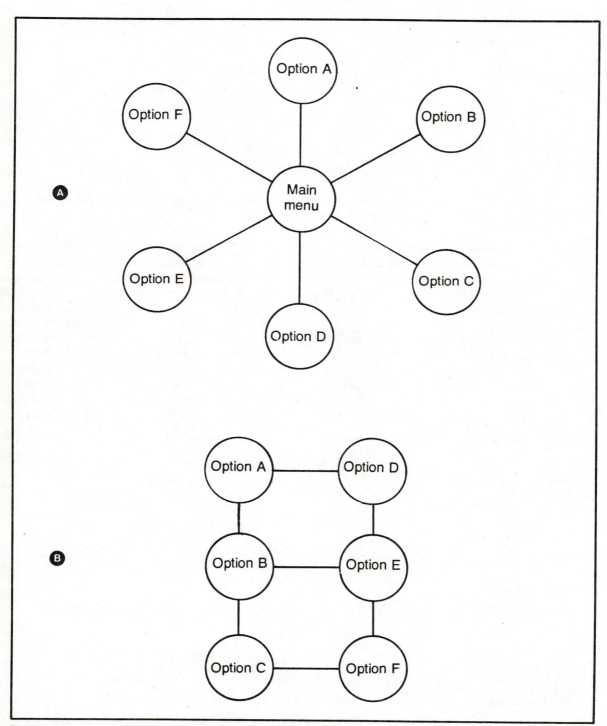

Fig. 6-21. Program control networks in the form of (A) ring, and (B) matrix.

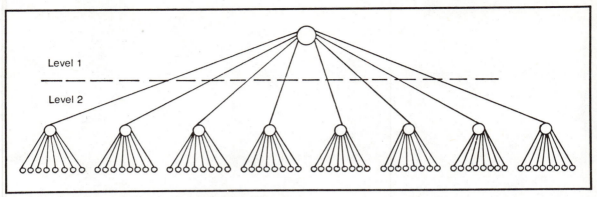

Fig. 6-22. A program control network of breadth 8 and depth 2.

Figure 6-25 shows a typical partial-screen menu. This menu is used for controlling what is on the display, obtaining help information, paging the display, or exiting the display. The characteristics of this menu are:

- It takes up two lines at the bottom of the screen.
- It is in inverse video.
- Menu options are selected with letters. The letters bear a mnemonic relationship to the options.

- Entries are single keystrokes, collected with the INKEY\$ (or GET) statement.
- The menu is untitled.
- There is no prompt.

A title and prompt could be included with the menu quite easily. Whether or not these are included depends mainly upon space availability. Since the menu is not the focus of interest on the screen—the information on the screen is, and the menu plays second fiddle—it is often necessary to reduce it to the bare minimum. This may mean leaving out title

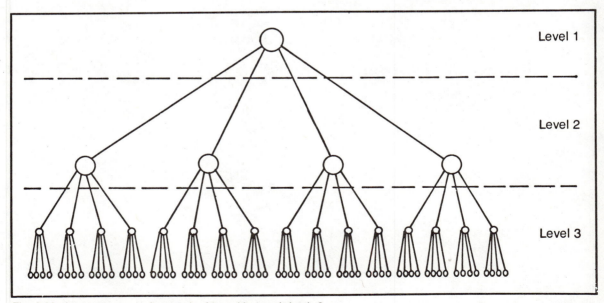

Fig. 6-23. A program control network of breadth 4 and depth 3.

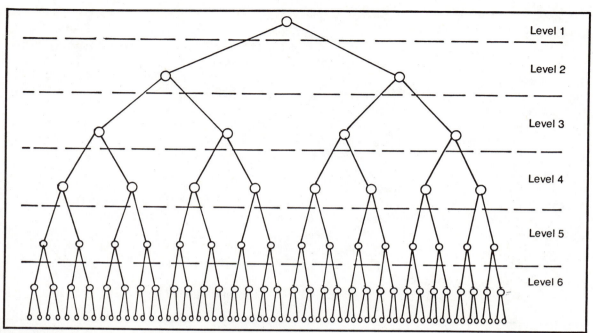

Fig. 6-24. A program control network of breadth 2 and depth 6.

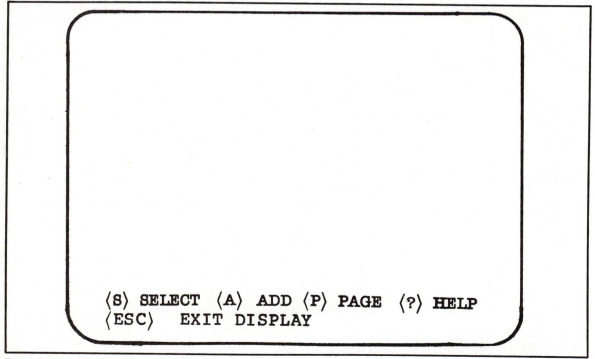

Fig. 6-25. Partial-screen menu consisting of two lines at the bottom of the display.

147

and prompt, and reducing option labels to single words.

These menus can appear anywhere on the screen and take almost any form. Figure 6-26 shows a menu that is compressed horizontally instead of vertically, and which appears centered at the right edge of the display. This menu is used to control the graphics appearing in the center of the display.

To round out the picture, Fig. 6-27 shows a menu that appears at the top of the screen. In general, the top of the screen is not the best place to locate a menu since this is where the title belongs. However, on some screens it makes sense.

In all of these menus, the option identifier is a single letter. Numbers could be used, but letters are preferable on menus such as these. The identifiers should bear a mnemonic relationship to the option label. Menu format—a block in inverse video with a flashing cursor at the right edge—is designed to make the menu clearly recognizable as such without title or prompt. The menu could, of course, be created without inverse video or flashing cursor, but without these cues it would not be as distinct.

The identifiers in these menus are linked to the labels in three different ways:

- Letter in brackets (Fig. 6-25) <A> ADD
- Equals sign (Fig. 6-26)   R = ROTATE
- Upper-lower case (Fig. 6-27) Quit

Any of these methods is effective, and mainly a matter of style. Once you have selected a method, however, stick with it consistently.

It is fairly easy to generate one of these menus either directly or with a subroutine. The subroutine technique will be shown, and you can adapt this to suit your particular needs. The subroutine allows you to generate a menu containing up to 24 lines,

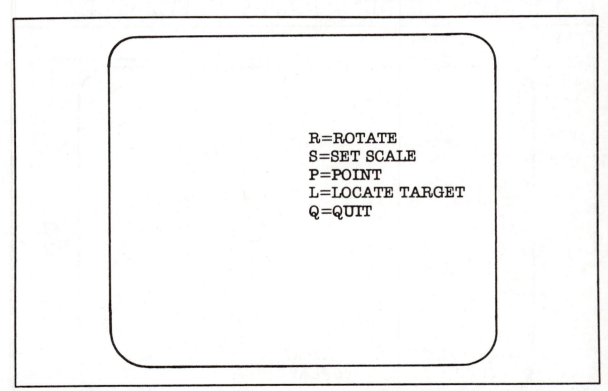

R=ROTATE
S=SET SCALE
P=POINT
L=LOCATE TARGET
Q=QUIT

Fig. 6-26. Partial-screen menu consisting of a block of options on the right edge of the display.

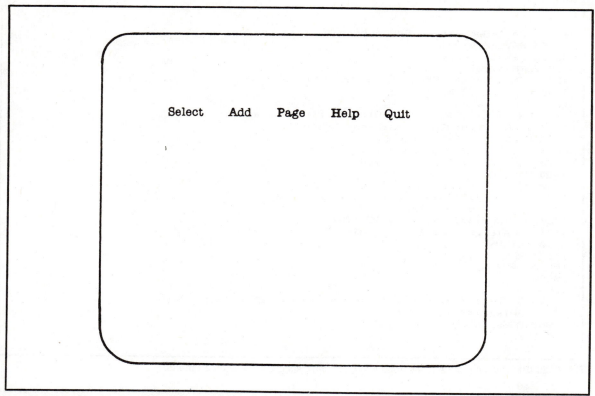

Select   Add   Page   Help   Quit

Fig. 6-27. Partial-screen menu consisting of one line at the top of the display.

in inverse video, anywhere on the screen. Figure 6-28 contains a subroutine in IBM PC BASIC for generating a partial-screen menu. Arguments of this subroutine are WIDE% (number of columns), V (starting row), H (starting column), N (number of lines), and OPT$(1) – OPT$(N) (text of menu). The subroutine consists of lines 4600 – 4740.

Since the subroutine must be able to create menus of different sizes, the number of menu lines, N, is a variable. The subroutine uses a FOR-NEXT loop to control how many rows are cleared and lines are printed. This work begins on line 4610 and ends on line 4690. Line 4630 clears the row, line 4640 positions the cursor at the beginning of the row, and line 4660 prints the Ath line of the menu in inverse video. Line 4680 then increments V by 1, so that the next row will be cleared and the line printed in the correct location when the FOR-NEXT loop

recycles. Line 4700 prints a flashing cursor, line 4720 uses INKEY$ to get the single character A$, and line 4730 displays the entry.

Note that this subroutine does not permit the user to verify the entry. Equivalent subroutines for the Apple and the C-64 are shown in Figs. 6-29 and 6-30, respectively.

To illustrate the subroutine's application, lines 10000 – 10060 contain the argument assignments and subroutine call necessary to generate the menu shown in Fig. 6-25. Lines 10010 – 10050 assign the arguments. This is a two-line menu and lines 10040 and 10050 define the menu's two lines. Line 10060 calls the subroutine to generate the menu. The only tricky part of this is to make sure that every line of the menu (except the last) is of the same length. The last line must have one character less to allow room for the flashing cursor.

```
0 REM Menu-Generating Subroutine (partial screen)
1 REM SAVE"FIG6-28",A
980 WIDE%=80
990 GOTO 10000
4600 REM--Partial Screen Menu Generator--
4610 FOR A=1 TO N
4620 LOCATE V,H
4630 PRINT SPACE$(WIDE%+1-H);:REM clear to end of line
4640 LOCATE V,H:REM reposition cursor
4650 COLOR 0,7:REM inverse
4660 PRINT OPT$(A);:REM print menu row A
4670 COLOR 7,0:REM normal video
4680 V=V+1
4690 NEXT
4700 COLOR 23,0:PRINT"_";:REM flash cursor
4710 COLOR 7,0:REM normal video
4720 A$=INKEY$:IF A$="" GOTO 4720
4730 LOCATE ,POS(0)-1:PRINT A$;:REM print entry
4740 RETURN
10000 REM--2-line menu--
10010 V=22
10020 H=5
10030 N=2
10040 OPT$(1)=" (A) Add      (M) Modify      (D) Delete  "
10050 OPT$(2)=" (Q) Quit                                "
10060 GOSUB 4600
10070 END
```

Fig. 6-28. IBM PC subroutine (lines 4600-4740) for generating a partial-screen menu.

```
0   REM   FIG 6-29
1   REM   MENU-GENERATING SUBROUTINE (PARTIAL SCREEN)
990   GOTO 10000
4600   REM --PARTIAL SCREEN MENU GENERATOR--
4610   FOR A = 1 TO N
4620   VTAB V: HTAB H
4630   CALL  - 868: REM  CLEAR TO END OF LINE
4640   VTAB V: HTAB H: REM  REPOSITION CURSOR
4650   INVERSE
4660   PRINT OPT$(A);: REM  PRINT MENU ROW A
4670   NORMAL
4680 V = V + 1
4690   NEXT
4700   GET A$
4710   PRINT A$
4720   RETURN
10000   REM --2-LINE MENU--
10010 V = 21
10020 H = 4
10030 N = 2
10040 OPT$(1) = " (A) ADD  (M) MODIFY  (D) DELETE "
10050 OPT$(2) = " (Q) QUIT                        "
10060   GOSUB 4600
10070   END
```

Fig. 6-29. Apple subroutine (lines 4600-4720) for generating a partial-screen menu.

```
4600 REM--PARTIAL-SCREEN MENU GENERATOR--
4610 FOR A=1 TO N
4620 SYS C0,1,V,H:REM CLEAR LINE
4630 SYS C0,0,V,H:REM POSITION CURSOR
4640 PRINT CHR$(18)OPT$(A);:REM PRINT MENU ROW A
4650 V=V+1
4660 NEXT
4670 POKE 204,0:REM FLASH CURSOR
4680 GET A$:IF A$="" GOTO 4680
4690 RETURN
10000 REM--2-LINE MENU--
10010 V=22
10020 H=5
10030 N=2
10040 OPT$(1)=" <A> ADD  <M> MODIF.  <D> DELETE      "
10050 OPT$(2)=" <Q> QUIT                             "
10060 GOSUB 4600
10070 END
```

Fig. 6-30. C-64 subroutine (lines 4600-4690) for generating a partial-screen menu. (Requires assembly-language subroutine loader; see Appendix B.)

SIMPLE CHOICES

After menus, the simple choice is a cinch. Here are some examples of control prompts that require the program user to make a simple choice:

- *Do you want to continue?* (y/n)
- *Do you want directions?* (y/n)
- *Are you sure?* (y/n)

In each of these examples, the user has come to some point in the program where a decision must be made. The easiest way to obtain the decision from the user is to display a short, two-choice question on the screen. The question may concern whether or not a hard-copy report should be generated, a file purged, or a particular program executed. A two-way question is much simpler to display than a two-way menu.

Of course, you could use a menu for getting the answer to such questions, but my feeling is that this is overkill. In general, it is best to reserve menus for situations that involve at least a three-way choice.

At the same time, you could use simple, two-way choices in place of menus, if you wanted to. Any program that can be written with menus can be rewritten so that it uses two-way choices instead. To illustrate, suppose that you start with the menu

shown in Fig. 6-7. You can restructure it as the following series of two-way questions:

- *Do you want to update your files?* (y/n)
- *Do you want to analyze your database?* (y/n)
- *Do you want to edit your database?* (y/n)
- *Do you want to reconcile your accounts?* (y/n)
- *Do you want to quit the program?* (y/n)

The way this works is as follows. When the program starts, the first question is posed. If the user types *y*, then that program is executed. Afterward, the first question is again posed.

If the user types *n* to the first question, the second question is posed. If the user types *n*, then the third question is posed.

And so on, until the last question is asked. If the user types *n* to that, then the series of questions begins over again at the first question. The questions continue to cycle in that manner, as long as the user responds *n* to each one.

If a program has more than a few options, this type of control is very cumbersome and slow. Can you imagine what it would be like if your program had a dozen different options and you were interested in doing number 11? And if you happened to press the wrong key when the right question popped up—then it would be kick-the-computer or

151

strangle-the-programmer time.

If your program has fewer than, say, half a dozen options, then simple choices may be a good way to control it. Answering a question is straightforward and in many ways easier than dealing with a menu. Even if your program does not use simple choices for overall control, it may use such choices for collecting answers to certain questions such as those posed earlier. In these situations, the simple choice is ideal.

The code for creating one of these prompts is straightforward and it is left to you to write your own routines.

TYPED CHOICES

Have you ever worked with a minicomputer or mainframe that required you to make use of a command language? You may have, for example, used UNIX or another sophisticated operating system that provided no menus or other on-screen prompting, but that required you to type in special system commands that you had already memorized. Command languages are very powerful. They let users tailor the tasks they want to perform very specifically. All users must know is what statements to type in and all the power of the computer is at their fingertips.

The drawback is that users must memorize everything beforehand. There are no helpful menus to jog the memory, no safety nets to correct errors or prompt users along in the right direction. Users are very much on their own. There is a penalty to pay for such power. Still, computer experts much prefer command languages to those with extensive on-screen prompting.

I'm not suggesting that you attempt to use BASIC code to simulate a command language. However, it is fairly easy to give program users the ability to select programs directly simply by typing in an abbreviation or name.

To illustrate, let us go back, for a moment, to the three-level, hierarchical menu network illustrated in Fig. 6-18. Recall that the user starts off at the Main Menu, selects an option from it to go to a level 2 menu, and then selects an option from that to go to a level 3 menu. Once at a level 3 menu, the user can select one of the eight displays: C1, C2, D1, D2, E1, E2, F1, or F2. (Note that these displays could be replaced by subprograms or other program functions.)

Now suppose that we simply eliminate the menus. Instead of using them, we will present a prompt that looks like this:

PROGRAM NAME:

To select a display, the user types its name—C1, C2, D1, etc. Let us write code to collect the keystrokes and assign them to a variable, and then use IF-THEN logic to switch control to the part of the program requested.

Figure 6-31 is a modified version of the (IBM PC) program shown earlier in Fig. 6-15. The program in Fig. 6-15 uses menus to switch control, but the one in Fig. 6-31 uses typed choices.

The LINE INPUT data-entry subroutine beginning at line 3010 was used in Fig. 6-31 to provide a convenient way to generate the required prompt. The Menu-Generation subroutine (starting at line 4200) has been eliminated, along with the menu generation code starting after line 10000. What remains of the old program are the dummy display-generating subroutines beginning at lines 14000, 15000, 17000, 18000, 21000, 22000, 24000, and 25000.

The new, controlling part of the program consists of lines 11000–11150. Lines 11020–11040 assign the arguments for generating the prompt that says "PROGRAM NAME" and printing it at row 12 and column 30 of the display. (Change column 30 to column 10 if you're using a 40-column display.) Line 11050 calls the LINE INPUT Data-Entry subroutine, which generates the prompt. After the subroutine call, lines 11060–11140 perform IF-THEN tests on the entry and switch control to the part of the program that contains the requested display. (The user types *QUIT* or *quit* to quit the program—see line 11140.) If all tests are failed, control falls through to line 11150, which sends it back to line 11000, which leads to regeneration of the prompt and another data entry.

If the user types a valid entry—say, C1—then one of the IF-THEN tests shifts control to the ap-

```
0 REM Non-Menu Network Code
1 REM SAVE"FIG6-31.BAS",A
980 WIDE%=80
990 GOTO 10000
1300 REM--Clear One Line--
1310 LOCATE V,H:REM position cursor
1320 PRINT SPACE$(WIDE%+1-H);:REM clear to end of line
1330 LOCATE V,H:REM reposition cursor
1340 RETURN
1500 REM--Center & Print Title--
1510 T=(WIDE%+1-LEN(T$))/2
1520 LOCATE ,T:REM position cursor horizontally
1530 COLOR 0,7:REM inverse
1540 PRINT T$
1550 COLOR 7,0:REM normal video
1560 RETURN
3010 REM--LINE INPUT Data Entry--
3020 GOSUB 1300:REM clear line & position prompt
3030 COLOR 0,7:REM inverse
3040 PRINT P$+":";:REM print prompt
3050 COLOR 7,0:REM normal video
3060 LINE INPUT A$
3070 RETURN
4010 REM--Temporary Pause Subroutine--
4020 LOCATE 23,WIDE%/2-13
4030 COLOR 16,7:REM inverse flash
4040 PRINT"[Press Space Bar to Continue]";
4050 COLOR 7,0:REM normal video
4060 A$=INKEY$:IF A$<>" " GOTO 4060
4070 PRINT
4080 RETURN
10000 REM--Data Entry--
11000 REM--Typed-in Display Selector--
11010 CLS
11020 V=12
11030 H=30
11040 P$="PROGRAM NAME"
11050 GOSUB 3010
11060 IF A$="C1" THEN GOSUB 14000
11070 IF A$="C2" THEN GOSUB 15000
11080 IF A$="D1" THEN GOSUB 17000
11090 IF A$="D2" THEN GOSUB 18000
11100 IF A$="E1" THEN GOSUB 21000
11110 IF A$="E2" THEN GOSUB 22000
11120 IF A$="F1" THEN GOSUB 24000
11130 IF A$="F2" THEN GOSUB 25000
11140 IF A$="quit" OR A$="QUIT" THEN CLS:END:REM END
11150 GOTO 11000
14000 REM--C1 Display--
14010 CLS
14020 T$="C1 DISPLAY"
14030 GOSUB 1500
14040 GOSUB 4010
14050 RETURN
15000 REM--C2 Display--
15010 CLS
15020 T$="C2 DISPLAY"
15030 GOSUB 1500
15040 GOSUB 4010
```

Fig. 6-31. IBM PC code for permitting user to select options directly, without using menus.

```
15050 RETURN
17000 REM--D1 Display--
17010 CLS
17020 T$="D1 DISPLAY"
17030 GOSUB 1500
17040 GOSUB 4010
17050 RETURN
18000 REM--D2 Display--
18010 CLS
18020 T$="D2 DISPLAY"
18030 GOSUB 1500
18040 GOSUB 4010
18050 RETURN
21000 REM--E1 Display--
21010 CLS
21020 T$="E1 DISPLAY"
21030 GOSUB 1500
21040 GOSUB 4010
21050 RETURN
22000 REM--E2 Display--
22010 CLS
22020 T$="E2 DISPLAY"
22030 GOSUB 1500
22040 GOSUB 4010
22050 RETURN
24000 REM--F1 Display--
24010 CLS
24020 T$="F1 DISPLAY"
24030 GOSUB 1500
24040 GOSUB 4010
24050 RETURN
25000 REM--F2 Display--
25010 CLS
25020 T$="F2 DISPLAY"
25030 GOSUB 1500
25040 GOSUB 4010
25050 RETURN
```

propriate part of the program by calling one of dummy display-generating subroutines. After the subroutine is executed, control returns to the line following the successful IF-THEN test, and eventually leads to a regeneration of the prompt.

Why would you want to control a program in this manner? The main reason is to increase speed. Clearly, it is more difficult to remember names and type them in than it is to look up the name of a program on a menu and type in a single number. However, if your program gets big enough, and has enough options, working your way through the menus takes a lot of time. If may be much quicker to type in the name and be done with it.

Obviously, this does not work well in every program, or for every program user. It is best for fre-

quent users who learn the program very thoroughly and can get by without menus.

COMBINING MENUS AND TYPED CHOICES

Would it ever make sense to combine menus and typed choices? Suppose, for example, that your program's Main Menu looks like the one shown in Fig. 6-32. This menu looks ordinary enough, but its last option is *Q-Query*. When a user types *Q*, the menu disappears and this prompt appears:

PROGRAM NAME:

Now the user can type the program name and call it in the manner described in the previous section.

On the other hand, if the user wants to go back

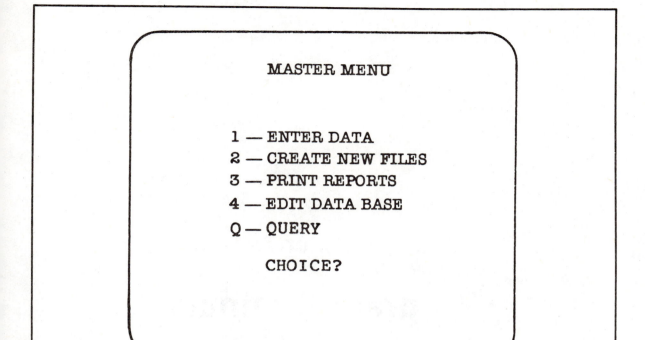

Fig. 6-32. Program control menu with Q—QUERY option.

to using menus, typing *MENU* puts the Main Menu on the display.

You get the idea. There are two ways to control the program, and the user can select either one. Why write a program that allows the user to do this? The advantage is that it lets the program be used at either a novice or expert level. The novice user can use menus. After using the program for a while, the novice becomes an expert. The menus can then be dispensed with. In short, the program grows with the user. This is a good quality for a program to have.

Still, not every program requires it. It begins to make sense when your program is complex and users spend a lot of time working with it. If both of these conditions are satisified, then users will probably benefit from being able to use menus or not, at their option.

Writing the code to permit dual control of a program is a simple extension of the techniques illustrated in this chapter. This is left to your creativity, imagination, and expert judgment.

Chapter 7

Program Chaining

Program chaining is a technique to link separate programs together. As programs grow in complexity, they also grow in size. Since your computer has a fixed amount of memory, there is a limit to how big a program can get before it uses up all available memory. In addition, the more variables you use, and the more files you load into memory, the less memory is left over for your program. You may reach a point where your program fits, but there is not enough room for the data you want to process, or vice-versa.

When you calculate everything beforehand and discover that both program and data will not fit into memory, you may decide to make the program smaller or to reduce the amount of data that it must process. In other words, you reduce the ambitiousness of your programming projects. If you do not anticipate this, and the last byte of memory gets gobbled up while your program is running, then your ambitiousness is reduced for you, as the screen stares silently at you. If you are lucky, an out-of-memory message appears on your screen. If not, your computer slips into a state of catatonia

and no longer responds to your ministerings.

Well, there is a solution to such problems. Instead of writing one long program, break it up into smaller programs that are loaded into memory separately. This leaves extra memory to play with. This technique is widely used in business programs and is referred to as *chaining*. When you break up one big program into two or more smaller ones, you are modularizing it on a global level. There are good and bad ways to do this modularization, and the good ones involve a bit more than slicing a listing in half with a pair of scissors. For this reason, the chapter begins with a discussion of some typical ways to modularize a program. This section applies to all computers, regardless of the particular statements required to chain.

The ease of chaining depends upon the specific computer and DOS being used. IBM PC DOS 2.1, for example, has powerful statements that make chaining easy. With Apple's DOS 3.3 and ProDOS, chaining is less straightforward, but still quite simple. Computers such as the C-64 lack the requisite chaining statements, and make chaining quite difficult; one gets the impression no one expected programmers to chain between C-64 programs. The final three sections of this chapter describe the essentials of chaining with these three computers. If you have one of them, read the discussion relating to it. If you have some other computer, then focus on the section for the IBM PC, since it is the most representative of the three.

PROGRAM MODULARIZATION

Modularization was first discussed in Chapter 3. That chapter stressed the importance of developing a program in a modular fashion, one part at a time, perfecting each part as you went. Later on, you link the various modules together to integrate them.

Some program developers prefer to break up their program into modules which are actually separate programs. One advantage of this is that, once you develop a module, it is easier to test and evaluate when it is separate from the rest of your program. You can make a copy of it on disk and give it to someone else to test more easily. In many ways, a program designed this way is easier to troubleshoot and maintain. When a problem occurs, it can usually be localized to the particular module that failed.

A drawback of this approach, however, is that it almost always takes up more disk space than developing a program as one continuous piece of code. Earlier in this book it was remarked that many programs make use of common subroutines, and that these subroutines might comprise as much as 50% or more of any given program. If you break your program up into separate modules, then many of these subroutines must be duplicated in each module, thereby taking up more disk space than if the program is in one piece.

Another advantage of developing a program as one piece is speed. If your program is broken up into separate modules, and you must chain between them, then it is always slower. Each time your program chains from module A to module B, it must load in the new module. Doing this takes time. If, instead of chaining, you simply send control to a different part of one long program, only a fraction

of a second is required. This is obviously much faster. While there may be certain advantages for the developer in creating a program consisting of separate modules, the loss of speed is an important disadvantage for the user. It is hardly an even trade. All things considered, speed for the user is far more important than convenience for the program developer. Unfortunately, you do not always have a choice. If you want to include certain features in your program, and you are memory-limited, you must modularize it and link the modules by chaining.

What is the best way to modularize a program? The answer depends upon the program, and you must do a little analysis to find the answer.

Start by noting the importance of speed. You must modularize the program in the way that allows the greatest speed. However, there is a trade-off:

- The bigger you make a module, the more time it takes to load that module during chaining.
- The bigger you make a module, the more you can put into it, and the faster the execution of any given subprogram within that module.

Alternatively, the shorter you make a module, the faster it loads but the less can go into it.

There are no hard-and-fast rules for how to divide a program into modules, but there are two very useful criteria to consider: the frequency of use of each subprogram, and dependencies between subprograms.

The more frequently a particular subprogram is used, the more important it is to provide quick access to it. It follows that it makes sense to combine the most frequently-used subprograms into a common module, if possible, so that the user does not have to chain to them separately.

If there are dependencies between subprograms—for example, between Data Entry and Data Base Edit—then combine them in a common module so that the user can move quickly between them without chaining.

To illustrate how you might apply these criteria

to actual problems, assume that your computer has 60K of usable memory and that you are at the initial design stage on two different programs. Each of these programs needs five subprograms. You have done an analysis and determined the amount of memory required by each subprogram, the probable frequency of use, and the dependencies between subprograms. The results of the analysis are shown in Table 7-1 (Program 1) and Table 7-2 (Program 2).

Start with Program 1. One way to modularize this program is shown in Fig. 7-1. Subprograms 1, 2, and 5 are included in a common module because of the high frequency of use of Subprograms 1 and 2 and the dependency between Subprograms 2 and 5. Subprograms 3 and 4 are each included in separate modules because of the large amount of memory each requires. The main part of the program, then, consists of three large modules, a sort of triad. Each of these modules is linked to the other two, and can chain to either one. This implies that the main menu (or other controlling mechanism) is duplicated in all three modules.

There is also a fourth module, Initialization, which is linked solely to the module containing subprograms 1, 2, and 5. This module is optional, but

Table 7-1. Results of Analysis of Program 1.

Subprogram	Memory (Kilobytes)	Frequency	Dependency
1	15	High	—
2	13	High	5
3	42	Low	—
4	44	Medium	—
5	19	Low	2

is often either convenient or necessary in a program that is modularized. The program begins at this module, which dimensions arrays, and does the other initialization preceding the working part of the program. By having it in a separate module, it can do its job and then get out of the way, without be carried as baggage in the working part of the program. Having it separate also helps avoid such inconveniences as redimensioned array errors.

Now consider Program 2. Table 7-2 shows that Program 2's memory, frequency, and dependency profile differs significantly from that of Program 1. The biggest difference is subprogram memory requirements. The subprograms are so large that none can be combined. Each subprogram must itself become a separate module. The resulting

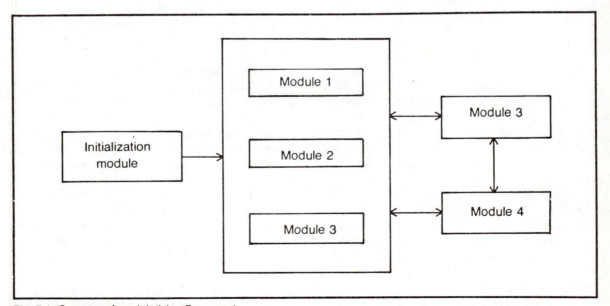

Fig. 7-1. One way of modularizing Program 1.

Table 7-2. Results of Analysis of Program 2.

Subprogram	Memory (Kilobytes)	Frequency	Dependency
1	42	High	—
2	41	Low	—
3	45	Low	—
4	44	Medium	—
5	49	Low	2

design is shown in Fig. 7-2. The central core of this design is a Menu module. When the program starts, the Initialization module loads the Menu module. From there, the user can access any other module. When the user finishes with one of these modules, he or she returns again to the Menu module. The next subprogram is then executed, the next, and so on.

These two examples are fairly typical of the way that subprograms are organized when chaining is used. Program 2 is, of course, the worst case—every subprogram gets its own module. Program 1 combines several subprograms into a few modules. Both of these designs use an Initialization module. This is optional, but generally good to include. Another important difference between Program 1 and Program 2 is where the Main Menu is located. In Program 1, it is duplicated in every module, and every module is linked to every other module. In Program 2, the Main Menu is in a separate module of its own, and only that module is shared among all modules.

If all or several of your subprograms use common subroutines, and if your DOS permits it, you may use the *overlay* technique. This consists of keeping one part of a program constantly in memory and then moving other parts in and out of memory as needed. For example, you might keep a core set of subroutines constantly in memory, while moving the controlling or "intelligent" parts of various subprograms in and out of memory when necessary. The technique is illustrated in Fig. 7-3.

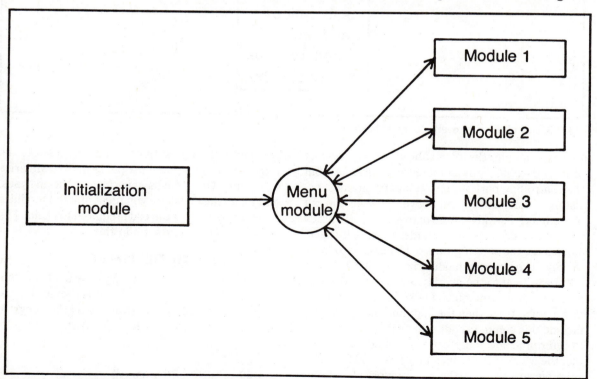

Fig. 7-2. One way of modularizing Program 2.

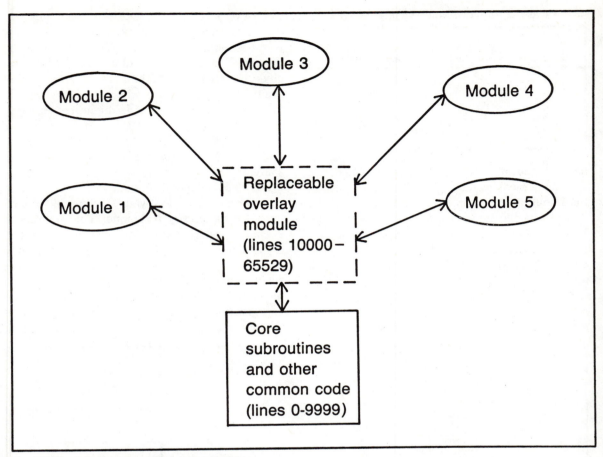

Fig. 7-3. Use of program overlay during chaining.

In this example, the core subroutines, consisting of lines 0 – 9999, stay in memory at all times, but the controlling portions of four subprograms, consisting of lines 10000 and above, move in and out of memory. The advantage of overlays is that they reduce the size of subprograms, save disk space, and enable the subprograms to be chained to more rapidly. The program modularization shown in Fig. 7-2 lends itself to the overlay technique if the subprograms use common code—such as subroutines and menus. If so, then the common module would include this common code. An analysis is required to determine how much code is common. It is clear that the Main Menu (which may be called from any subprogram) should be kept in memory at all times to speed access to it.

These examples, though simple, illustrate the types of analyses you must perform to modularize a program. Once you have performed the analyses, and made the decision, you must link the modules together by writing the code required to chain. The next section tells how to do this.

CHAINING WITH THE IBM PC

The IBM PC makes it very easy to chain from one program to another. All that is required is the CHAIN statement. To illustrate, enter this program and save it to disk as PROGA.BAS:

```
10   REM—Program A—
20   CLS
30   PRINT "Program A"
40   CHAIN "PROGB"
```

Now enter this program and save it to disk as PROGB.BAS:

```
10   REM—Program B—
20   CLS
30   PRINT "Program B"
```

Now run PROGA.BAS and see what happens. What should happen is that PROGA chains to PROGB, and *Program B* appears on your display.

Very simple, and this is the essence of chaining. There are a few complications, however. First, if you simply chain from Program A to Program B, the values of all numeric and string variables will be lost. To illustrate this concretely, let us build a little demonstration program. Figure 7-4 is a somewhat more ambitious version of PROGA.BAS, although this, too, is simple. Lines 210 – 250 assign values to five variables: C1%, C2, C3#, C$, and WIDE%. Lines 4010 – 4080 contain a familiar subroutine to insert a pause in the program until

the space bar is pressed. Lines 10000 – 10020 clear the screen and display the title "Program A." Lines 10040 – 10080 display the assigned values of the five variables. Line 10090 calls the temporary pause subroutine. And line 10110 chains to PROGB. Take a few minutes to enter this program, and save it to disk as PROGA.BAS. Several variations of this program will be created to illustrate different aspects of chaining.

After saving PROGA, create PROGB from PROGA by deleting lines 0 – 4080 and 10090 – 10110 and adding new lines 0, 1 and 10020 (see Fig. 7-5).

With both programs saved to disk, run PROGA and see what happens. What should happen is this: When you run PROGA, it clears the screen, displays the correct variable assignments, and waits for you to press the space bar. When you do, PROGA chains to PROGB. When PROGB executes, the values of variables it displays differ from their assignments in PROGA—all numeric variables have the value 0, and C$ is the null string.

```
0 REM Fig 7-4
1 REM SAVE"PROGA.BAS",A
210 C1%=10
220 C2=.5
230 C3#=.333333432674408#
240 C$="sea string"
250 WIDE%=80
990 GOTO 10000
4010 REM--Temporary Pause Subroutine--
4020 LOCATE 23,WIDE%/2-13
4030 COLOR 16,7:REM inverse flash
4040 PRINT"[Press Space Bar to Continue]";
4050 COLOR 7,0:REM normal video
4060 A$=INKEY$:IF A$<>" " GOTO 4060
4070 PRINT
4080 RETURN
10000 REM--Display Program I.D. & Data--
10010 CLS
10020 PRINT"Program A"
10030 LOCATE 10
10040 PRINT "C1%=";C1%
10050 PRINT "C2=";C2
10060 PRINT "C3#=";C3#
10070 PRINT"C$=";C$
10080 PRINT"WIDE%=";WIDE%
10090 GOSUB 4010
10100 REM--Chain to Program B--
10110 CHAIN"PROGB"
```

Fig. 7-4. IBM PC Program A.

```
0 REM Fig 7-5
1 REM SAVE"PROGB.BAS",A
10000 REM--Display Program I.D. & Data--
10010 CLS
10020 PRINT"Program B"
10030 LOCATE 10
10040 PRINT "C1%=";C1%
10050 PRINT "C2=";C2
10060 PRINT "C3#=";C3#
10070 PRINT"C$=";C$
10080 PRINT"WIDE%=";WIDE%
```

Fig. 7-5. IBM PC Program B.

Transferring Variables during Chaining

In some programs, losing the values assigned to variables may not pose problems, although in most programs it is convenient to carry some (if not all) of the values along. You can do this in two different ways, both quite easy. The first is to use COMMON statements; the second to use the ALL parameter in the CHAIN statement. Let us start with the COMMON statement.

The COMMON statement enables you to define which variables to carry from the first program to the second during chaining. The syntax of the COMMON statement is as follows:

COMMON *variable 1, variable 2, . .*

For example, to transfer the numeric variables C1% and C2 from PROGA and PROGB, insert this COMMON statement:

COMMON C1%,C2

This statement may appear anywhere in the program, so long as it is executed prior to the CHAIN statement. To illustrate how this works, load PROGA and insert this line:

10105 COMMON C1%,C2

Save the modified PROGA as PROGA'. Run it and see what happens when PROGB executes. The values of C1% and C2 should be safely carried to PROGB, but the values of the other variables should be lost.

So much for COMMON. Now let us demonstrate the ALL parameter. The ALL parameter will cause all variables to be transferred from the first program to the second. The ALL parameter is added following the CHAIN statement. It is the third parameter following the file name, and so two commas must separate it from the file name. For example, to transfer all variables from Program A to Program B, change line 10110 of Program A to read as follows:

10110   CHAIN "PROGB",,ALL

Make this change to Program A and save the resulting program to disk as Program A". Now run Program A" and see what happens. All variables should make it safely through to Program B.

Obviously, it is much easier to use the ALL parameter than to insert COMMON statements in your program. However, there may be cases when you do not want to transfer all variables from the first program to the second. In fact, the only variables that you need to transfer are the global variables that are used throughout the program. There is not much point in transferring local variables, since they do not really carry any useful history with them. Use of COMMON statements permits you to reset certain numeric variables to zero and string variables to the null string. This feature may come in handy.

Using Program Overlays

During chaining, you can retain part or all of

Program A in memory after loading in Program B. To do so, you must add three parameters to the CHAIN statement. These parameters are MERGE, *number of line* to begin execution at in Program B, and DELETE *line range* in Program A. The syntax of the CHAIN statement with these additional parameters is as follows:

CHAIN MERGE *"filename", start line,* ALL, DELETE# *line range*

For example, to chain to Program C, start at line 10000, transfer all variables, and retain lines 0 – 9999 of Program A, you would use this statement:

10110 CHAIN MERGE "PROGC", 10000, ALL, DELETE 10000 – 10110

Insert this line into Program A and save the result as Program A'''.

Now load PROGB and convert it to PROGC by adding this line.

10090 GOSUB 4010

This new line calls for a subroutine that is not in Program C, but that will be transferred there from Program A'''. Run Program A''' and see what happens. Variables should transfer safely, and the subroutine call should work without causing an error condition. List PROGC and verify that the subroutine has been transferred to PROGC. This example illustrates the essence of the overlay technique. Though the example transferred only one simple subroutine, you can extend it to much larger and more complex programs that involve transferring hundreds of lines of code from the first program to the second.

This discussion touched on the highlights of the CHAIN statement, and is far from complete. Your BASIC manual provides additional information; refer to it for details.

Program Verification

The chaining technique described above works fine if the program being chained to is present on disk when your drive goes looking for it. If it is not there, then a disk error occurs and your system crashes.

You will not have this problem if all of your subprograms are on one disk that is never removed from your drive. In that case, there is never a danger of removing the disk that contains the subprogram that your drive is looking for.

It gets trickier, however, if your program requires *disk swapping*. Disk swapping is the popular name for putting one disk in your drive for a while, pulling it out, putting another in, putting the first back in, putting another in, and so on. Disk swapping is required when all of the files required by your program are not on the same disk. Your subprograms may take up too much space to fit on one disk, for example.

And even if your program should not require disk swapping, you never know what a user might do during the program. The user may, for whatever reason, have the wrong disk in the drive when it is time to chain.

Fortunately, it is fairly easy to keep your system from crashing. You can do this by including an ON ERROR GOTO statement and error-handling routine in the program. When your computer executes a CHAIN statement, it looks for the to-be-chained-to program on the disk. If the program is there, chaining occurs. However, if the program is not there, DOS sets an error condition and retains the first program in memory. In other words, your program is never lost in the twilight zone between Program A and Program B.

Since having the wrong disk in the drive is a human error, and one of the more common types that is likely to occur, you may want to give it special handling by having your program look for the error code and provide a specific error message and recovery action when such an error occurs. The error in this case is number 53, "File not found in line number X". Refer to the discussion of error-handling routines in Chapter 3 for details.

CHAINING WITH THE APPLE

It is relatively easy to link two programs together with the Apple. The method differs depending upon whether or not you want to retain variables in memory, and which DOS is being used. The various chaining alternatives are discussed in separate sections below.

Simple Chaining

The simplest chaining situation is a transition from one program to another without retaining the variables used in the first program for use in the second. This type of chaining is useful when a clear break is being made between the first program and the second. The second program starts as if from scratch, just as if you type in a direct RUN command through the keyboard. To link programs this way, have the final line of Program 1 print a Ctrl + D (that is, CHR$(4)), followed by a semicolon, followed by the RUN command and the name of the program to be chained to within quotation marks, like this:

```
24500 PRINT CHR$(4);"RUNPROG2"
```

To illustrate the technique, let us create two programs and use simple chaining to link them together. Enter the program shown below and save it to disk as PROG1.

```
1    REM PROGRAM 1
10   HOME
20   PRINT "PROGRAM 1"
30   A = 5.631
40   A$ = "A STRING"
50   PRINT CHR$(4);"RUNPROG2"
```

PROG1 will clear the screen, display the message *PROGRAM 1*, assign the real variable A and the string variable A$, and then load and run a program called PROG2.

Now type in Program 2, shown below, and save it to disk as PROG2.

```
1    REM PROGRAM 2
10   HOME
20   PRINT "PROGRAM 2"
30   PRINT "A = ";A
40   PRINT "A$ = ";A$
50   END
```

Now run PROG1 and see what happens.

What should happen is that Program 1 will display the message *PROGRAM 1* briefly, and then load Program 2, which will display the message *PROGRAM 2*, and show the assignments of A and of A$; as far as Program 2 is concerned, A is equal to zero and A$ is equal to the null string.

When simple chaining is used, nothing is retained from the first program when the second program begins executing. All arrays must be redimensioned, functions redefined, error-handling routines created anew.

Very simple. This works nicely if you do not care about transferring variables. More often than not, however, you will want to make the transfer. Transferring variables during chaining is done differently, depending upon whether you are using an early version of DOS (3.2 or 3.3) or ProDOS, as described below.

Transferring Variables during Chaining

DOS 3.2 or 3.3. In order to transfer variables during chaining, your program must make use of the machine-language CHAIN program, which is located on the Apple system master disk. The first step in building a program that will chain this way is to transfer the CHAIN file to the disk containing the program that will do the chaining. Make the transfer with a file-copying program such as FID or FILEM. Once the CHAIN file is available, you can access it and perform the chain by having the final line of Program 1 PRINT a Ctrl + D, followed by a semicolon, followed by the statement BLOAD CHAIN, A520 within quotation marks, like this:

```
24500   PRINT CHR$(4);"BLOAD CHAIN,A520"
```

The above line activates the CHAIN program as a prelude to chaining. The following line of the program CALL the CHAIN program and contains the name of the program to be chained to, such as PROG2. For example:

```
24510   CALL 520"PROG2"
```

It is important that the quotation remark preceding

the name of the second program follow the number 520 without any separation. No space, semicolon, or comma must come between the two or the chain will not work properly.

To illustrate the technique, let us modify PROG1 by changing line 50 and adding line 60. Load PROG1, type in these two lines, and then save the new program to disk as PROG1'.

```
50   PRINT CHR$(4);"BLOAD CHAIN,A520"
60   CALL 520"PROG2"
```

Now run PROG1' and see what happens.

What should happen is that the variables are successfully transferred and displayed by PROG2. When chaining is done this way, variables are all that transfer from the first program to the second. It is not necessary to redimension arrays used earlier; in fact, doing so will result in a redimensioned array error. However, it is necessary to redefine functions, and to create error-handling routines again. Also, it's generally advisable to duplicate Reset key deactivation code, if such code is used in the program.

ProDOS. ProDOS offers a considerable improvement and simplification in chaining technique over earlier versions of DOS. ProDOS adds a CHAIN statement to the BASIC language which can be used directly, without loading a separate CHAIN program. The syntax of the CHAIN statement is as follows:

CHAIN *program name* [,@ *line number*] [,S *slot number*] [,D *drive number*]

The items between brackets are optional, and the only required information is *program name*. The @ parameter defines the line in the second program at which the program is to begin execution. The *slot number* and *drive number* define, respectively, the slot and drive of the disk on which the second program is to be found.

To illustrate the technique, type in Program 1", shown below (based on Program 1, described earlier).

```
1   REM PROGRAM 1"
```

```
10   HOME
20   PRINT "PROGRAM 1"
30   A = 5.631
40   A$ = "A STRING"
50   PRINT CHR$(4);"CHAIN PROG2"
```

Save this program to disk as PROG1". Now type in PROG2, which was shown earlier in the discussion of simple chaining.

When both programs are saved to disk, run PROG1" and see what happens. What should happen is that the variables are successfully transferred, and displayed, by PROG2.

You can test the *line number* parameter by modifying line 50 of PROG1" to start running PROG2 at line 30 instead of the first line of PROG2. Simply change line 50 of PROG1" as follows:

```
50   PRINT CHR$(4);"CHAIN PROG2, @30"
```

Now run PROG1" again and it will begin execution of PROG2 at line 30, displaying the values of A and A$.

When chaining is done this way, variables are all that transfer from the first program to the second. It is not necessary to redimension arrays used earlier; in fact, doing so will result in a redimensioned array error. However, it is necessary to redefine functions, and to create error-handling routines again. Also, it's generally advisable to duplicate the Reset key deactivation code, if such code is used in the program.

In addition to its CHAIN statement, ProDOS also has STORE and RESTORE statements, which may come in handy in programs that do chaining. The STORE statement saves the names and values of all variables in use in a program to a disk file. The RESTORE statement reads this file and places the names and values back into memory. Refer to *BASIC Programming with ProDOS* for details.

Program Verification

The chaining technique described above works fine if the program being chained to is present on disk when your drive goes looking for it. If it is not there, then a disk error occurs and your system crashes. You prevent crashes by including an

ONERR GOTO statement and error-handling routine in the program, as described in Chapter 3. Since having the wrong disk in the drive is a human error, and one of the more common types of errors that is likely to occur, you may want to give it special handling by having your program look for the error code and provide a specific error message and recovery action when such an error occurs. Error in this case is number 6, "FILE NOT FOUND."

CHAINING WITH THE C-64

It is very easy to link two C-64 programs together if all you want to do is go from one program to the next and are not concerned with transferring variables or arrays. A little more is required to transfer variables and arrays. And still more is required to transfer strings. In short, there are three progressively more powerful ways to chain, depending upon your goal. This section discusses each of these in turn.

Going from Program A to Program B

The C-64 *Programmer's Reference Guide* advises, on page 49, that you can use the LOAD statement to chain two programs together. The procedure described there is simple. Just include the following as the last line executed during the first program:

LOAD "PROGRAM B NAME", 8

PROGRAM B NAME is, of course, the name of the second program. If you add this line, and then RUN Program A, you will see that Program B LOADs and begins executing. No problem . . . unless you want to transfer the values assigned to the variables, arrays, and strings used in the first program. Unless you are lucky, these values turn to garbage when the second program starts.

Actually, a little more than luck is involved. The deciding factor as far as variables and arrays are concerned is whether the second program is smaller than the first. If it is, then the variables and

```
10 REM PROGRAM A
20 A=100
30 A(5)=555.55
40 A$="A STRING"
50 A$(5)="A STRING OF FIVE"
60 LOAD"PROGRAM B",8
```

Fig. 7-6. C-64 Program A.

arrays transfer nicely, although the strings are usually lost. However, if you do not care about the strings, then there is no problem. In short, if the first subprogram in your program is the largest, and you do not care about transferring strings, then the LOAD statement, as described above, is the answer.

To illustrate this simple way to chain, try it for yourself. Figure 7-6 contains a little program that assigns a real variable (A), one element of a real array (A(5)), a string (A$), and one element of a string array (A$(5)). You do not have to worry about dimensioning the arrays, since BASIC does it automatically. Type the listing and save it to disk as PROGRAM A.

Line 60 of Program A loads PROGRAM B. The listing of Program B is shown in Fig. 7-7. This program attempts to print the values of the four variables assigned by Program A. Enter Program B and save it to disk as PROGRAM B.

Now load and run Program A and see what happens.

Your C-64 should have suffered a serious case of amnesia, and may also have felt that one or more of the array variables had a bad subscript. As this exercise illustrates, you can go from Program A to Program B by simply including a line at the end of the first program that loads the second. But, as this also shows, you will lose the real and array variables you were using, and may encounter some redimensioned array errors.

Transferring Variables and Arrays

If you want to transfer variables and arrays (non-string) from one program to the next, things get a bit more involved. The following explains why C-64 chaining involves what it does.

```
10 REM PROGRAM B
20 PRINT"A=";A
30 PRINT"A(5)=";A(5)
40 PRINT"A$=";A$
50 PRINT"A$(5)=";A$(5)
60 REM************************************
70 REM************************************
```

Fig. 7-7. C-64 Program B.

First, as you are aware, your C-64 has several kilobytes of working memory area. Different parts of this area are assigned to hold different information. Usually, a programmer can leave it to the operating system to worry about what is located where, and simply ignore it. Unfortunately, your C-64's operating system lacks the smarts to manage things properly when you attempt to link two programs together and pass the variables. It is pretty smart, but not that smart. If you try to make it do this job for you, you find that it has reached its "level of incompetence," to use the term coined by an author named Peter a few years ago.

Here is why. When you load a program, it is assigned a particular range within your program's memory. When you later enter data—variables, arrays, strings—they are assigned to areas of memory above the program. As long as the program stays put, everything is fine. However, if you load a new, larger program, it may extend up into the areas reserved for variables, arrays, and strings, thereby destroying them. This is what happened in the little exercise with Program A and Program B.

The solution comes in two steps. First, protect the variables and arrays. Second, protect the strings. All that is required to protect the variables and arrays is a very simple trick. As you saw, in chaining from Program A to Program B, Program B overwrote the memory area containing variables, arrays, and strings. Suppose that Program A were bigger than Program B? In that case, Program B would no longer extend into the wrong memory area.

The problem encountered earlier in attempting to chain from Program A to Program B was caused by Program B being slightly bigger than Program A. You can fix part of the program by changing Program A to the form shown in Fig. 7-8. This (Program A′) is identical to Program A except for lines 70 and 80, which do nothing more than add a few bytes to Program A′ and thereby make it bigger than Program B. Modify Program A to look like Fig. 7-8 and then save it to disk as PROGRAM A′. Now run Program A′ and see what happens.

This time the values assigned to the real variable and array make the trip successfully to Program B, but the strings do not make it, and the character color changes due to some string confusions. Still, this exercise illustrates that you can pass the values of variables and arrays if Program A′ is bigger than Program B.

```
10 REM PROGRAM A′
20 A=100
30 A(5)=555.55
40 A$="A STRING"
50 A$(5)="A STRING OF FIVE"
60 LOAD"PROGRAM B",8
70 REM************************************
80 REM************************************
```

Fig. 7-8. C-64 Program A′.

167

I'm not suggesting that you add dummy lines to your first program to make it bigger than the second. Though the example just given illustrates the idea, doing it this way is not very efficient. Besides, there is another way to do it. Your C-64 measures the size of a program when it loads it, and stores this value in memory. It also decides where to put the variables, arrays, and strings, and stores these in memory. The respective values are stored as two bytes each in low-byte high-byte format. If you are unfamiliar with this, the following formula allows you to compute the decimal value from a low-byte and high-byte pair:

Decimal Value = LO + 256 * HI

For example, if LO is 150 and HI is 15, then Decimal Value = 150 + 15 * 256, or 3990. As a practical matter, the LO byte contributes much less to the total and can be safely ignored if you add a safety factor—1 or 2—to the HI byte.

Your C-64 uses the memory locations shown in Table 7-3 to store several pointers that are important during chaining. When the C-64 executes a program, it allocates various memory areas to the variables, arrays, and strings, and stores the pointers to the memory areas in locations 45 through 52. The allocated areas are always above the program itself. Now, if you load your largest program, and peek at the values of memory locations 45 and 46, you can see where it has allocated the lowest of these areas in the largest program. Knowing this value, you can take it back to your first program and poke the value in there, and thereby do the allocation yourself instead of letting your C-64 do it.

Table 7-3. Memory Locations of Pointers for Variables, Arrays, and Strings.

Pointer	Low Byte	High Byte
Start of Variables	45	46
Start of Arrays	47	48
End of Arrays	49	50
String Storage	51	52

```
10 REM PROGRAM A''
11 POKE 46,9
12 POKE 48,9
13 POKE 50,9
14 POKE 52,9
20 A=100
30 A(5)=555.55
40 A$="A STRING"
50 A$(5)="A STRING OF FIVE"
60 LOAD"PROGRAM B",8
```

Fig. 7-9. C-64 Program A''.

To illustrate the use of the peeks and pokes, load Program B and type in and record the value you obtain by printing the following statement:

PEEK (46)

(You should get 8.)

Now add 1 to this value (9), and add lines 11 – 14 to the original Program A shown in Fig. 7-8. The new program (Program A'') is shown in Fig. 7-9. Save this program to disk as Program A''. Then run it and see what you get when Program B executes. What should happen is that the real variable and array survive, but the strings, once again, get lost during the trip.

When you poke the value into locations 46, 48, 50, and 52 what you are doing is telling the computer that the poked value is where the top of the program is located and it can begin putting variables, arrays, and strings above that. It does not argue, but follows you order obligingly, allowing itself to be tricked.

A word of caution: Be careful how you save a subprogram that assigns its own values to memory locations 46 through 52. Your C-64 is not smart enough to know that you have tricked it. If your subprogram only takes 2K of memory, but you have tricked your C-64 into thinking it takes up 22K, it allots 22K of disk space when it saves the subprogram. You can waste a lot of disk space this way. Do not ever save such a program immediately after you have run it. Clear memory first and load the subprogram from scratch. This resets the memory pointers, and allows the program to be saved in the amount of space that it actually needs.

```
10 REM PROGRAM A'''
11 POKE 46,9
12 POKE 48,9
13 POKE 50,9
14 POKE 52,9
20 A=100
30 A(5)=555.55
40 A$="A STRING"
45 A$=A$+""
50 A$(5)="A STRING OF FIVE"
55 A$(5)=A$(5)+""
60 LOAD"PROGRAM B",8
```

Fig. 7-10. C-64 Program A'''.

Transferring Strings and String Arrays

Your C-64 does not have as much respect for strings as it does for variables. They probably know how Rodney Dangerfield feels. Although an area of memory is allocated to string storage, not every string receives the call, and most of them go through the meat grinder when you chain. The reason is that BASIC leaves strings in the program area, rather than storing them in a separate area—unless the program does certain things to them. You can assure that strings receive the respect they deserve by concatenating all strings with the null string. For example, Set A$ = A$ + "".

To illustrate how this works, Fig. 7-10 is a modified version of Fig. 7-9 in which lines 45 and 44 have been added to concatenate the strings and string array element with the null string. Type in these two lines to Program A'', and then save the program to disk as Program A'''.

Run it and see what happens. If all worked according to plan, both variables and strings should have found their way safely to Program B.

The foregoing illustrates that it is possible to preserve the identity of strings by concatenation. It follows from this that if you do not concatenate strings, they are not preserved. A string that is not preserved does not turn into the null string, but may take on an astonishing shape if you attempt to use it later on. If you have a color monitor and have been faithfully following the keyboard exercises described in this chapter, then you probably saw the character color of your display change when some non-preserved strings were printed during Program B. This and stranger things can happen. The lesson is that, if your choose not to preserve a string, do not attempt to use it later on unless you first redefine it. If you use it without doing this, you may be in for some interesting surprises.

Chapter 8

File Handling

This chapter concerns disk files. Its primary focus is on data files. These are the files that the serious programmer uses to store data entered by the user through the keyboard. Later on, the files are read back in and the user's earlier entries come back to life. Many—perhaps most—serious programs use data files. It is important to know how to handle them properly, efficiently, and with minimum complications.

There is a good deal more to file handling than simply being able to create a file, write to it, and then read it back into memory. This is the heart of the matter, but not enough to allow you to write a program that handles files safely or well. You also need to be able to plan your files intelligently, deal with error conditions, prompt the user to make necessary disk swaps, and design a control structure to read and write the files efficiently. This chapter covers these subjects. Knowing them makes your life as a programmer easier, and allows you to write programs that are safe for users.

Once you have mastered the techniques for reading and writing files, dealing with disk swaps,

and so forth, you may forget a lot of what you worked so hard to learn. You can become quite competent at writing these routines if you work with them often enough. If you do not, then you go through the normal process of learning decay, which is the fancy term for forgetting. Then, when you want to write a new program, you must learn everything all over again. There is, of course, an easier way: Use subroutines.

This tune was played before, and there is nothing new about it. However, the volume of the song should be turned up a few notches for this chapter. File handling code is often complex, and that is why it is especially important to use subroutines to deal with files. Once you have a good set of these in your library, you can pull them out and adapt them to a new application. It makes life much easier.

There is another aspect to this, as well. If you have ever attempted to translate a program from one dialect of BASIC and DOS to another—say, from the Apple II to the IBM PC—then you know what an adventure it can be. File handling code differs from computer to computer. Common denominators seem to be the OPEN and CLOSE statements, but these are embedded in a variety of syntaxes, depending upon the computer. Most computers have both sequential and random access files of one kind of another. PRINT and INPUT statements (or close relatives) are widely used to send data to and read data from files, respectively. However, once you begin to delve into a particular DOS, these similarities seem minor, and you find it necessary to concentrate on the many unique requirements of that DOS.

The difficulty of translating is influenced a good deal by how the program was first designed. If it was built around subroutines, translation is much easier. The reason for this is not hard to understand. The control code of such a program is at a fairly high level. Much of it consists of statements setting arguments and making subroutine calls. These are very similar from BASIC to BASIC. That is, a GOSUB 3000 means the same in virtually any dialect of BASIC. In short, using subroutines makes it easier to translate your program.

This chapter assumes you are familiar with the fundamentals of using both sequential and random access files on your computer system. If you are a beginner or have limited recent experience in the area, review some introductory material before proceeding. The discussion is illustrated primarily with examples of IBM PC file handling code, which may or may not resemble the code used on your computer. Illustrations of equivalent Apple and C-64 code are also presented, but without detailed explanations. Detailed explanations of Apple and C-64 file handling code are presented in Appendix A and B, respectively.

This chapter is not a good place to learn the fundamentals of file handling. If you do not have an IBM PC, try not to be put off by the focus on IBM PC code. Although the discussion is illustrated with it, the concepts presented are generalizable across all computer systems. The chapter shows how to plan files, document files, decide whether to use a sequential or random access file in an application, develop subroutines to write and read files, and manage your files both safely and effi-

ciently. Ignore the inapplicable specifics—and especially such wonders as LSET, RSET, MKI$, and MKD$—and concentrate on the five more general concepts just noted.

This chapter covers several different topics. It begins with a discussion of file planning. The next two sections cover sequential files and random access files, respectively. Each of these two sections discusses relevant options on the IBM PC BASIC command, key file-handling statements, the design of subroutines to write and read files, and file documentation. The final section covers efficiency and safety in writing and reading files.

FILE PLANNING

It is very important to plan your files carefully before you start writing code. If you do not do this properly, you may find yourself modifying their structure, adding new ones, deleting others, and in a state of confusion. During the development of a program that uses files, you need the code to write and read them early on. Much of the early coding work makes assumptions about those files. Consequently, changes to them have a ripple effect throughout the design and have significant time, work, and error consequences. Plan carefully, and do it early.

Sequential versus Random Access Files

There are two types of files: sequential, and random access. A *sequential file* has one record and is loaded into memory or written out to disk all at once. Sequential files are commonly used for storing arrays. However, a sequential file can be as short as one character, and in fact such files come in handy for certain applications. The prime characteristic of a sequential file is not its length or what is stored in it, but that its entire contents are handled at one time. When your program reads it, it reads it all at once. When it writes it, it writes it all at once. Sequential files are useful for storing directories, indexes, and other information that can be considered (more or less) one-of-a-kind, However, if your program must deal with a number of different data sets, then it is better to use a random access file.

A *random access file* is like a card file. The file consists of records, and each record has its own unique record number. You can read or write one record, without reading or writing the entire file. Random access files are required when your program must deal with several different data sets—for example, identically formatted personnel records of different people, price histories of different stocks, or market analyses of different real estate properties.

Opening and Closing Files

IBM BASIC permits you to have as many as 15 files open simultaneously. To have more or fewer than three files open, you must set the /F: files option on the BASIC (or BASICA) command when loading the language, as described later in this chapter. Each additional file takes up more memory—188 bytes in the file control block plus a minimum of 128 bytes (and usually more) for the file buffer. The /S: buffer size option is important for random access files. The /S: option sets the size of the buffer used for sending data to or receiving data from a random access file. The default value of buffer size is 128 bytes. The record length used in a random access file must not exceed the buffer size or an error condition will occur. This means that, if you intend to use records longer than 128 bytes, you *must* set the /S: option when BASIC is loaded. If you do not set a BASIC option, BASIC allows you to have three files open at once—that is, the default is three. (The best way to set the BASIC option is with a batch file. The user should not be required to type in extensions to the BASIC command that, if left out, will cause problems during the program.)

(Apple DOS permits you to have as many as 16 files open simultaneously. The DOS default is three files; that is, you can open up to three files without using the MAXFILES statement. If you wish to open more than three files, then your program must execute a MAXFILES statement early in the program. MAXFILES should be the first line of the program, since its execution changes memory pointers and will probably disrupt GOTO and GOSUB and certain other instructions.)

As a general rule, the fewer files open at any time, the better. One good reason is the memory overhead in having more than one file open. If your program uses 10 different files, decide whether it is really necessary for all of these to be open at once. If not, determine the minimum number that your program needs to function effectively. If it is fewer than 10, set the BASIC (or MAXFILES) option appropriately and save some memory. Note also that you can have as many files as you want in a program, and every one of them can use the same file number. The only constraint is that no two files with the same file number can be open simultaneously.

As you read on in this chapter, you will note that all of the file write and read subroutines both open and close a file. DOS does not require that this be done. You can, for example, have your program open a file at the beginning of the program, go on to other business, and not close it until the end. The CLOSE statement, when executed, forces the file to be written to disk. Some file writing may occur before this, but CLOSE assures that the job gets finished. Until the file is closed, there is some danger that a program interrupt—user error, power loss, or program error—will cause data to be lost or a file to be damaged. Thus, in general, it is good practice to close a file unless there is a need for it to be open. This need is most obvious when you are reading or writing the file. At other times, it is more questionable, especially when you consider the importance of protecting the user's files.

In some programs there is a need to have one or more files open for long stretches of time. If you do want to do this, then modify the file write and read subroutines given later in this chapter by removing the CLOSE statements. Close the files in the control code of your program, rather than having a subroutine do it automatically.

File Documentation

Once you have decided what types of files you need (sequential or random access) lay them out on paper. It is not difficult to write a file handling subroutine (one for writing or reading a file), but you must take many details into account. You should not be worrying about these details when you sit down before your computer to write the code. Sort them out beforehand. The actual writing of the file handling code should be as mechanical a task as possible. You should also be able to base your new routines on a standard formula. Writing a program is not like writing a novel. Instant inspiration is more a hazard than a blessing. Systematic, step-by-step working habits get you to the goal more quickly, and with fewer errors, than the programmer's muse.

The more variables stored in your files, the more important it is to plan them. If you store only a few variables, then record layouts and computer memory or disk storage requirements are not a great concern. However, if you store large amounts of data in a file, then these matters grow greatly in importance. This is particularly true for random access files, since you cannot write good file-handling code without completely planning each record beforehand.

The best way to plan your files is to document them. There are many different ways to document files, the simplest and most popular of which is probably the form shown in Fig. 8-1. This documentation identifies record field, length, and relevant assignment variables, and is adequate for some purposes. It is far from complete documentation, however, and does little to help a programmer create code to write and read a file, or decipher file han-

dling code that is already written. These are the two programming tasks that file documentation should be designed to support. To do this, the documentation must provide several additional pieces of information. Here are some things that this documentation should tell the programmer:

- Type of file—sequential or random access.
- File name.
- Flags used with the file—for example, a flag used to control whether or not to write or read a file.
- File number.
- Line numbers for calling file write and read subroutines, if such subroutines are used.
- Descriptions of record fields, arrays/variables representing each field, field lengths, number of elements in each array, and number of bytes in each record.
- If a random access file, the record number argument variable, such as R%; record length; number of records; and the variables used in FIELD statements.

A suggested format for documenting a sequential file is shown in Fig. 8-2, and a similar format for a random access file is shown in Fig. 8-3. The next section will provide detailed information on completing this form for sequential files, and the section following for random access files.

FILE DOCUMENTATION

Field Description	Array/Variable	Length
NAMES	A$(A)	24
PRICES	A(A)	8
⋮	⋮	⋮
⋮	⋮	⋮
⋮	⋮	⋮
ITEM COUNT	K4%	6

Fig. 8-1. A simple documentation format such as this is widely used, but contains little information about the file.

```
                    FILE DOCUMENTATION

Type file : SEQUENTIAL
File name : NAME.SEQ
Flag      : F%
File no.  : I
Write line: 6000
Read line : 6250


                      FILE CONTENT

                    Array/      Max.
Field Description   Variable    Arg.     Length    No.Bytes
-----------------   --------    ------   ------    --------

NAMES               A$(A)        64        24       1536
PRICES              A (A)        64         8        512
      |                 |         |         |          |
      |                 |         |         |          |
      |                 |         |         |          |
ITEM COUNT          K4%          I          6          6
```

Fig. 8-2. Suggested documentation format for a sequential file.

You should document your files before you create the code that handles those files. Documentation, in short, is an act of planning. In order to prepare such documentation, you must have a full understanding of sequential and random access files, topics that are covered in the next two sections.

SEQUENTIAL FILES

This section is divided into two parts, covering code for creating subroutines to write and read sequential files, and file documentation.

Write and Read Subroutines

In creating write and read subroutines for sequential files, these conventions are followed:

- File handling subroutines use line numbers 6000 through 8999.

- The write subroutine always precedes the read subroutine.
- There is a line increment of 250 (more or less) between write and read subroutine.

There is nothing magic about these rules, but they help us keep things straight. Write and read subroutines are always adjacent, and their line numbers are not far apart. In working with one, we are never far from the other.

Writing the File. A sequential file cannot be read unless it exists, and it is created when it is first written. Thus, the first requirement for using a file is to write it. To write the file, your program must do three things: open the file, send data to it, and close the file.

You open a file by using an appropriate file-opening statement. With the IBM PC, there are two acceptable ways to do this, but it is best to learn and use just one, rather than to alternate between two (consistency principle). And, if one must be chosen, it is best to select the one that is the most straightforward (simplicity principle). The syntax of the simplest file-opening statement for a sequential file is as follows;

OPEN *"d:filename"* FOR OUTPUT AS #*n*

The parameters of this statement are:

- *d*—Disk drive indicator (A or B). If this term is left out, the file will be written to the default drive.
- *filename*—File name. This, like the name of any file, may contain up to eight characters plus a three-character extension.
- *n*—file number. This will be a number between 1 and 15, and it cannot exceed the maximum number of files set in the /F: option of the BASIC command, or 3, if the /F: option has not been set.

Assume that you want to open a file named SEQFILE, using file number 1. Further, assume that the disk it is on may be in either drive A or drive B and so it is necessary to make the disk drive indicator **d** a variable that can be set with the program. The following statement will open SEQFILE, and also permit drive A and B to be specified as the string variable DRIVE$:

OPEN DRIVE$ + ":SEQFILE" FOR OUTPUT AS #1

Once the file has been opened, data can be sent to it using PRINT#, PRINT# USING, or WRITE#

FILE DOCUMENTATION

```
Type file  : RANDOM
File name  : NAME. RND
Flag       : F%
File no.   : I
Write line : 7000
Read line  : 7250
No. recs.  : 999
Rec. arg.  : R%
```

FILE CONTENT

Field Description	Program Array/ Variable	Buffer Array/ Variable	Max. Arg.	Length	No. Bytes
NAMES	A$(I-5)	F0$(I-5)	5	24	120
PRICES	A (I-5)	FI$(I-5)	5	4	20
'	'	'	'	'	'
'	'	'	'	'	'
'	'	'	'	'	'
ITEM COUNT	K4%	F9$	I	2	2

RECORD LENGTH = 252

Fig. 8-3. Suggested documentation format for a random access file.

statements. PRINT# statements are cumbersome to use because program code must provide special delimiters between adjacent items as they are sent to the file. Similar problems exist with PRINT# USING, but this statement permits you to format data in the same manner as you would when printing data to the screen with the PRINT USING statement. When either of these two statements is used to send numeric data to a file, a space is added at the start of a positive number, just as when printing a positive number to the screen with the PRINT statement.

The easiest and simplest way to send data to the file is with the WRITE# statement. This automatically provides delimiters between adjacent items as they are sent to the file, provided a comma or a carriage return follows each item. In sum, use WRITE# and leave PRINT# and PRINT# USING alone, if you can.

The syntax of the WRITE# statement is as follows:

> WRITE# *file number, variable 1, variable 2, . . .*
> *variable k*

For example, to send the variables A, B$, and C% to file number 1, you would use this expression:

> WRITE #1, A,B$,C%

When this statement sends data to the file, it inserts a comma between each variable, and a carriage return/line feed after the last item. The comma and carriage return/line feed serve as *delimiters*, separating adjacent characters when the file is read. Within the file, quotation marks are added at the start and end of each character string, and real and integer variables are written to the file as straight ASCII (non-encoded) characters. No space is added to the beginning of a positive number, as it is with PRINT# or PRINT# USING. For example, if the variables A, B$, and C% have the values 1.2345, "Tweedledum & Tweedledee," and − 32768, then the portion of the file that the above WRITE# statement creates will look like this:

. . . ,1.2345, ''Tweedledum & Tweedledee'', − 32768 . . .

If an array must be written to the file, the best way is with a FOR-NEXT loop. For example, to write elements 0 through 5 of the real array A(n) to the file, use code like this:

```
6070   REM-real array-
6080   For A = 0 to 5
6090   WRITE#1,A(A)
6100   NEXT
```

After the data have been sent to the file, the file must be closed with the CLOSE statement. The syntax of this statement is as follows:

> CLOSE# *file number*

For example, to close file number 1, use the statement CLOSE#1. The CLOSE statement can be used without a file number, but if it is, then it will close all files and devices currently open. Thus, it is best to include the file number parameter.

To combine these pieces together, let us create a subroutine that will write SEQFILE. Assume that SEQFILE consists of three arrays—string, real (single precision), and integer—and three sets of string, real, and integer variables. The resulting subroutine is shown in Fig. 8-4.

Line 6020 opens the file. Lines 6030 – 6140 write the three arrays to the file, using FOR-NEXT loops. Lines 6160 – 6180 write the three sets of variables to the file, using WRITE# statements, with each variable separated from those adjacent to it by a comma. And line 6190 closes the file with a CLOSE statement.

Note that, if you do not want to close the file within the subroutine, line 6190 can be deleted from the subroutine and placed elsewhere in program code. Under some conditions, the CLOSE statement can be left out, since BASIC will automatically close all files when it executes an END, NEW, RESET, SYSTEM, or RUN command. It is best practice to close the file, however, rather than leaving it to these commands.

Equivalent subroutines for the Apple and C-64

```
0 REM Sequential File Write Subroutine
1 REM SAVE"FIG8-4.BAS",A
6010 REM--Sequential File (Write)--
6020 OPEN DRIVE$+":SEQFILE" FOR OUTPUT AS #1
6030 REM-string array-
6040 FOR A=1 TO 5
6050 WRITE#1,A$(A)
6060 NEXT
6070 REM-real array-
6080 FOR A=1 TO 5
6090 WRITE#1,A(A)
6100 NEXT
6110 REM-integer array-
6120 FOR A=1 TO 5
6130 WRITE#1, A%(A)
6140 NEXT
6150 REM-variables-
6160 WRITE#1,A0$,A1$,A2$:REM string
6170 WRITE#1,A0,A1,A2:REM real
6180 WRITE#1,A0%,A1%,A2%:REM integer
6190 CLOSE#1:REM close file
6200 RETURN
```

Fig. 8-4. IBM PC subroutine to write or create the sequential file SEQFILE.

```
0    REM    FIG 8-5
1    REM   SEQUENTIAL FILE WRITE SUBROUTINE
10   D$ =  CHR$ (4): REM   CTRL-D
20   D = 1: REM   DISK DRIVE
6010   REM --SEQUENTIAL FILE (WRITE)--
6020   PRINT D$;"OPENSEQFILE,D";D
6030   PRINT D$;"WRITESEQFILE"
6040   REM -STRING ARRAY-
6050   FOR A = 1 TO 5
6060   PRINT A$(A)
6070   NEXT
6080   REM -REAL ARRAY-
6090   FOR A = 1 TO 5
6100   PRINT A(A)
6110   NEXT
6120   REM -INTEGER ARRAY-
6130   FOR A = 1 TO 5
6140   PRINT A%(A)
6150   NEXT
6160   REM -VARIABLES-
6170   PRINT A0$: PRINT A1$: PRINT A2$: REM    STRING
6180   PRINT A0: PRINT A1: PRINT A2: REM     REAL
6190   PRINT A0%: PRINT A1%: PRINT A2%: REM    INTEGER
6200   PRINT D$;"CLOSESEQFILE"
6210   RETURN
```

Fig. 8-5. Apple subroutine to write or create the sequential file SEQFILE. (Refer to Appendix A for a complete explanation of this subroutine.)

```
6010 REM--SEQUENTIAL FILE (WRITE)--
6020 OPEN 2,8,2,"@0:SEQFILE,SEQ,W":REM OPEN FILE
6030 REM-STRING ARRAY-
6040 FOR A=0 TO 5
6050 PRINT#2,A$(A)
6060 NEXT
6070 REM-REAL ARRAY-
6080 FOR A=0 TO 5
6090 PRINT#2,A(A)
6100 NEXT
6110 REM-INTEGER ARRAY-
6120 FOR A=0 TO 5
6130 PRINT#2,A%(A)
6140 NEXT
6150 REM-VARIABLES-
6160 PRINT#2,A$
6170 PRINT#2,A0
6180 PRINT#2,A%
6190 CLOSE 2:REM CLOSE FILE
6200 RETURN
```

Fig. 8-6. C-64 subroutine to write or create the sequential file SEQFILE. (Refer to Appendix B for a complete explanation of this subroutine.)

are shown in Fig. 8-5 and 8-6, respectively.

Reading the File. The procedure for reading a sequential file—like that for writing one—has three parts: open the file, read in data, and close the file. The parts for writing and reading a file are very similar; in fact, similar enough so that any pro-grammer with common sense first creates the write subroutine, and then uses the screen editor to convert it to a read subroutine. More on this later.

Figure 8-7 contains a subroutine for reading the sequential file created by the subroutine shown in Fig. 8-4. The only difference between the two

```
0 REM Sequential File Read Subroutine
1 REM SAVE"FIG8-7.BAS",A
6250 REM--Sequential File (Read)--
6260 OPEN DRIVE$+":SEQFILE" FOR INPUT AS #1
6270 REM-string array-
6280 FOR A=1 TO 5
6290 INPUT#1,A$(A)
6300 NEXT
6310 REM-real array-
6320 FOR A=1 TO 5
6330 INPUT#1,A(A)
6340 NEXT
6350 REM-integer array-
6360 FOR A=1 TO 5
6370 INPUT#1, A%(A)
6380 NEXT
6390 REM-variables-
6400 INPUT#1,A$,B$,C$
6410 INPUT#1,A0,A1,A2
6420 INPUT#1,A0%,A1%,A2%
6430 CLOSE#1:REM close file
6440 RETURN
```

Fig. 8-7. IBM PC subroutine to read the sequential file SEQFILE.

178

subroutines other than line numbers is the file-opening statement, and the substitution of INPUT# statements for WRITE# statements. The file-opening statement now looks like this:

OPEN DRIVE$ + ":SEQFILE" FOR INPUT AS #1

The word OUTPUT (appearing in the opening statement for the write subroutine) has been changed to INPUT. As this subroutine is nearly the image of the one previously discussed, I leave it to you to sort out.

Equivalent subroutines for the Apple and C-64 are shown in Figs. 8-8 and 8-9, respectively; see Appendix A or B for detailed explanations.

Converting a Write Subroutine to a Read Subroutine. It is easy to convert a write subroutine to a read subroutine (or to do the opposite, if you are the contrary type). There are two basic approaches. The first is to copy the write subroutine alone to a separate file, renumber it, convert it, and then merge it with the original program.

The second approach is to work within the same program by going through the write subroutine, line by line, changing the line numbers, and producing a duplicate of the write subroutine at a different line range. Either way works and is faster than creating the second subroutine from scratch. The first approach has the advantage of relying less on your ability to keep track of two sets of line numbers simultaneously, and is probably somewhat less error-prone. The second approach is faster for short subroutines. Either way works.

Sequential File Documentation

A suggested format for documenting sequential files was presented in Fig. 8-2. To show how this format can be used to document an actual file, let us examine the documentation for SEQFILE, the file whose write and read subroutines were illustrated earlier in this section. This documentation is shown in Fig. 8-10. Figure 8-10 shows that type of file is sequential and file name is SEQFILE. No Flag has been defined, and so this line is blank.

```
0    REM    FIG 8-8
1    REM    SEQUENTIAL FILE READ SUBROUTINE
10   D$ =   CHR$ (4): REM  CTRL-D
20   D = 1: REM  DISK DRIVE
6250    REM  --SEQUENTIAL FILE (READ)--
6260    PRINT D$;"OPENSEQFILE,D";D
6270    PRINT D$;"READSEQFILE"
6280    REM -STRING ARRAY-
6290    FOR A = 1 TO 5
6300    INPUT A$(A)
6310    NEXT
6320    REM -REAL ARRAY-
6330    FOR A = 1 TO 5
6340    INPUT A(A)
6350    NEXT
6360    REM -INTEGER ARRAY-
6370    FOR A = 1 TO 5
6380    INPUT A%(A)
6390    NEXT
6400    REM -VARIABLES-
6410    INPUT A0$,A1$,A2$: REM    STRING
6420    INPUT A0,A1,A2: REM    REAL
6430    INPUT A0%,A1%,A2%: REM    INTEGER
6440    PRINT D$;"CLOSESEQFILE"
6450    RETURN
```

Fig. 8-8. Apple subroutine to read the sequential file SEQFILE. (Refer to Appendix A for a complete explanation of this subroutine.)

179

File number is 1. The file Write subroutine starts at line 6010 and the file Read subroutine at line 6250.

The field descriptions are given for each variable. A$(A) represents Names, A(A) Prices, and so forth. The appropriate array or variable is given opposite each field description. The maximum arguments of the three arrays used in the read and write subroutines are each 5, as indicated in the Max. Arg. column.

The numbers appearing in the Length column require a little explanation. Recall that the contents of a sequential file are stored as a series of ASCII characters, with delimiters between adjacent characters. The length of each field depends upon the type of field and what goes in that field.

You must estimate field length based on both the type of field and probable content of the field. Make liberal estimates. The value of No. Bytes is calculated by multiplying the field length + 1 (1 is added to account for the delimiter) by the number of fields. If an array is used, the number of bytes is calculated with this formula:

No. Bytes = (Field Length + 1)* Number of Array Elements

If the field is not part of an array, No. Bytes is simply the field length plus 1. Note that the number of array elements differs by 1 depending on whether or not element 0 is used. (Length of number fields increases by one for positive numbers written to file with PRINT# or PRINT# USING statements.)

RANDOM ACCESS FILES

This section is divided into two parts, covering the code for creating subroutines to write and read random access files, and file documentation.

Write and Read Subroutines

In creating write and read subroutines for random access files, the same conventions are followed as for sequential files, namely:

- File-handling subroutines use line numbers 6000 – 8999. Since the sequential file subroutines used lines in the 6000 range, the range above 7000 will be used for random access files.
- The write subroutine precedes the read subroutine.

```
6250 REM--SEQUENTIAL FILE (READ)--
6260 OPEN 2,8,2,"@0:SEQFILE,SEQ,R":REM OPEN FILE
6270 REM-STRING ARRAY-
6280 FOR A=0 TO 5
6290 INPUT#2,A$(A)
6300 NEXT
6310 REM-REAL ARRAY-
6320 FOR A=0 TO 5
6330 INPUT#2,A(A)
6340 NEXT
6350 REM-INTEGER ARRAY-
6360 FOR A=0 TO 5
6370 INPUT#2,A%(A)
6380 NEXT
6390 REM-VARIABLES-
6400 INPUT#2,A$
6410 INPUT#2,A0
6420 INPUT#2,A%
6430 CLOSE 2:REM CLOSE FILE
6440 RETURN
```

Fig. 8-9. C-64 subroutine to read the sequential file SEQFILE. (Refer to Appendix B for a complete explanation of this subroutine.)

```
                      FILE DOCUMENTATION


    Type file : SEQUENTIAL
    File name : SEQ FILE
    Flag      : -
    File no.  : 1
    Write line: 6010
    Read line : 6250




                         FILE CONTENT
```

Field Description	Array/ Variable	Max. Arg.	Length	No. Bytes
NAMES	A$(A)	5	24	125
PRICES	A (A)	5	12	65
AGES	A%(A)	5	6	35
ITEM 1	A0$	1	12	13
ITEM 2	A1$	1	12	13
ITEM 3	A2$	1	12	13
VALUE 1	A0	1	8	9
VALUE 2	A1	1	8	9
VALUE 3	A2	1	8	9
COUNT 1	A0%	1	6	7
COUNT 2	A1%	1	6	7
COUNT 3	A2%	1	6	7
			TOTAL	312

Fig. 8-10. Documentation for sequential file SEQFILE (IBM PC version).

- There is a line increment of 250 between write and read subroutines.

Writing the File. In IBM PC BASIC, a random access file is created by opening the file. Once the file has been opened, it exists and can be read, even if no data have been written to it previously. In this respect (as well as in many others), random access files differ from sequential files. Attempting to read a sequential file which has not previously been written produces error condition 53 (file not found), but not so with random access files. Still, there is not much point in reading an empty file, and so the logical place to start is by writing the file.

Dealing with random access files is considerably more cumbersome than dealing with sequential files. The main difference is the complexity of the code required to write and read random access files. It is not simply a matter of opening a file, sending data to it, and then closing it (as with a sequential file). Writing or reading a random access file involves much more than this.

One other major difference between the two types of files is the size of the record that can be used. A sequential file can be as long as you want to make it—up to the entire storage capacity of a disk, or until the variables use up all available computer memory. One record in a random access file may, in principle, be up to 32,767 bytes long, but the code gets increasingly complex if a record gets longer than about 1000 bytes.

The main advantage of a random access file is the ability to reach any part of the file very quickly. This speed is possible because the data in the file are stored as individual records, and those records consist of encoded binary data that can be written and read more quickly than the ASCII characters of sequential files.

To write to the file, an IBM PC program must do five things:

- Open the file.
- Allocate space in the file buffer.
- Move data into the buffer.
- Write data from the buffer to the disk.
- Close the file.

Opening the File. You open the file by using an appropriate file-opening statement. There is one acceptable way to do this for random access files, and it works for both writing and reading the file. The same file-opening statement can be used for both. The syntax of this statement is as follows:

OPEN "*d:filename*" AS #*n* LEN = *record length*

The parameters of this statement are:

- *d*—Disk drive indicator (A or B). If this term is left out, DOS uses the default drive.

- *filename*—File name. This, like the name of any IBM PC file, may contain up to eight characters, plus a three-character extension.
- *n*—File number. This will be a number between 1 and 15, and it cannot exceed the maximum number of files set in the /F: option of the BASIC command, or 3, if the /F: option has not been set.
- *record length*—This is the combined length of all of the fields which are to be written to the file. This value is computed by adding up the length of each field. String fields are as long as the number of characters they contain. Numeric fields are stored in encoded binary form and take fewer bytes than the number of ASCII characters they consist of. Double-precision numbers take 8 bytes, single-precision numbers take 4 bytes, and integers take 2 bytes. Record length cannot exceed 128 bytes unless the /S: buffer size parameter of the BASIC command has set it to a higher number.

The following is the file-opening statement for a file whose name is RANDFILE, file number of 1, and record length of 126:

OPEN "RANDFILE" AS #1 LEN = 126

This statement will open the file for the default drive. The drive can be specified as a variable by modifying the file-opening statement as follows:

OPEN DRIVE$ + ":RANDFILE" AS #1 LEN = 126

Allocating Space in the File Buffer. Once the file has been opened, the next step is to allocate space in the buffer for the variables that are to be written to the file. Space allocation is performed with the FIELD statement. Like the file-opening statement, the FIELD statement is required for both writing and reading of the file. Consequently, it makes sense to combine the file-opening and FIELD statements into a subroutine that can be called from both the file write and file read subroutines.

The syntax of the FIELD statement is:

FIELD# *file number, length* **AS** *string variable 1, length* **AS** *string variable 2 . . .*

The parameters of this statement are:

- *file number*—The file number declared in the file-opening statement (1 in the example given above).
- *length*—The length of the string variable representing the field.
- *string variable*—All variables listed in FIELD statements must be string variables. These variables are generally used only in the FIELD statement and not elsewhere in the program. Numbers must be converted to the string variables representing them in the FIELD statement with MKD$, MKS$, and MKI$ statements (see below). The lengths alloted to these variables in FIELD statements are determined according to these rules:

> String length = number of characters
> Double-precision number = 8
> Single-precision number = 4
> Integer = 2

To illustrate, suppose that a random file contains four variables:

> F0$—Represents a name, 16 characters long.
> F1$—Represents a double-precision number, 8 bytes long.
> F2$—Represents a single-precision number, 4 bytes long.
> F3$—Represents an integer, 2 bytes long.

This FIELD statement allocates the necessary space in the buffer:

FIELD#1, 16 as F0$, 8 AS F1$, 4 AS F2$, 2 AS F3$

BASIC permits you to use as many FIELD statements as you like in a program, but only one of these statements can be active at one time. The total of all the field lengths given in the FIELD statement cannot exceed the parameter following LEN in the file-opening statement. If the total is larger, a Field Overflow error occurs.

The variables used in a FIELD statement should not be assigned new values elsewhere in the program. Doing so will disrupt the pointers in the file buffer by moving the reassigned variable from the buffer into string space. It does no harm to display the variables on the monitor or to print them in a report. However, the best and safest practice is not to use the variables except in FIELD statements or when moving data into the file buffer with LSET or RSET statements (see below). By avoiding their use outside these places, you reduce the proliferation of variable names in the main part of the program and make the program more readable. You also reduce the risk of accidental reassignments. The easiest way to keep things straight is to use one set of variables in the FIELD statement and a second set in the rest of the program. It is a good idea to keep these field variables simple, and logically related to one another. For example, use F0$, F1$, F2$, and so on. If you intend to store array data in the record, use an array such as F$(1) – F$(n).

Moving Data into the Buffer. Once the FIELD statement has been executed, the next step is to move data into the buffer. This and the next step are performed only when writing a file. Data are moved into the buffer with LSET or RSET statements. The syntax of these statements is:

> **LSET** *buffer$* = *program$*
> **RSET** *buffer$* = *program$*

Buffer$* is the variable used in the FIELD statement. *Program$ is the name of this variable as used elsewhere in the program. If the program variable is a number, it must be converted to *program$* with an MKD$, MKS$, or MKI$ function (see below).

LSET left-justifies buffer$ in the field, and RSET right-justifies it.

If *buffer$* and the program variable are both strings, then the two strings are simply set equal to one another, after the LSET or RSET statement. For example, if *buffer$* is F0$ and *program$* = FOWL$, then the LSET statement looks like this:

LSET F0$ = FOWL$

If the program variable is a double-precision number, then the MKD$ function must be used to convert it to a string. For example, if the program variable is LONGNUMB# and buffer$ is F1$, then the LSET statement looks like this:

LSET F1$ = MKD$(LONGNUMB#):REM double-precision conversion

Similarly, if the program variable is a single-precision number or an integer, the MKS$ or MKI$ function is used, respectively, like this:

LSET F2$ = MKS$(MIDNUMB):REM single-precision conversion
LSET F3$ = MKI$(NODEC%):REM integer conversion

Writing Data from the Buffer. Once the data has been moved into the buffer, the buffer is ready to write to the file. This is done with the PUT statement. The syntax of this statement is as follows:

PUT# *file number, record number*

The *file number* is the file number used in the file-opening statement. It is 1 in the examples given above. The *record number* may be any number between 1 and 32767.

For example, to PUT the data into record number 33 of file number 1, use this statement:

PUT#1,33

Since *record number* is usually a variable, it may be represented as an integer variable in the PUT statement:

PUT#1, RECORD%

Closing the File. The final step in writing the file is to close it with a CLOSE statement of the form CLOSE# *file number*. This statement would be used to close file number 1:

CLOSE#1

As noted in the discussion of sequential files, the CLOSE statement can be used with or without a file number, but it is best to use the file number.

Let's combine these five steps—open file, allocate space in buffer, move data into buffer, write data from buffer, and close file—to create a subroutine that will write an actual file. The name of this file is RANDFILE, its file number is 1, and its length is 126 bytes. This file will be used to store the data in the program variables A$(0) – A$(5), A0$, A0#, A0, and A0%. Record number will be specified with the integer variable RECORD%.

Figure 8-11 shows the file-writing subroutine that is created from these ingredients. This subroutine starts on line 7000 and actually consists of two separate subroutines. The bottom subroutine, going from lines 7170 – 7210, performs the first two steps (open file, allocate space in buffer), and the top subroutine, going from lines 7000 – 7160, performs the last three (move data into buffer, write data, close file). Line 7010 of the top subroutine calls the bottom subroutine. (The bottom subroutine will also be used by the field read subroutine described later in this chapter.)

Line 7010 calls the subroutine at line 7170. Line 7180 contains the file-opening statement. Line 7200 contains a FIELD statement that allocates space for the buffer variables F0$ – F9$ in the file buffer. Line 7210 ends the bottom subroutine and returns control to line 7020 of the top subroutine.

Lines 7030 – 7120 move data into the file buffer. These lines contain a series of LSET statements which convert program variables to the buffer variables used in the FIELD statement. String assignments are made directly, and number assignments are made with MKD$, MKS$, and MKI$ functions.

Line 7140 PUTs the data defined in the FIELD

```
0 REM Random-Access File Write Subroutine
1 REM SAVE"FIG8-11.BAS",A
7000 REM--Random File (Write)--
7010 GOSUB 7170:REM open file & define field
7020 REM-Move Data into Random File Buffer-
7030 LSET F0$=A$(0):REM start unloading array
7040 LSET F1$=A$(1)
7050 LSET F2$=A$(2)
7060 LSET F3$=A$(3)
7070 LSET F4$=A$(4)
7080 LSET F5$=A$(5):REM finish unloading array
7090 LSET F6$=A0$:REM string
7100 LSET F7$=MKD$(A0#):REM double-precision real
7110 LSET F8$=MKS$(A0):REM single-precision real
7120 LSET F9$=MKI$(A0%):REM integer
7130 REM-Write Record-
7140 PUT#1, RECORD%
7150 CLOSE #1:REM close file
7160 RETURN
7170 REM--Open File & Define Data Fields--
7180 OPEN DRIVE$+ ":RANDFILE" AS #1 LEN=126
7190 REM-Define Data Fields-
7200 FIELD#1,16 AS F0$,16 AS F1$,16 AS F2$,16 AS F3$,16 AS F4$,
     16 AS F5$,16 AS F6$,8 AS F7$,4 AS F8$,2 AS F9$
7210 RETURN
```

Fig. 8-11. IBM PC subroutine to write or create random access file RANDFILE.

statement into record number RECORD% of file number 1. Line 7160 closes the file.

Equivalent subroutines for the Apple and C-64 are shown in Figs. 8-12 and 8-13, respectively; see Appendix A or B for details.

Reading the file. There are five steps in reading an IBM PC random access file: open the file, allocate space in the file buffer, move data from the file into the buffer, close the file, and convert buffer variables into program variables. Step 5 is optional if the variables read from the file are not reassigned, but required if they are. In either case, it is highly advisable.

The first two steps of reading a file are the same as the first two steps of writing a file. These two steps were described earlier and are performed by the subroutine consisting of lines 7170 – 7210 in Fig. 8-11.

Getting Data from the File. Step 3, moving data from the file into the buffer, is performed with the GET statement. This statement is similar to the PUT statement, but does just the opposite. PUT moves data from the buffer into the file, and

GET moves data from the file into the buffer. The syntax of the GET statement is as follows:

GET# *file number, record number*

For example, to get data from the record number 9 of file number 1, this statement would be used:

GET#1, 9

Since record number is usually a variable, a form of the GET statement similar to the following is more common:

GET#1, RECORD%

The file is closed with the CLOSE statement, which has already been described.

Converting Buffer Variables into Program Variables. The fifth step, converting buffer variables into program variables, is done with assignment statements. If the program variable is a string, then all that the assignment statement re-

```
0   REM    FIG 8-12
1   REM   RANDOM-ACCESS FILE (WRITE) SUBROUTINE
7000   REM   --RANDOM-ACCESS FILE (WRITE)--
7010   PRINT D$;"OPENRANDFILE,L400,D";D
7020   PRINT D$;"WRITERANDFILE,R";R
7030   REM -STRING ARRAY-
7040   FOR A = 1 TO 5
7050   PRINT A$(A)
7060   NEXT
7070   REM -REAL ARRAY-
7080   FOR A = 1 TO 5
7090   PRINT A(A)
7100   NEXT
7110   REM -INTEGER ARRAY-
7120   FOR A = 1 TO 5
7130   PRINT A%(A)
7140   NEXT
7150   REM -VARIABLES-
7160   PRINT A0$: PRINT A1$: PRINT A2$: REM    STRING
7170   PRINT A0: PRINT A1: PRINT A2: REM    REAL
7180   PRINT A0%: PRINT A1%: PRINT A2%: REM    INTEGER
7190   PRINT D$;"CLOSERANDFILE"
7200   RETURN
```

Fig. 8-12. Apple subroutine to write or create random access file RANDFILE. (Refer to Appendix A for a complete explanation of this subroutine.)

```
7000 REM--RANDOM FILE (WRITE)--
7010 GOSUB 8000:REM CALCULATE RL & RH
7020 OPEN 15,8,15
7030 OPEN 6,8,6,"RANDFILE"
7040 PRINT#15,"P"CHR$(6)CHR$(RL)CHR$(RH)
7050 REM-STRING ARRAY-
7060 FOR A=0 TO 5
7070 PRINT#6,A$(A)
7080 NEXT
7090 REM-REAL ARRAY-
7100 FOR A=0 TO 5
7110 PRINT#6,A(A)
7120 NEXT
7130 REM-INTEGER ARRAY-
7140 FOR A=0 TO 5
7150 PRINT#6,A%(A)
7160 NEXT
7170 REM-VARIABLES-
7180 PRINT#6,A$
7190 PRINT#6,A0
7200 PRINT#6,A%
7210 CLOSE 6
7220 CLOSE 15
7230 RETURN
```

Fig. 8-13. C-64 subroutine to write random access (i.e., relative) file RANDFILE. (Refer to Appendix B for a complete explanation of this subroutine.)

quires is an equals (=) sign. For example, to convert the buffer variable FO$ into the program variable FOWL$, use this statement:

FOWL$ = FO$

If the program variable is a number, then a CVD, CVS, or CVI function is required to convert the string variable in the buffer into the appropriate double-precision, single-precision, or integer variable in the program. These assignment statements illustrate the procedure:

LONGNUMB# = CVD(F1$):REM convert string to double-precision number
MIDNUMB = CVS(F2$):REM convert string to single-precision number
NODEC% = CVI(F3$):REM convert string to integer

Once the variables have been converted, they can be used in the program for any purpose, including reassignment.

Figure 8-14 shows a subroutine that will per-form these five steps and read the file that was written by the subroutine shown earlier in Fig. 8-11.

The read subroutine begins on line 7250. Line 7260 calls the subroutine on lines 7170–7210 which opens the file and allocates buffer space. (This subroutine is also used by the file write subroutine shown in Fig. 8-11.) Line 7270 moves data from the file into the file buffer. Lines 7300–7390 convert the buffer variables into program variables.

Equivalent subroutines for the Apple and C-64 are shown in Figs. 8-15 and 8-16, respectively; see Appendix A or B for details.

Random File Documentation

As the previous section demonstrated, random access files are more complex than sequential files, and there are many things for you to keep track of. This makes adequate file documentation all the more important. A random access file requires you to keep track of several additional items, such as the record number argument variable, record length, number of records, and the buffer variables

```
0 REM Random-Access File Read Subroutine
1 REM SAVE"FIG8-14.BAS",A
7170 REM--Open File & Define Data Fields--
7180 OPEN DRIVE$+ ":RANDFILE" AS #1 LEN=126
7190 REM-Define Data Fields-
7200 FIELD#1,16 AS F0$,16 AS F1$,16 AS F2$,16 AS F3$,16 AS F4$,
     16 AS F5$,16 AS F6$,8 AS F7$,4 AS F8$,2 AS F9$
7210 RETURN
7250 REM--Random File (Read)--
7260 GOSUB 7170:REM open file & field statement
7270 GET#1, RECORD%:REM read record
7280 CLOSE#1
7290 REM-Convert File Variables to Program Variables-
7300 A$(0)=F0$:REM start loading array
7310 A$(1)=F1$
7320 A$(2)=F2$
7330 A$(3)=F3$
7340 A$(4)=F4$
7350 A$(5)=F5$:REM finish loading array
7360 A0$=F6$:REM string
7370 A0#=CVD(F7$):REM double-precision real
7380 A0=CVS(F8$):REM single-precision real
7390 A0%=CVI(F9$):REM integer
7400 RETURN
```

Fig. 8-14. IBM PC subroutine to read random access file RANDFILE written by subroutine shown in Fig. 8-11.

```
0    REM    FIG 8-15
1    REM    RANDOM-ACCESS FILE (READ) SUBROUTINE
7250    REM --RANDOM-ACCESS FILE (READ)--
7260    PRINT D$;"OPENRANDFILE,L400,D";D
7270    PRINT D$;"READRANDFILE,R";R
7280    REM -STRING ARRAY-
7290    FOR A = 1 TO 5
7300    INPUT A$(A)
7310    NEXT
7320    REM -REAL ARRAY-
7330    FOR A = 1 TO 5
7340    INPUT A(A)
7350    NEXT
7360    REM -INTEGER ARRAY-
7370    FOR A = 1 TO 5
7380    INPUT A%(A)
7390    NEXT
7400    REM -VARIABLES-
7410    INPUT A0$,A1$,A2$: REM    STRING
7420    INPUT A0,A1,A2: REM    REAL
7430    INPUT A0%,A1%,A2%: REM    INTEGER
7440    PRINT D$;"CLOSERANDFILE"
7450    RETURN
```

Fig. 8-15. Apple subroutine to read random access file RANDFILE created by subroutine shown in Fig. 8-12. (Refer to Appendix A for a complete explanation of this subroutine.)

```
7250 REM--RANDOM FILE (READ)--
7260 GOSUB 8000:REM CALCULATE RL & RH
7270 OPEN 15,8,15
7280 OPEN 6,8,6,"RANDFILE"
7290 PRINT#15,"P"CHR$(6)CHR$(RL)CHR$(RH)
7300 REM-STRING ARRAY-
7310 FOR A=0 TO 5
7320 INPUT#6,A$(A)
7330 NEXT
7340 REM-REAL ARRAY-
7350 FOR A=0 TO 5
7360 INPUT#6,A(A)
7370 NEXT
7380 REM-INTEGER ARRAY-
7390 FOR A=0 TO 5
7400 INPUT#6,A%(A)
7410 NEXT
7420 REM-VARIABLES-
7430 INPUT#6,A$
7440 INPUT#6,A0
7450 INPUT#6,A%
7460 CLOSE 6
7470 CLOSE 15
7480 RETURN
```

Fig. 8-16. C-64 subroutine to read random access (i.e., relative) file RANDFILE written by subroutine shown in Fig. 8-13. (Refer to Appendix B for a complete explanation of this subroutine.)

188

used in FIELD statements. Nonetheless, you can still use a documentation format similar to that for sequential files. Formats for documenting sequential and random access files were presented in Figs. 8-2 and 8-3, respectively, and the documentation for the sequential file SEQFILE was shown in Fig. 8-10. You may want to compare the two documentation formats and note similarities and differences. The following discussion assumes that you are familiar with both formats, and focuses on the unique features of documentation for random access files. And, once again, both of these formats are "suggested," which means that you should feel free to adapt them to suit your own working style and needs.

Figure 8-17 contains the documentation for RANDFILE, the random access file whose write and read subroutines were described earlier in this section. At the top of the form, Type file is shown as Random, rather than Sequential. Two additional items, No. recs. and Rec. arg., are added at the bottom of the block. Number of records is 99 and the Record argument is the integer variable RECORD%.

On the lower part of the form, one heading—Buffer Array/Variable—has been added to document the relationship between the arrays and variables used in the program and those used in the buffer during disk access.

The entries beneath the Length heading are based on the type of variable listed to the left, in the Buffer Array/Variable column, according to rules given earlier. Number of bytes, respectively, of different variables types are: strings (length of

FILE DOCUMENTATION

```
Type file : RANDOM
File name : RANDFILE
Flag      : -
File no.  : I
Write line: 7000
Read line : 7250
NO. RECS. : 99
REC. ARG. : RECORD %
```

FILE CONTENT

Field Description	Program Array/ Variable	Buffer Array/ Variable	Max. Arg.	Length	No. Bytes
NAMES	A$(0)-A$(5)	F0$-F5$	5	16	96
LABEL	A0$	F6$	I	16	16
EPSILON	A0#	F7$	I	8	8
COST	A0	F8$	I	4	4
DAY	A0%	F9$	I	2	2

RECORD LENGTH = 126

Fig. 8-17. Documentation for random access file RANDFILE (IBM PC version).

string), double-precision numbers (8 bytes), single-precision numbers (4 bytes), and integers (2 bytes).

The entries in the No. Bytes column are the product of the entries in the Max. Arg. and Length row to the left. For example, in the top row, number of bytes (96) is calculated by multiplying the maximum argument (6) by the length of each element (16). Since delimiters (such as commas) are not used to separate items in IBM PC random access files, no extra byte is added (as it is with sequential files). (The DOSs of some computers—such as those of the Apple and C-64—store data in random-access files in the same manner as in sequential files, in ASCII format and with field separators. Check the DOS manual of your computer for storage formats.)

EFFICIENCY AND SAFETY IN FILE HANDLING

When accessing files, you need to consider both efficiency and safety. We'll discuss three areas where this is important: file verification, writing files, and reading files.

File Verification

Any time your program must access a disk drive, the risk of operator error is high. The operator may fail to insert, or may inadvertently remove, a disk that should be in the drive. Then, when your program instructs the drive to read a data file or chain to another program, the file is not there and the program can crash.

The solution to the problem is to use an error-handling routine of the type described in Chapter 3. Do include one! It is your program's best insurance against disaster and against some operator's plaintive call asking you how to recover the four hours' worth of data that were entered before the program crashed. Sometimes operators are not plaintive, but get downright aggressive about these matters; we leave that to your imagination. Enough said.

To Write or Not to Write

When should you write a file? More specifically, at what point in your program code should you call the subroutine that writes a data file? The answer to this question is more elusive than it might seem at first. There are two main factors to consider. The first of these is efficiency, and the second is safety.

Efficiency dictates that you write a file only when necessary. Writing a file involves a time delay. It also produces disk wear. Suppose that your program has a data-entry section that collects several items of data from the user. Your program can write the complete file each time the user enters a data field, but this is not very efficient. It is more efficient to wait until the user enters all fields, and then write.

On the other hand, you have the safety factor. You must write the file often enough so that, in case of a power failure, program interruption, or some other unforeseen event, all of the user's work in entering data does not go to waste.

Obviously, these two factors—efficiency and safety—are somewhat in conflict. You must balance them some way to decide how to handle file writing in your program.

To further complicate the matter, in some programs filing writing should be performed automatically by the program, and in others it should occur only when the user tells the program to write the files. Which way you do this depends mainly upon the long-term value of the data the user is working with. For example, if the program is used to build some sort of permanent database, then file writing should usually be done automatically to protect against the user's forgetting to do so. On the other hand, if the program is used to perform some sort of analysis—for example, to evaluate alternative real estate investments—then the user may or may not want to save the data left over at the end. In this case, the file should be written only when the user gives an explicit command to do so.

Making the efficiency-safety tradeoff and deciding whether or not to write files automatically require a careful analysis, and we have no simple formula to offer you here. The foregoing is intended mainly to raise your consciousness about these issues and the importance of considering them during design.

While there are no simple formulas for making these design tradeoffs, there are some simple guidelines that can help you write files efficiently and safely, regardless of what tradeoffs you make.

First, never write an existing file unless it has first been read. If you permit your program to do otherwise, then old data may be overwritten. In some cases this may be what the user wants. If so, make sure the user is given the chance to verify the choice of overwriting the file before proceeding.

Second, never write a file unless it needs to be written to. If the file has been opened and used in the program, but no change has been made to it, there is no need to rewrite it. How do you know whether a change has been made? Here, at last, we arrive at the subject of *write flags*. A write flag is a string or variable that your program sets when a data entry is made. It follows that, if no entry is made, no flag is set. Later on, when it comes time to write the file, your program uses this flag to test whether or not to proceed. For example, suppose that you have this data-entry routine in your program:

```
3400   REM—Data entry—
3410   FLAG$ = "UP"
3420   INPUT "Type in your name:";NAMES$
```

Line 3410 sets the Write Flag; that is, defines the string FLAG$ = "UP." This means that the data-entry routine has been executed. The flag is not set otherwise. Now, when your program calls the write subroutine, include a line such as 6410 in it:

```
6400   REM—Write file—
6410   IF FLAG$< >"UP" THEN RETURN
```

The write subroutine is not executed unless FLAG$ is "UP." (Incidentally, the RETURN at the end of line 6410 should really be a GOTO to the RETURN statement in the subroutine to conform with good programming practice, but it is a little easier to illustrate this way.) Be sure to reset FLAG$ = " " after the file has been written.

Now, a bit about safety. If your program writes files automatically, it is a good idea to have it do so before chaining to another subprogram, when exiting a data-entry module, and when the user quits the program (for example, by selecting the last option on the main menu). Chaining is always a bit risky, no matter how carefully it is done, and it is best to have those data entries stored in a file when your program starts to walk the tightrope.

If your program has a data-entry module (usually a good idea), then the logical time to write the file is when leaving that module. Presumably, the user enters it to make changes, and leaves it to do something else. Anything can happen afterward, so write the file, and get the user off the hook.

If your program takes care of file writing within a data-entry module, then there is no need to worry about signing off with the data still unwritten. Otherwise, this is about the most obvious place to write the file. Be honest—have you ever quit a program after a data-entry session and then realized that you forgot to write the file? Remember what it felt like?

The Well-Read File

Just as you want to be both efficient and safe in the way you handle file writing, you must be concerned with these two factors when it comes to reading files.

Do not read a file unless necessary. If your program has several different files, and makes use of different ones at different times or in different parts of the program, map out the various requirements and manage them carefully. For example, suppose that your program is organized into three modules. Module 1 requires a file called DATA. Module 2 requires a file called DATA and another called CATEGORIES. Module 3 requires files DATA, CATEGORIES, and BONUS. To assure that you read only the files necessary, insert some file reading control logic to assess which files have been read, check which files need reading, and read the necessary files.

There are a number of other variations on this same theme, but they all boil down to the idea of reading only when necessary.

Chapter 9

Documentation

Most programmers regard documentation as a necessary evil and about as exciting as a telephone book, the Dewey decimal system, or the table of organization of a large bureaucracy. However, this is a misperception—at least in the eyes of one young novice programmer who took enough interest in it to seek the Ultimate Truth on the subject. This programmer (his name was Fred) trekked many miles and underwent many difficult trials in search of answers. Through his efforts, he discovered the existence of the High Guru of Programming, who resides in an ashram on a mountaintop in the Far East. Fred obtained an audience with the master, and the following is the substance of their conversation, transcribed from the original parchment transcript. Figure numbers have been added to integrate the master's drawings into this chapter, but the content of the dialogue is otherwise unchanged.

Their conversation took place in a great hall. Fred sat on the floor. The master—an elderly man with long, gray beard, dressed in saffron robes— sat in the lotus position atop a high, golden pedestal. Herewith, their conversation.

SYSTEM DOCUMENTATION

"Tell me, master—what is system documentation?"

"A general definition is that it is information that tells how a program works. It is written by programmers for programmers. It consists of information inside a program in the form of remarks and of written information that is outside of the program."

"Why should I document my program?"

"For two reasons. First, to communicate to other programmers how your program works. This will enable them to fix it if something goes wrong or if they want to modify it. Second, because you will forget. Without documenting your program, you will forget many of its details—what the variables stand for, program control flow, how different subroutines work."

"When should I document my program?"

"Before, during, and after you have written it. The more you do before, the better. When you plan a program, you can document many things: variable assignments, the design of files, record layouts, what flags are used. Some documentation is best prepared when coding the program. This is the time to put remarks in code, for example. Also, if you add new functions, arrays, or variables, or change file or record layouts, document them as your code.

"After you finish your program, wrap up loose ends. Clean up your documentation. Do what you should have done earlier, but did not have time to."

"Pray, tell, master, how should I use remarks in my program?"

"Use them freely, liberally—like the signs that mark the streets, parks, monuments, buildings, tunnels, movie houses, singles' bars, art galleries, public utilities, dumps, and famous citizens' homes in a city. Leave no mysteries. Tell your secrets. Label your program modules, submodules, subsubmodules, and so forth. Label your subroutines. Describe the action. Tell what is going on inside your program."

"How much of my program should be remarks?"

"Somewhere between 10 percent and 30 percent of all program statements should be remarks." [The master does not equivocate.—EDITOR]

"But won't this make my program slower and use up valuable memory?"

"Yes and no. Even if you use many remarks, they do not have a significant effect on program speed. Remark statements are executed quickly. They affect memory in proportion to the number of remarks you use. If memory and speed are serious problems in your program, compile it or compress it by using a file-compression utility. But always keep the source code version of the program for changes."

"What written documentation should I prepare?"

"That depends on how complex your program is and whether you are preparing the documentation for yourself or others. The more complex the program, the more documentation you need. If you are writing it for other programmers, you need more than if it is for yourself. Select what you need from this list:

- List of functions and their definitions (Fig. 9-1)—Tell what each function does and what its arguments stand for.
- Lists of variables (Fig. 9-2)—List each global variable and tell what it stands for. List local variables alphabetically.
- List of arrays and what each stands for (Fig.

```
               PROGRAM FUNCTIONS

FUNCTION     PURPOSE
--------     -----------------------------------
FN C1 (X)    Rounds X to one decimal place
FN C2 (X)    Rounds X to two decimal places
FN D(R)      Calculates data file number based on record
             number R
-

-

-

FN Z(Z)      Locates last byte in final field of record Z
```

Fig. 9-1. Suggested format for documenting user-defined functions.

```
DEFINITIONS OF PROGRAM VARIABLES

    VARIABLE     PURPOSE
    --------     ---------------------------
    M            Menu name
    M$           Menu number
    O            Presentation order
    T            Trial number (1-8)
    I            Target number (1-16)
    J            Data argument
    T            Time increment
```

Fig. 9-2. Suggested format for documenting program variables.

9-3)—Do this just like your listing of variables. If you want to simplify things, make one list that includes variables and arrays.

- Subroutine table (Fig. 9-4)—Prepare tables that give the function (what the subroutine does), arguments, and line number of each subroutine.
- File descriptions—Provide detailed descriptions of content and variables, strings, and arrays used. [See Chapter 8 for details—EDITOR]
- Flow charts—Do not use these for everything. Use them to explain parts of the program where the control flow is complex."

"Are there any ways to simplify things?"

"One trick for preparing lists of functions, variables, or arrays is to make up a dummy program. List each item on a separate line, followed by a remark giving its definition (Fig 9-5). This is easier to update than paper documentation.

"Another trick is to create a dummy program called "subroutines" that contains a consolidated listing of all your subroutines. If your program consists of several subprograms, it is easier to document your subroutines once in your common subroutine listing than to document each subprogram separately."

"Do you have any other advice to offer, master?"

"Yes. Be conscientious about documentation. Be compulsive about details. Be consistent. The programmer you save may be yourself."

```
DEFINITIONS OF PROGRAM ARRAYS

    ARRAY        PURPOSE
    --------     ---------------------------
    M$(4)        Menu options
    V%(21)       Row number
    H%(21)       Column number
    T$(12)       Target names
    R%(128)      Minimum number of responses to targets (1-128)
    T(8)         Total time per trial
```

Fig. 9-3. Suggested format for documenting program arrays.

```
--------------------------------------------------------------------
Title          : "Deluxe GET" Data Entry
Function       : Prints prompt in reverse video and
                 collects keyed entries from user
Line no.       : 3010
Arguments      : V - screen row (1-24)
                 H - screen column (1-80)
                 P$ - prompt

Returns        : User entry as A$
Side effects   : V, H, P$, A$ assignments affected
--------------------------------------------------------------------
```

Fig. 9-4. Suggested format for documenting program subroutines.

"Thank you, master. You have been very helpful. I have one final question. How can I make my life meaningful?"

"That is not my department. I suggest you find yourself a good shrink. However, you will be doing yourself and other programmers a service by documenting your programs carefully."

USER DOCUMENTATION

User documentation is the information that tells people how to use your program. Usually it is in written form and is labeled a User's Guide or something similar. However, you can also have documentation within your program. A help screen

is one example of such documentation.

In the last few years, people involved in the microcomputer industry have been paying increased attention to user documentation. Program publishers, particularly, have come to realize that the quality of a program's documentation may very well decide its fate. If its documentation is good, then program purchasers will be able to learn about the program quickly and use it efficiently. On the other hand, if the documentation is poor, then they must stumble along on their own and learn by trial and error. When they are forced to do this, often they feel frustrated, angry, and cheated enough to return their program to the computer store, issu-

```
1 REM SAVE"FIG9-5",A
10 REM--"Dummy" Program--
20 REM for documentation purposes only
30 REM--Variables & Arrays--
40 H%(21):REM column number
50 I:REM target number (1-16)
60 J:REM data argument
70 M:REM menu name
80 M$:REM menu number
90 M$(4):REM menu options
100 O:REM presentation order
110 R%(128):REM minimum number of responses
120 T:REM time increment
130 T$(12):REM target names
140 V%(21):REM row number
```

Fig. 9-5. Dummy program consisting of list of variables and arrays and REMark lines containing relevant information.

ing a vote of no confidence in the publisher. Does this sound familiar? You may have done this yourself. I have.

On the other hand, if you write programs strictly for yourself, you probably do not really need a user's guide. You have what is necessary in your head. User's guides are important when you write programs that others use, or that you have ambitions of publishing.

The logical person to write a program user's guide is the program's author. This does not always work out well, however. First, many programmers do not like to write documentation, or feel that they are not very good at it. A few hard-headed programmers do not actually see the need for it. Since they understand how their program works so thoroughly, it may be difficult for them to take the point of view of a program user who is completely naive about it. As a consequence, the program may be poorly documented, if at all.

On the positive side, the user documentation being prepared for commercial microcomputer programs is definitely improving. There is also a good deal more awareness these days about the importance of such documentation. This awareness is having its effect on the consciousness of programmers.

Writing a user's guide or designing help screens for your program is no party. The subject itself does not cause one's pulse to quicken with excitement, either. Still, this is a very important subject for you or anyone who writes computer programs.

It is important, for example, to Fred, the novice programmer who was introduced earlier in this chapter. You may recall that Fred, in a quest for information concerning system documentation, sought out and visited the High Guru of Programming, from whom he learned a version of the Sublime Truth (or something like that) concerning system documentation.

Since our current subject is of similar ilk, let us rejoin Fred as he once again confronts the Master. You will recall that Fred has trekked many miles and undergone many trials to reach the High Guru. The scene is as before: Fred sits on the floor

of the great hall and the master—an elderly man with a long, gray beard, dressed in saffron robes—sits in the lotus position atop a high, golden pedestal. Once again, the questioning begins:

"Tell me, master what is user documentation?"

"User documentation explains your program to users. It comes in two forms: external and internal.

"External documentation is on paper. Internal documentation is within the program. It consists of help screens, directions, and other information that helps the user with the program."

"Why should I provide user documentation?"

"Idiot! If you do not, how is the user to know what to do with your program? People do not pick up such information by ESP, you know.

"Besides preparing good user documentation is a humane, social act. It is an attempt to communicate information to others and to spare them the frustration, pain, and anger of attempting to use a program without fully understanding it.

"Do you grasp these concepts?"

"Yes, master. I humbly beg your forgiveness for my stupidity."

"The master forgives all."

"You mentioned two types of documentation, master—external and internal. Which is best?"

"It is not an either-or question. Both have advantages and disadvantages. Look at them as complementary.

"Internal documentation is good for presenting reminders, warnings, quick reference information, and other things that the user might want to know on the spot without having to look in a manual. It is not very good for presenting long and detailed descriptions of how a program works, or other information that requires extended text.

"Your external documentation, or user's guide, should be the bible for your program. Put the details in it."

"Should some information go in one and not the other?"

"There is no simple answer to this question. It depends on your program. However, in general, the best practice is to make sure that your external documentation contains everything, even what is in the internal documentation. Another way of looking at it is that the internal documentation contains highlights of the external documentation."

"Where should I start in preparing user documentation?"

"The same place you start in designing your program. At least I hope you do. Do you follow?"

"With the user, master?"

"Good! I have hope for you.

"Decide who your user will be. Try to determine as much about the user as you can—age, intelligence, education, computer sophistication, and so forth. It is impossible to know everything, of course. But the type of program you are writing gives you a good idea. For example, the guide for your game program should be written as if to a child, since many users will be children. The guide for your real estate investment analysis program should be written to an adult with financial sophistication, but not great computer sophistication. Your assembly language programming utility should be written as if to a sophisticated programmer.

"Know thy audience, and write accordingly."

"What should I put in my written user's guide?"

"This depends upon the type of program. The more complex the program, the more you should include.

"Every user's guide needs a section that tells how to set the program up. It explains what hardware is required to use the program, any special software requirements, and how to get the program up and running.

"Many user's guides contain a tutorial. A tutorial is a step-by-step lesson that leads the user by the hand through the program. It tells the user to do certain things at the computer, and thereby demonstrates the program's features. It also helps the user build confidence by using the program successfully. In complex programs such as word processors, database managers, and such, a tutorial is required. Simpler programs do not require it as much. But is always a good idea to include a tutorial anyway.

"Every user's guide should contain reference information that explains how to use the program.

This differs from a tutorial in that it is comprehensive and does not actually demonstrate every detail of the program with the user participating. However, it contains the same basic source information—in greater detail, of course—and from it the user can figure out how to work the program. The reference information should cover such things as the required procedures for executing the program's functions, descriptions of commands, and all the other technical details required for using the program. One way of thinking of it is as containing the program's *procedures* and *vocabulary*. The procedures are the steps the program user must take to make the program do its job. The vocabulary is the content of commands, special terminology used in the program, and the names of everything.

"Just providing this information is not enough, however. You must also make it easy for the user to find and make effective use of what is there. Make sure you include a table of contents and an index. These are extra work for you, but they make it much easier for the user.

"In writing your guide, remember the value of concrete examples. You cannot simply explain how to perform some program function abstractly. You must make it real to the reader by using specific examples that illustrate your concepts."

"Tell me about internal documentation, master."

"First, make it voluntary, not required, for the user to review such information. A help screen helps the user the first time he or she sees it, but not the fourth time, and certainly not the 50th. Let the user decide when to look at help information.

"Make appropriate help information available where and when the user needs it. Do not put all your help information in one part of the program where it must be accessed at one time. Rather, distribute it throughout the program so that the user can get the answer to the question being asked while using the program. For example, if the user is performing some complex data-entry function, and gets confused, make it possible to access a help screen in that part of the program."

"What kinds of information should be included in internal documentation?"

"The most obvious things to put there are simple things such as warnings, directions for performing a procedure, a brief explanation of how the particular part of the program works, or lists and definitions of relevant program vocabulary (such as names of commands, programs, and such). You might, for example, make it possible for the user to call up a help screen with such information by pressing one of the function keys. Things such as this might be regarded as reference information.

"You can also be more ambitious. You might, for example, create an animated demonstration that shows on the screen how the program works. You know, have the program type in the entries, generate the screens, and the like—and every once in a while display a screen with a written explanation of what is going on. A demonstration such as this leaves the user more or less passive, watching what is happening, but not really participating in the action.

"What is much nicer is to have an interactive tutorial that is a sort of animated extension of the written tutorial in the user's guide. You might create a set of screens that enable the user to try out various aspects of the program, all the while providing feedback on the screens themselves or with separate screens that interpret the user's entries and tell what to do next."

"Thank you, master. I am ready to begin now. Do you have any final advice for me?"

"The user.

"Think of the user before you start writing, and as you write your documentation. Also think of the user after you have finished the job. If you can, try out your attempts on users and listen to what they say. Modify your documentation based on their comments.

"Remember, your documentation is for users. It is not enough for you or your sophisticated programmer friends to like what you have done. Your users must like it, too."

"I have listened, learned, and will abide by what you say, master. I have another question."

"Ask it."

"How did you become so wise?"

"I was born that way. Any other questions?"

"Yes, master. You do not have any electricity up here in the ashram. How do you run your computers?"

"We do not have computers. We had one once, but it distracted us from our contemplations, and so we painted it gold and made it into the pedestal on which I sit."

"But then, master, how do you know so much about computers?"

"Recognize, novice, that in life some things are simply unexplainable."

Appendix A

Apple II-Series
Addendum to Chapter 8

This appendix applies strictly to the Apple II series of computers. It contains a discussion of file write and read subroutines for the Apple. It is suggested that Apple programmers review the material in this appendix concurrently with Chapter 8.

The appendix is divided into two parts. The first covers sequential files; the second, random access files.

SEQUENTIAL FILES

A sequential file cannot be read unless it exists, and it is created when it is first written. Thus, the first requirement for using a file is to write it.

Writing the File

To write the file, your program must do three things: open the file, send data to it, and close the file.

You open a file by using an appropriate file-opening statement. The file-opening statement must be preceded by a printed Ctrl + D. Ctrl + D is

typically defined as a character string early in the program to avoid printing its CHR$ form in file handling routines. That is, Ctrl + D is defined as a string such as D$—a logical mnemonic—like this:

```
10   D$ = CHR$(4)
```

After D$ has initially been defined, it can be used throughout the program as needed. Some programmers define D$ to include a carriage return character—CHR$(13)—like this:

```
10   D$ = CHR$(13) + CHR$(4)
```

The reason for doing this is to assure that the file will be opened properly if the file-opening statement is executed following a line that does not contain a carriage return. For example, if an attempt is made to open a file following a line that prints a string with a semicolon at the end (to suppress the carriage return), then the file will not open. Similar problems occur if you attempt to open a file immediately after a GET statement. Including the

CHR$(13) as part of D$ prevents such problems, but has the side effect of causing the screen to scroll as each D$ is printed. In general, the best practice is to define D$ simply as CHR$(4), and then to make sure that you never attempt to execute a file-handling statement without first issuing a carriage return in program code. (You will know you have blown it when you see your file-opening statement printed on the screen and the disk drive does nothing.)

The syntax of the simplest file-opening statement is:

PRINT D$;"OPEN*filename*"

The only parameter of this statement is *filename*, which is the file name—a character string. For example, to open a file named SEQFILE, this statement would be used:

10   PRINT D$;"OPENSEQFILE"

This statement will open SEQFILE on the default drive and slot.

Drive number and slot number can be included in the opening statement, if needed, like this:

PRINT D$;"OPEN*filename,Ddrive,Sslot*"

With this more elaborate syntax, *drive* is drive number (1 or 2) and *slot* is slot number (1-6). For example, to open SEQFILE in drive number 1 and slot number 6, this statement would be used:

10   PRINT D$;"OPENSEQFILE,D1,S6"

Since different program users may have put the file being accessed into different drives and slots, it is best to make drive number and slot number user-defined parameters. This can be done by modifying the file-opening syntax like this:

10   PRINT D$;"OPENSEQFILE,D";D;"S,";S

Here, D is the number of the drive and S is the number of the slot. Most program users will use one or two disk drives in a single slot—typically slot

6—and for most purposes it is adequate to omit the "S,";S parameter, giving you a general file-opening statement like this:

10   PRINT D$;"OPENSEQFILE,D";D

This appendix will use this type of file-opening statement in all examples. If your code does not require the D parameter, then you can omit it from your code. Similarly, if your code needs to define slot number as well as drive number, add the S parameter, as illustrated above.

After the file has been opened, a second statement must be executed to indicate whether the file will be written to or read. The syntax of the statement to show that the file is to be written to is as follows:

PRINT D$;"WRITE*filename*"

For example, to set up SEQFILE to write, this statement would be used:

20   PRINT D$;"WRITESEQFILE"

(Note that drive number and slot number parameters are not required in this statement.)

In sum, to open SEQFILE to write, these lines would be used:

10   PRINT D$;"OPENSEQFILE,D";D
20   PRINT D$;"WRITESEQFILE"

Once the file has been opened, data can be sent to it using PRINT statements. Each print statement sends a separate item of data to the file. Each item should have its own PRINT statement. (It is possible to send several items of data to a file with a single statement by separating them with commas, but inadvisable, since they are sent to the file as they would be to the separate print fields of the screen—with extra spaces and without their separators. The resulting file will contain much empty space and cannot be read properly, since its data items are not properly separated.) For example, to send the variables A, B$, and C% to SEQFILE, you would use expressions of this form:

```
30   PRINT A
40   PRINT B$
50   PRINT C%
```

When these statements send data to the file, a carriage return character is inserted between each variable, which serves as a delimiter, separating adjacent characters when the file is read.

If an array must be written to the file, the best way is with a FOR-NEXT loop. For example, to write elements 0 through 5 of the real array A(n) to the file, use code like this:

```
60   REM—REAL ARRAY—
70   FOR A = 0 TO 5
80   PRINT A(A)
90   NEXT
```

After the data have been sent to the file, the file must be closed with the CLOSE statement. The syntax of this statement is as follows:

PRINT D$;"CLOSE*filename*"

For example, to close SEQFILE, use the statement PRINT D$;"CLOSESEQFILE". The CLOSE statement can be used without a file number, but if it is, then it will close all files currently open. Thus, it is best to include the *filename* parameter.

Let's combine these pieces together to create a subroutine that will write SEQFILE. Assume that SEQFILE consists of three arrays—string, real, and integer—and three sets of string, real, and integer variables. The resulting subroutine is shown in Fig. 8-5 (see Chapter 8).

Reading the File

The procedure for reading a sequential file, like that for writing one, has three parts: open the file, read in data, and close the file. Figure 8-8 (see Chapter 8) contains a subroutine for reading the sequential file created by the subroutine shown in Fig. 8-5.

Except for line numbers, the two subroutines are very similar. The file-opening and closing statements are identical. The line following the file-opening statement contains READ instead of WRITE. All PRINT statements have been changed to INPUT statements. Note also that the variables read by lines 6410 – 6430 are separated by commas and do not have separate INPUT statements; it is perfectly acceptable to read a file this way, although it is not acceptable to write one with data elements separated by commas. As this subroutine is nearly the image of the one previously discussed, it is left to the reader to sort out.

RANDOM ACCESS FILES

A random access file is created by opening the file and writing data to it. Simply opening the file creates the file on disk and adds its name to the file directory. However, an attempt to read the file—which is empty—will in all probability produce an End of Data error.

Writing the File

The main differences between the code for sequential and random access files are the statements that open the file and tell DOS whether the file is to be written or read. The syntax of the file-opening statement is:

PRINT D$;"OPEN*filename,*L*record length,*D*disk drive,*S*slot number*"

This statement is a close relative of that for opening sequential files, the only difference being that a *record length* must be declared following L. Moreover, if we dispense with the *slot number* parameter, as was done with the sequential file code, the syntax is simplified further.

To illustrate, let us create the statement to open RANDFILE, which has a record length of 357 bytes. Although record length was computed to be 357 bytes, let us set it to 400 to allow a safety margin. Further, let us ignore slot number and make the *disk drive* parameter a variable. The following statement will meet the requirements just defined:

```
7010   PRINT D$;"OPENRANDFILE,L400,D";D
```

In addition to opening the file, program code must tell whether the file is to be written or read. The syntax of the required statement is as follows:

PRINT D$;"WRITE*filename,R*record number"

Record number is obviously the number of the record that is to be written. For example, to write record number 5 of RANDFILE, this statement would be used:

7020   PRINT D$;"WRITERANDFILE,R5"

And, as before, record number can (and should) be defined as a variable for convenience in accessing records. This is how it is done:

7020   PRINT D$;"WRITERANDFILE,R";R

So much for opening the file and setting whether the file is to be written to or read. The rest of the file handling code is identical to that for sequential files. Data are sent to the file with PRINT statements, and the file is closed with a statement like this:

PRINT D$;"CLOSE*filename*"

In the example of interest, this file-closing statement would be used:

7110   PRINT D$;"CLOSERANDFILE"

Figure 8-12 (see Chapter 8) contains a subroutine to open the random access file RANDFILE, send data to it, and then close it.

Reading the File

The code to read a random access file is very similar to that for writing it. The opening and closing statements are identical for both purposes. The statement following the file opening statement differs. When the file is to be read, we must substitute READ for WRITE. PRINT statements become INPUT statements. Figure 8-15 (see Chapter 8) is the listing of a subroutine that will read the subroutine written by the subroutine shown in Fig. 8-12.

Appendix B

Commodore 64 Addendum to Chapters 4, 5, and 8

T his appendix applies strictly to Commodore 64 computers. It contains additional discussion of topics covered in Chapter 4, 5, and 8. Subjects covered include cursor control, clearing a line or range of lines, using INPUT# for data entry, and file write and read subroutines.

The first two subjects extend the discussion in Chapter 4, the third that in Chapter 5, and the last that in Chapter 8. It is suggested that C-64 programmers review the material in this appendix concurrently with the relevant chapter.

CURSOR CONTROL

Cursor control with the C-64's BASIC 2.0 is possible but cumbersome. To move the cursor to a particular absolute vertical and horizontal position on the screen, three statements are required:

- Move the cursor to the home (top left) position by printing CHR$(19) or CHR$(147).
- Move the cursor down the required number of rows by printing CHR$(17)—equivalent to

pressing Cursor Down key.
- Move the cursor across the required number of columns by printing CHR$(29)—equivalent to pressing cursor right key.

By combining these three statements, you can create subroutines to move the cursor to any position on the screen. This works, but is slow.

Another technique for cursor control is to create character strings consisting of quoted Cursor Down or Cursor Right keystrokes, and then to take substrings of these and print them. This has the effect of moving the cursor the number of spaces equal to the length of the substring. If you want to stick with BASIC, then you can use one of these techniques.

A better way to control the cursor is to use assembly-language subroutines. These are faster and more powerful than what you can do with BASIC. Before you can use these subroutines you must first load them into memory. Figure B-1 is the listing of lines of code which read DATA state-

```
500 REM--LOAD ASSEMBLY LANGUAGE SUBROUTINES--
510 C0=49152
520 READ B
530 POKE C0,D:C0=C0+1
540 IF D=0 THEN READ D:POKE C0,D:C0=C0+1:IF D=0 GOTO 880
550 GOTO 520
560 DATA 173,72,160,133,20,173,73,160
570 DATA 133,21,160,6,169,96,153,232
580 DATA 3,177,20,153,231,3,136,208
590 DATA 248,160,3,169,0,153,252,3
600 DATA 136,16,250,32,121,0,201,0
610 DATA 240,26,201,58,240,22,230,122
620 DATA 208,2,230,123,200,132,251,32
630 DATA 232,3,164,251,165,20,153,252
640 DATA 3,184,80,223,24,173,252,3
650 DATA 42,42,42,42,42,42,144,1
660 DATA 42,141,252,3,56,32,240,255
670 DATA 173,253,3,240,2,170,202,142
680 DATA 253,3,173,254,3,240,2,168
690 DATA 136,140,254,3,192,40,176,30
700 DATA 173,253,3,201,26,176,23,169
710 DATA 255,44,252,3,112,23,8,174
720 DATA 253,3,172,254,3,24,32,240
730 DATA 255,40,240,110,80,7,169,161
740 DATA 141,204,5,208,101,16,5,169
750 DATA 25,141,255,3,173,255,3,208
760 DATA 6,173,253,3,141,255,3,205
770 DATA 253,3,144,226,201,26,176,222
780 DATA 173,254,3,201,40,176,215,206
790 DATA 255,3,169,0,133,251,169,4
800 DATA 133,252,174,253,3,240,16,24
810 DATA 165,251,105,40,133,251,165,252
820 DATA 105,0,133,252,202,208,240,172
830 DATA 254,3,169,32,145,251,200,192
840 DATA 40,144,247,152,160,0,24,101
850 DATA 251,133,251,144,2,230,252,238
860 DATA 253,3,173,255,3,205,253,3
870 DATA 176,224,96,0,0
880 C0=49152
```

Fig. B-1. C-64 assembly-language subroutine loader which gives access to SYScalls for various screen-clearing and cursor-positioning operations.

ments and then POKE into memory the values comprising the machine-language subroutines.

These subroutines use an area of memory from decimal 49152 up. This memory area may be used by your BASIC and DOS extension or other software and interfere with the proper use of the subroutines. Two solutions are to relocate the subroutines or to deactivate the software. Relocation is very simple. Line 510 contains the statement C0 = 49152. This is the starting point in memory of the subroutines. Various values are poked into this decimal location and into higher locations in memory until line 540

reads a value of D = 0, which signals the end of the DATA statements (see line 870).

Now, let us try out an assembly language subroutine. You call one of these subroutines with the SYS command, followed by the subroutine's parameters. The syntax is as follows:

SYS *C0,OPCODE, parameter 1, parameter 2*

C0 is the memory location (decimal) at which the machine language subroutine is accessed, that is, decimal location 49152. *OPCODE* is a value between 0 and 4 that tells the computer which type of subroutine you are calling. The OPCODE for the cursor-positioning subroutine is 0. With an OPCODE of 0, *parameter 1* is the cursor's vertical position (1 – 24), measured down from the top of the display. *Parameter 2* is the horizontal position (1 – 40), measured over from the left edge of the display. Putting together these pieces, a call for the cursor-positioning subroutine looks like this:

SYS C0,0,V,H

V is the cursor's vertical position and H is its horizontal position. For example, to move the cursor to row 15 and column 23, use the statement SYS C0,0,15,23 in your program.

Since this is an assembly language subroutine, it is much faster than BASIC. It gives the C-64 programmer access to a cursor-positioning statement equivalent to the IBM PC's LOCATE.

CLEARING A SINGLE LINE

You can clear part or all of a single line by using the assembly-language subroutine (see Fig. B-1) with an OPCODE of 1. The syntax of the line-clearing subroutine is as follows:

SYS C0,1,V,H

This SYScall clears to the end of a line from cursor location V (vertical position) and H (horizontal position). For example:

SYS C0,1,22,20   clears columns 20 – 40 of row 22
SYS C0,1,4   clears all of row 4

Use this call directly in code or in a subroutine. Lines 1300 – 1320 of Fig. 4-10 (see Chapter 4) are the subroutine form of this SYScall.

CLEARING TO END OF SCREEN

You can clear from the cursor position to the end of the screen by using an OPCODE of 3. The syntax of the to-end-of-screen clearing subroutine is as follows:

SYS C0,3,V,H

This SYScall clears to the end of the screen from cursor location V (vertical position) and H (horizontal position). Some examples:

SYS C0,3,1,1   clears the entire screen
SYS C0,3,15   clears everything from row 15 down
SYS C0,3,15,20   clears everything to the right of column 20 in row 15, and all of rows 16 – 25

Use this call directly in code, or in subroutines. Lines 1350 – 1370 of Fig. 4-14 (see Chapter 4) are the subroutine form of this SYScall.

CLEARING A RANGE OF LINES

You can clear a range of lines by using an OPCODE of 4. The syntax of the range-of-lines-clearing subroutine is as follows:

SYS C0,4,V1,0,V2

This SYScall clears all lines between vertical locations V1 (top vertical position) and V2 (bottom vertical position). For example:

SYS C0,4,1,0,10   clears rows 1 through 10
SYS C0,4,15,0,17   clears rows 15 through 17

A subroutine form of this SYScall is shown in Fig. 4-17 (see Chapter 4).

USING INPUT# FOR DATA ENTRY

Most C-64 programmers are unaware that it is possible to collect data from the keyboard with the INPUT# statement. This statement is most commonly used to read in data from data files. Before it works, the program must OPEN a file and specify a device from which data are to be read in. The OPEN statement has this syntax:

OPEN *file number, device number*

For reading or writing a data file, *file number* is some number between 2 and 14, and *device number* is 8 (drive #1) or 9 (drive #2).

The keyboard has a device number (1), and so you can OPEN a file and read in data from it. To illustrate, let us set file number to 1 and write a little program to OPEN and read the keyboard. Here it is:

```
10   OPEN 1,0
20   PRINT "ENTER DATA: ";
30   INPUT #1,A$
40   PRINT
50   CLOSE 1
```

If you try this program out, you discover that the INPUT# statement works much like the INPUT statement except for the following differences:

- No question mark prints on the screen, although there is a flashing cursor.
- Pressing the Return key with no typed entry has no effect.

In other respects, the two forms of INPUT work identically. Using INPUT# requires additional code to do the following:

- Open and close the keyboard for input.
- Print the prompt—INPUT# does not permit an embedded prompt string.
- Print a carriage return after the entry has been taken (line 40)—INPUT# does not do this automatically.

Since INPUT# does not respond to a null entry, it cannot inadvertently pick up its variable's previously assigned value (as it will with C-64's INPUT statement). To illustrate, add this line to the listing shown above:

```
5   A$ = "OLD ASSIGNMENT"
```

Now run the program. Press the Return key with no typed entry.

As you discover, what happens is that the cursor flashes contentedly away, and ignores the Return key press. The only way to move on is to type in a more substantial entry—one or more characters. Type in a letter and press Return and the display responds.

Using the INPUT# in a program requires slightly more code than using INPUT, but the extra effort is well worth it in terms of increased error protection and more professional-appearing data entry prompts. INPUT# is the preferred method to collect keystrokes in the majority of C-64 programs. It is the C-64 equivalent of the IBM PC's LINE INPUT statement (see Chapter 5).

WRITING SEQUENTIAL FILES

Figure 8-6 (see Chapter 8) contains the code for creating and writing a sequential file called SEQFILE. The write subroutine consists of lines 6010 – 6200. Let us go through this subroutine line by line.

Line 6020 contains the file OPEN statement. The syntax of this statement is as follows:

OPEN *file number, device number, channel number,* "@0:*file name,*SEQ,W"

File number and *channel number* do not have to be the same, but it simplifies things to make them the same. Think of them both as *file number*, and forget about *channel number*. These can be any numbers between 2 and 14. Figure 8-6 uses *file number* and *channel number* of 2. *Device number* is 8 if the disk is in drive 1, or 9 if it is in drive 2. Figure 8-6 uses Device Number 8. Filename is whatever you choose to call the file—it is SEQFILE in Fig. 8-6. SEQ stands for SEQuential. W means Write (or use R for Read). Put all this together and you come up with line 6020.

So much for opening the file. From here on it gets easier. Lines 6040 – 6180 contain PRINT# statements that PRINT the data into the file. The number following the PRINT# statement is the *channel number* (2), as used in the OPEN statement on line 6020.

Lines 6040 – 6140 print three string, real, and

integer arrays to the file. Each array is printed with a FOR-NEXT loop. Each element of the array can be printed separately, but this is not as efficient as using a FOR-NEXT loop.

Lines 6150 – 6180 print string, real, and integer variables to the file. Each item must have its own PRINT# statement, as in line 6160. It is possible to print several items to the file with a single PRINT# statement by separating the items with commas. For example, you can print all three items with this statement:

PRINT#2,A$,A0,A%

Do not do this. The reason is that, when DOS prints this to the file, it separates each item by eight spaces, just as if printing information to separate fields on your display. This leaves a lot of extra, wasted space in the file.

Line 6190 contains the CLOSE statement, which CLOSE the file. Line 6200 contains the RETURN, which marks the end of the subroutine. When you want to create the file, make sure that arrays have been dimensioned and then just give a GOSUB 6010. There is one additional requirement. DOS has a problem with null strings—strings whose content has not yet been defined. To illustrate, if you write an undefined string to a file, C-64 DOS acts like nothing is there. It does not put a separator (,) between the null string and the next item. This means that the file is not properly created.

The solution to this problem is to define every element of the array before writing that array to a file. DOS does not have this problem with real or integer arrays, so you do not have to assign their values before writing the file.

READING SEQUENTIAL FILES

The procedure for reading a sequential file also has three steps: OPEN file, INPUT# data, and CLOSE file. Figure 8-9 (see Chapter 8) contains a subroutine for reading the sequential file created by the subroutine in Fig. 8-6.

Line 6260 opens the file for reading. This line is identical to the OPEN file statement used in the write subroutine except that the last character is R (for Read) instead of W (for Write).

Lines 6280 – 6420 read in the data from the file with INPUT# statements. The INPUT# statement is analogous to the PRINT# statement used in the write routine. However, in using the INPUT# statement, no harm is done by INPUT#ing several variables on the same line, separated by commas. The number following the INPUT# statement is the *channel number*, as used in the OPEN statement on line 6260. Line 6430 closes the file. And line 6440 ends the subroutine with a RETURN statement.

RANDOM ACCESS FILES

The C-64 can use two different types of random access files. These may, for the sake of discussion, be called Type 1 and Type 2. Type 1 files require you to worry about blocks, sectors, tracks, pointers, and other matters that most computers leave to their operating systems, although these files can be handy if you do machine-language programing. Type 2 files are much easier to work with since they are similar to standard BASIC random access files. This appendix covers Type 2 files (sometimes called ''relative'' files), but not Type 1 files. Most serious programs can be written very nicely with Type 2 files, and these files are also much easier to use.

To create a random access file, you must insert specific lines of code in your program to perform the act of file creation. The syntax of the required code is as follows:

OPEN *file number, device number, channel number,* ''*filename,*L,'' + CHR$(*record length)*

Let us make *file number* and *channel number* identical and set them to 6. *Device number* for one drive is 8. *Filename* is ''RANDFILE.'' *Record length* is 198. The code required to create the file is as follows:

```
20000   OPEN 6,8,6,"RANDFILE,L,"
          + CHR$(198)
```

There is no point in putting this code into a subroutine since it is only executed once. Locate it in your program where the file is to be created. For example, to create the file at line 20000, include these lines in your program:

```
20000   OPEN 6,8,6,"RANDFILE,L," +
        CHR$(198)
20010   CLOSE 6
```

The code for writing and reading a random access file has some similarities to that for a sequential file, and also some differences. In both cases, code is required to open and close the file at the start or end of a write or read operation. However, for a random access file, two channels must be opened—the command channel, and the channel to transmit the file data through. The syntax of the file OPEN statement for a random access file is simpler than that for a sequential file; it is shorter, does not require an R (read) or W (write) code, and is identical for both write and read operations. Finally, the PRINT# statements and INPUT# statements are identical in form for both sequential and random access files.

Three lines are required to OPEN the command channel, OPEN the file, and position the file pointer to read the required record.

The syntax of the statement for OPENing the command channel is:

OPEN *file number, device number, channel number*

Use 15 for *file number. Device number* is 8 for drive 1 or 9 for drive 2. Thus, using drive 1, this statement OPENs the command channel:

OPEN 15,8,15

The syntax of the statement for OPENing the file is:

OPEN *file number, drive number, channel number, "filename"*

Assume *file number* and *channel number* of 6 and a *filename* of RANDFILE. This statement will OPEN the file:

OPEN 6,8,6 "RANDFILE"

The tricky part, actually, is to position the file pointer—locate the record to be read. The syntax of this statement is as follows:

PRINT#15,"P"CHR$(*channel number*)
CHR$(*Rec.No.Lo byte*)CHR$(*Rec.No.Hi byte*)

Since the file contains many records, a statement (this one) must identify the record of interest. In this statement, the command channel (15) is used to direct DOS to the desired record. The "P" stands for Position; that is, the position the file pointer must go to to read the record.

CHR$ (*channel number*) identifies the channel number. In this example, *channel number* is the same as *file number* (6).

The next two CHR$ terms identify the record number in low-byte high-byte form. The actual record number, R, is computed from Rec.No.Lo (LR) and Rec.No.Hi (RH) according to this formula:

$$R = RL + 256 * RH$$

This is not the easiest way to indicate Record Number, but it does work. To illustrate how, let us consider a few examples. To find record number 50, use this statement:

PRINT #15,"P"CHR$(6)CHR$(50)CHR$(0)

To find record number 257, use this statement:

PRINT #15,"P"CHR$(6)CHR$(1)CHR$(1)

To find record number 720, use this statement:

PRINT #15,"P"CHR$(6)CHR$(208)CHR$(2)

If your file has fewer than 256 records, then forget about RH and set RL to R. That is, use this kind of statement in your code:

PRINT #15,"P"CHR$(6)CHR$(R)CHR$(0)

If your file has more than 255 records, then you must provide both arguments, RL and RH.

Assume that you want to locate record number 10 in RANDFILE. These lines will OPEN the file and position the pointer as required:

```
10  OPEN 15,8,15:REM OPEN COMMAND
    CHANNEL
20  OPEN 6,8,6:REM OPEN FILE
30  PRINT#15"P"CHR$(6)CHR$(10)CHR$(0)
    :REM POSITION POINTER
```

After OPENing the file in this manner, and positioning the record pointer, data may either be written to the file with PRINT# statements or read from the file with INPUT# statements. After so doing, the file is closed by closing both of the channels.

To illustrate, Fig. 8-13 (see Chapter 8) is the listing of a subroutine for writing RANDFILE. Let us go through this subroutine line by line.

Line 7010 calls subroutine 8000, which converts the single record number R to the low-byte/high-byte record numbers RL and RH. This conversion could be done in the file write subroutine itself, but since it is required in all subroutines that write or read random access files, it is more efficient to keep it separate.

Line 7020 OPENs the command channel. Line 7030 OPENs file channel 6. Line 7040 positions the record pointer. Lines 7050 – 7200 print data to the record with PRINT# statements. Line 7210 CLOSEs the file channel and line 7220 CLOSEs the command channel.

The only difference between the code for writing and reading a file is that PRINT# and INPUT# statements are substituted for one another. Figure 8-16 (see Chapter 8) is the listing of the subroutine for reading the random access file just described. Compare it with the listing shown in Fig. 8-14.

Index

Index

Other Bestsellers From TAB

☐ **469 PASCAL PROBLEMS WITH DETAILED SOLUTIONS—Veklerov**

Now this unique self-teaching guide makes it amazingly easy even for a novice programmer to master Pascal. With a total of 469 problems ranging from the most basic to advanced applications, the guide provides a unique learning opportunity for anyone who wants hands-on understanding of the Pascal language and its programming capabilities. 224 pp., 23 illus. 7″ × 10″.

Paper $14.95   **Hard $21.95**
Book No. 1997

☐ **TRUE BASIC® —A COMPLETE MANUAL**

Written by microcomputer programmer and consultant Henry Simpson, this invaluable guide covers all the main features of True BASIC including commands, statements, and functions, program control, input/output, file-handling, and even graphics. Simpson even supplies you with example programs that demonstrate all the programming functions that can be performed by True BASIC as opposed to Microsoft BASIC. 208 pp., 53 illus. 7″ × 10″.

Paper $14.95   **Hard $22.95**
Book No. 1970

☐ **SERIOUS PROGRAMMING FOR THE IBM® PC™/XT™/AT®**

Here's your key to learning how programs can be developed and designed for your own specific purposes to really do the job you need accomplished. You'll cover different aspects of program design, including using subroutines to build an effective subroutine library of your own. You get special tips on learning to write a user's guide and creating help screens. 208 pp., 113 illus. 7″ × 10″.

Paper $14.95   **Hard $21.95**
Book No. 1921

☐ **THE BASIC COOKBOOK—2nd Edition**

Covers every BASIC statement, function, command, and keyword in easy-to-use dictionary form—highlighted by plenty of program examples—so you can cook up a BASIC program in just about any dialect to do any job you want. Whether your interests are business, technical, hobby, or game playing, this revised 2nd edition of our all-time bestselling BASIC guide contains exactly what you want, when you want it! 168 pp., 57 illus.

Paper $7.95   **Hard $12.95**
Book No. 1855

☐ **TRUE BASIC® PROGRAMS AND SUBROUTINES**

Explore the powerful, built-in features of True BASIC—a new language that is destined to standardize microcomputer programming. Now professional programmer and consultant John Clark Craig shows you hands-on how True BASIC can make your programming easier and less time-consuming than traditional languages. You'll discover the features that make True BASIC unmatched: coherent syntax, compiled operating speed, greatly improved graphics capabilities, structured language features, and portability. 224 pp., 50 illus. 7″ × 10″.

Paper $16.95   **Hard $24.95**
Book No. 1990

☐ **SERIOUS PROGRAMMING FOR YOUR APPLE® II/IIe/IIc**

Here's your opportunity to advancing far beyond ineffective trial and error programming methods and learn the secrets of writing programs that accomplish exactly what you want them to—for business, educational, and other practical purposes. Taking a simple and straightforward approach, this guide leads you through the process of program development, step-by-step. Author Henry Simpson provides all the guidelines and techniques to give you the understanding needed to develop your own serious applications programs. 192 pp., 104 illus. 7″ × 10″.

Paper $12.95   **Hard $18.95**
Book No. 1960

☐ **FROM FLOWCHART TO PROGRAM—Todd**

Master the skills of effective, "bug-free" programming with this practical approach to program design and development. Using the flowcharting system of structuring a program, you'll learn step-by-step how to break down the program logically, enabling you to tackle even large-scale programs with confidence. It's your key to writing programs, that are easier to debug, easier to change and expand, easier to understand, and faster in execution. 192 pp., 190 illus. 7″ × 10″.

Paper $12.95   **Hard $19.95**
Book No. 1862

☐ **SERIOUS PROGRAMMING FOR THE COMMODORE 64—Simpson**

Serious programming means writing programs that are user friendly, well documented, and designed to take full advantage of all of the resources offered by the BASIC language, your DOS (disk operating system), and assembly language routines. And that's what you'll find here—everything you need to get more programming power from your C-64! 208 pp., 124 illus. 7″ × 10″.

Paper $9.95   **Hard $15.95**
Book No. 1821

Other Bestsellers From TAB